DORIAN SOLOT and MARSHALL MILLER are the founders of the Alternatives to Marriage Project, a national nonprofit organization that advocates for equality and fairness for unmarried people. Their work has been widely featured on national television, radio, and newspapers, including *NBC News, CNN, National Public Radio, USA Today, Time,* and *The New Yorker.* They are also popular lecturers and workshop presenters who educate audiences around the country. Brown University graduates, Dorian and Marshall are themselves in a committed nine-year unmarried relationship. They live in the Boston area with their two cats, and can be contacted at www.unmarriedtoeachother.com.

unmarried TO EACH OTHER

UNMARRIED
to each other

The Essential Guide to
Living Together
as an Unmarried Couple

Dorian Solot and Marshall Miller

MARLOWE & COMPANY
NEW YORK

UNMARRIED TO EACH OTHER: *The Essential Guide to
Living Together as an Unmarried Couple*
Copyright © 2002 by Dorian Solot and Marshall Miller
Owing to limitations of space, acknowledgments
for permission to reprint previously published material
may be found on page 263.

Published by
Marlowe & Company
An Imprint of Avalon Publishing Group Incorporated
161 William Street, 16th Floor
New York, NY 10038

This book addresses various topics of interest to unmarried partners,
including legal and financial issues. While it contains general
information about the law, it cannot provide advice for your specific
legal situation. For this, seek the assistance of a knowledgeable
attorney licensed to practice law in your state.

Library of Congress Cataloging-in-Publication Data
is available.

ISBN 1-56924-566-5

9 8 7 6 5 4 3 2

DESIGNED BY PAULINE NEUWIRTH, NEUWIRTH & ASSOCIATES

Printed in Canada
Distributed by Publishers Group West

To our own and each other's families,

for their infinite love, wisdom, and open arms.

CONTENTS

unmarried TO EACH OTHER

INTRODUCTION

YES, WE'RE UNMARRIED TO EACH OTHER

COHABITATION IS EVERYWHERE. Living together may once have been scandalous, but today it's the way most people begin partnered life with the person they love. From bustling cities to leafy suburbs, on small-town streets and winding dirt roads, people are living with unmarried partners. There are eleven million cohabitors in the United States today, a 1,000 percent increase since 1960.[1] If unmarried couples all lived in the same city, it would have a population larger than New York City and Chicago combined.

Like Jenna and Wyatt, most cohabitors eventually marry. The pair met in college on the East Coast but didn't start dating until a few years later in California, when a mutual friend encouraged Wyatt to give Jenna a call. After six months of dating two or three nights a week, Jenna says they were telling each other, "I don't want to commute anymore, I want to see you all the time. I want to be with you." Wyatt was talking marriage, but Jenna wasn't ready to get engaged yet. They found an apartment, adjusted to the rhythms of life together, and had their first major fights. Jenna remembers that before moving in together, "we used to call each other 'the treat at the end of the week.' Now we realized we weren't the treat at the end of the week anymore—we were every day." As the months went by, "we learned volumes about each other," and soon

Jenna realized that despite her earlier hesitation, she, too, wanted to get married. Though they already share their lives, they'll soon have an outdoor wedding on the college campus where they first met.

Others see marriage further in the future. Carmen expects that some day she'll probably marry her partner, Alex, who has lived with her and her daughter Jasmine for the last four years. Carmen's family is Puerto Rican, and she calls Alex her *marido*, a Spanish word that can mean husband, common-law husband, or live-in boyfriend. "Living together is the same thing as being married," she says. "The only thing is you don't have a ring on your finger, and you don't have the documents. As long as you are together, you are a family." Now twenty-two, Carmen says she'd like to marry when she's older.

For Duncan and Lydia, on the other hand, marriage isn't in the cards. Married once before, Duncan can remember when, "if you wanted to be with someone, you had to be married." Now that hotel check-in clerks no longer request matching I.D.s, he says, it's been easy for him and Lydia to share their lives, their cooking and cleaning, and their vacations for the last eleven years. They describe themselves as pragmatists, not radicals. "I don't have a banner or a flag. I don't march around saying being unmarried is the right way to live. But on the other hand, I feel totally comfortable," Lydia says.

Raymond and Brian, unmarried partners as well, own a home together in Michigan and share their land with their goats, burros, geese, ducks, chickens, birds, fish, cat, and dog. Raymond and Brian plan to spend the rest of their lives together, just as both their sets of parents did—so far, they've celebrated eighteen years and counting. If same-sex marriage were legalized they'd consider it, but they'd prefer a big picnic to a fancy wedding. Their biggest concerns about marital status relate to legal issues like hospital visitation and inheritance. It frustrates them that it would cost $250 for Brian to be able to get a library card at the university where Raymond works, even though spouses get free cards.

You may be part of this dramatic increase. Maybe you're thinking about moving in with your sweetheart—or have done so recently—as a step along the path toward matrimony. Perhaps you're in a long-term relationship with someone you love dearly but don't plan to marry. Perhaps marriage isn't an option for you because you're in a same-sex relationship, or because of your financial situation. Maybe you're married but want to better understand your friends and loved ones who aren't.

At the heart of this book are stories from over one hundred unmarried people who generously agreed to share their successes and challenges, ups and downs, practical advice, and views on life. We spoke with them on living room sofas, at local diners, on park benches, and by telephone. We met their dogs and their kids, admired photos of their commitment ceremonies, listened and asked questions as they shared their experiences. They range in age from their twenties to their seventies and are diverse in terms of race, class, sexual orientation, geographic location, and the duration of their relationships, which ranged from one year to thirty-two.

As we explore in chapter 2, the reasons they're not married vary tremendously, ranging from a desire to "try out" the relationship to deeply-held philosophical beliefs to practical considerations and legal barriers. Some eagerly look forward to marrying, a few are vigorously opposed to the idea, and most fall somewhere in between. The one thing everyone we interviewed had in common was a belief that unmarried perspectives need to be shared.

ABOUT THE INTERVIEWEES

WE FOUND THE people interviewed for this book through newspapers and newsletters, postings online, and word of mouth. In addition to the one hundred people who participated in formal interviews, several dozen additional people told their stories in shorter interviews, phone calls, and e-mails. Of those in the in-depth interview group, who make up our primary sample, 18 percent are in their twenties, 35 percent in their thirties, 20 percent in their forties, 14 percent in their fifties, and 12 percent age sixty or above. Thirteen percent of this sample are people of color (5 percent African-American, 3 percent Asian-American, 2 percent Latino or Hispanic, and 2 percent multiracial). Eighty-seven percent are in relationships composed of different-sex couples, 8 percent are same-sex couples, and 5 percent have three or more adults in their family. As a group they represent twenty states, from Vermont to Georgia to Nebraska to California. On average, the people we interviewed are somewhat older and have higher incomes than cohabitors overall. While we sought out varied viewpoints and experiences, our sample is not statistically representative. *Unmarried to Each Other* contains both real names and pseudonyms (and last initials when people have the same first name), as requested by the interviewees.

In the one to four years since we conducted the original interviews, most of the people we spoke with have stayed in touch with us informally. Their lives have changed, of course: they've moved and had babies, some have married, and others separated. A striking majority are still together and unmarried, which makes our sample somewhat different than cohabitors overall, most of whom marry within a couple years of living together. Clearly, though, our sample has figured out how to make unmarried relationships work, the subject of this book. The collective knowledge of cohabitors with particularly strong, resilient relationships can teach us all how to stay together successfully.

DINING AT THE BUFFET

One way to understand the difference between married and unmarried relationships is to compare a sit-down steak dinner to a buffet. With the former, you know you'll get your steak, some kind of potato, and a vegetable on the side. It may not be identical to the steak dinner at the restaurant across town, but they'll resemble each other reassuringly. A buffet, on the other hand, is all about options. You may be able to choose that identical steak, potato, and vegetable off the buffet table, but you can also pile your plate with pasta primavera or choose roast turkey with your veggies. It's unlikely that any two people eating from the buffet will end up with dinners that look exactly the same.

Formal marriage, with its license, ceremony, white dress, wedding rings, honeymoon, and babies is like a steak dinner. There's comfort in knowing the basic expectations so you can proceed with planning your life. Unmarried relationships, on the other hand, are like a buffet. You can think creatively about the form and function of your relationship. You might still choose to trade rings or have babies, or you might create a relationship that's profoundly "alternative" in some way. You can choose a religious ceremony and get married "in the eyes of God," but bypass filing for a marriage license at City Hall. Whether the steak dinner marriage is something you're not allowed to order (if you're a gay couple, for instance), something you're putting off until later (for cohabitors in a "trial period"), or something you choose to forgo altogether, the combinations from the buffet are unlimited. Despite real differences between the married and unmarried menus, most people in unmarried relationships can put together a plate that meets their needs.

This doesn't mean that all marriages follow a predictable form and all unmarried relationships are unorthodox. Married people are also free to modify their "meal" by making a special request when they place their order—perhaps they want to be married on a mountaintop instead of in a church, or choose not to have children. And unmarried couples can lead very "traditional" lives, right down to taking the same last name and arranging for the woman to stay home to care for the kids. In fact, there's a lot of overlap between these two groups, since most cohabitors eventually marry, and most people marrying today have lived together first.[2] What the analogy illustrates are the different expectations and choices that each group sets out with. While both ultimately have many of the same options, those at the unmarried buffet are confronted with an array of choices that can be simultaneously overwhelming and liberating.

The image of an assortment of people serving themselves from the buffet is a reflection of the diversity that increasingly represents the American family. Just as our population represents many races and ethnicities, people choose to form families in many ways. A seven-year-old girl came up with our favorite definition of "family." She said, "A family is a bunch of people, or not so many, who love each other."[3] Typical neighborhoods today include single people and step-families, adoptive families and single parent families, cohabitors and foster families, interracial couples and interfaith couples, childfree and parenting marriages, and gay, lesbian, bisexual, and transgender families—all alongside the married mom, dad, and their kids model. Forty-four percent of American adults aren't married,[4] and we live among married people as their friends, neighbors, children, parents, and coworkers. Like married people, unmarried ones pay taxes, put out recycling bins, and fall in love.

YES, WE'RE UNMARRIED TO EACH OTHER

Our own story began at Brown University, where we met as prospective student and tour guide, got to know each other better as student mediators, and eventually started to sit together in an anthropology class. Casual conversation shifted to e-mail flirtation, to a date at a local restaurant, then to months of shared meals and meandering conversations that would last late into the night. Despite all those hours of talking, neither of us can recall the first time we discussed our feelings on marriage. At some point in those first years we must have established that getting married wasn't something that particularly interested either of us, although we weren't—and still aren't—against marriage.

Fast forward a couple of years to a house in Providence, Rhode Island, when we were living together with a gaggle of recent college graduates, an assortment of mismatched furniture, and a front hall full of bicycles. Although our own conversations about marriage apparently weren't noteworthy enough to be remembered, we clearly recall the subject being brought up by relatives and friends who hinted and sometimes asked quite openly when we'd announce our big news. Over and over again we were reminded that although being unmarried suited us, the arrangement didn't fit society's expectations.

After graduation, Marshall was self-employed as a freelance writer and Dorian worked for an organization that found adoptive homes for abused children. If we'd been married, Dorian would have automatically been able to add Marshall to her health insurance plan at work. But since we weren't, and since Dorian's workplace did not offer domestic partner benefits, joint health insurance wasn't an option. Dorian began a series of thoughtful, polite conversations with, and letters to, the director of the agency where she worked, pointing out that we had been in a relationship longer than one of the married employees, and that the organization's own policy forbade discrimination on the basis of marital status. The director, in turn, continued the discussion with the organization's board of directors. After many months of advocacy and negotiation, the board gave its final answer: no. Marshall was forced to buy health insurance elsewhere.

Not long after, we were beginning the stressful process of looking for an apartment. From a convenience store pay phone in a Boston suburb, we started calling landlords who had advertised in the local paper. The very first call went something like this:

> Dorian: Hi! We saw your ad about the apartment in the newspaper, and we
> wanted to find out more about it.
> Landlord: How many people?
> Dorian: Two. We're a couple.
> Landlord: Are you married?
> Dorian: No.
> Landlord: When are you getting married?

We were stunned. At the time we weren't savvy enough to point that out that the landlord's questions were illegal according to Massachusetts law. Rather than pushing our luck with a landlord so openly uncomfortable with our relationship, we decided to look elsewhere.

Around the same time an article appeared in the newspaper detailing the plight of a Rhode Island man who wanted to adopt his domestic partner's child. He'd been living with the boy and his mother as a family for many years, and had gone to court for permission to adopt him. The man and the mother wanted to ensure that he could sign the boy's field trip permission slips, or take him to the emergency room if he got hurt at a Little League game. It would be the kind of run-of-the-mill stepparent adoption that courts grant every day. On this day, though, the judge refused to hear the case. He told the man, "Come back when you're married." The decision left the child without a legal tie to the man who was already his dad in every other way.[5]

The worst part was what happened next: absolutely nothing. No letters to the editor ran in the newspaper. No rallies were organized in front of Family Court. No experts expressed outrage that the best interests of the child had been ignored, or pointed out the inequities facing unmarried parents everywhere. There was no flurry of phone calls condemning the decision, and no outpouring of support for the family. National organizations like the American Association of Retired Persons (AARP) and the National Association for the Advancement of Colored People (NAACP) speak out on behalf of their constituencies all the time, but there was no equivalent organization speaking out for people in unmarried relationships.

For a while it seemed as though we encountered marital status discrimination everywhere we turned. Although our relationship was happy and committed, we felt bombarded with the message that it didn't count. The inequity frustrated us, and we were surprised by the lack of relevant information and support. We knew we hadn't invented the unmarried relationship—in fact, we'd both grown up knowing relatives and close friends of our parents and grandparents, both gay and straight, who had stable, long-term unmarried relationships. We figured if we just looked for it hard enough, we would find the book that would unlock the secrets to unmarried survival, and the organization that represented people like us.

At the library down the street we searched the card catalog and the Internet for books about unmarried couples—and turned up only a handful of legal guides. Legal issues are, indeed, important for unmarried people since our relationships aren't automatically protected like marriages are. But what was missing, not just from the library but from the culture at large, was a body of thought that addressed the social and emotional aspects of being in an unmarried relationship. There was nothing that could begin to help anyone deal with Great-Aunt Ethel's questions, figure out whether "significant other" beats "boyfriend," or decide whether marriage was a prerequisite for having children. After years of talking and dreaming, we finally decided that if the book were going to exist, we needed to write it.

We also believed that if unmarried partners were to receive recognition and fair treatment, there needed to be a grassroots movement. We had seen political movements achieve broad new rights for women and African-Americans, for the disabled, for gay, lesbian, bisexual, and transgender people. It was time to take action. In 1998 we announced that we were starting a national nonprofit organization, the Alternatives to Marriage Project (AtMP). At the top of our to-do list was to begin the interviews that would become the core of this book, so we could hear what cohabitors around the country were saying. At the same time, we headed back to the library to learn what academic researchers could teach us about cohabitation.

There's something magical about putting a name to a social phenomenon in which so many people already take part. In the years since AtMP got its start, thousands of people have contacted the organization for information, support, and community. In the first few months after we launched its website we started to receive a steady of stream e-mails that read, "I am so glad I discovered your existence! I will be sending a donation to you very soon! I would be interested in creating a group in my area to promote your organization's views in the legal and social arenas," and "I'm thrilled to have found you. Thanks for existing. Can't wait to read more!" Now AtMP's mailing list has grown to represent every state and several dozen countries, and its website and publications are a place where journalists, policymakers, and researchers turn for information and perspectives not found elsewhere. The Alternatives to Marriage Project has become a leading voice responding to the public policy debates that swirl around marriage and cohabitation, and our members and volunteers are regularly interviewed by television, radio, and print journalists.

At the beginning of one live radio interview, the host peered across the table at us: "So, you're Dorian, and you're Marshall and you're both unmarried." We agreed. Her next question took us by surprise: "Are you unmarried to each other?" We realized she didn't know whether we were two co-workers from the same organization, or a couple. We were delighted. How fitting: unmarried to each other described us perfectly.

ABOUT THIS BOOK

Each chapter in *Unmarried to Each Other* explores a subject that is important to unmarried partners. Because of their diversity, not everything in the pages ahead will apply equally to every reader. The personal stories might reassure someone who feels like she's the only woman on earth not pining for an engagement ring,[6] whereas someone who's been worrying about how to create a legal safety net for his family might turn to the practical information in chapters 6 and 9. Understanding the historical and social context of unmarried relationships (chapter 11) might reassure one person, while another is just looking for ideas about how to plan her commitment ceremony (chapter 8).

A few thoughts on language. The word marriage has legal, religious, and social meanings. When we talk about marriage in *Unmarried to Each Other* we are referring to legal marriage. Some couples who have not or cannot get legally married consider themselves married, like Marvin and Roberta, who had a church wedding but choose not to marry legally for financial reasons. Calling themselves married is entirely reasonable, since in many eras throughout history it was the couple's and community's perception of the relationship, not the piece of paper, that determined whether a given couple was married. But legally, no matter which religious blessings they have received and how many times Roberta introduces Marvin as her husband, they're still an unmarried couple, and that's how we understand them in this context.

There are so many stereotypes about gender in relationships that it can be difficult to talk about the subject without tripping over pronouns. We use both "he" and "she" in examples throughout the book, but in most cases either pronoun could apply. There are also linguistic challenges to describing the different kinds of unmarried partnerships that exist. While marital status discrimination means a lesbian couple may face many of the same issues as a heterosexual unmarried one, their situations also differ. We mostly use the terms "same-sex couples" and "different-sex couples" when a specific point is relevant to one or the other. We prefer to avoid "opposite-sex," because we believe that men and women are similar in many ways, not opposites, and that gender is more complex than two opposite categories.[7]

Even "unmarried" has its drawbacks: it defines who we *are* by what we *lack* relative to the presumed norm—even though the average American now spends the majority of his or her lifetime unmarried.[8] But we think it has some advantages, too. "Cohabiting" isn't a term most people use in everyday life. Many unmarried partners tell us they don't like the word "single" because it implies that they're alone, and it can mislead policy discussions (like those that focus on "births to single mothers," 40 percent of which are to two-parent cohabiting households where the parents are single only in a legal sense).[9] Fundamentally, we *are* describing not being married in a culture that still assumes all couples are or should be married to a different-sex partner. Until the English language catches up with social reality, "unmarried" will have to do.

UNMARRIED PIONEERS

In the first few months of our research we interviewed Wendy and Dan, a Vermont couple of eighteen years who commented that even though they knew they weren't the first long-term unmarried relationship, they sometimes felt like pioneers. Wendy said that in their early years together, she and Dan would have loved to have a map of the territory, a sense of what other couples had already "plowed through." Given how many millions of partners around the world are living together, she said it would have been valuable to hear other people say, "Oh, yes, we did that, too!" or "Oh, here's how to do that and not get in trouble later."

As we show in chapter 11, relationships outside formal definitions are hardly anything new. But since most of us have never experienced life in a culture that treats cohabiting couples and married ones alike, the territory is new *to us*. The people we interviewed have learned the terrain remarkably well, though. Their collective wisdom and accumulated experience is vast.

Despite how common it has become, in many places it is still radical to say that it's OK to live together without being married. Many people are surprised to realize that commitment cannot be measured in wedding rings, and that family can no longer be understood by birth and marriage records alone. Thanks to the many pioneers in thriving relationships and families, the world increasingly supports our vibrant diversity and emerging voice.

ONE

SHALL WE LIVE TOGETHER?

Considering Cohabitation

THERE ARE THOUSANDS of websites, shelves of books, stacks of glossy bridal magazine articles, and even listings of retreats and classes designed to help engaged couples and newlyweds with their relationships. The assumption, of course, is that the months following the wedding will be the couple's first experience sharing a home, and that they'll need extra guidance as they adjust to their new lives together. But these days, most couples who get married are already living together.[1] Whether or not they ultimately marry, cohabitors are already dealing with many of the same problems and challenges that married couples face—without the benefit of any up-front guidance.

Even though almost half the population of the United States under age forty-five lives with an unmarried partner at some point, including a substantial majority among younger generations,[2] there's a stunning lack of information about how to cohabit well from the start. If prospective live-ins turn up any advice at all it's likely to be, "Don't do it." This recommendation isn't particularly helpful to the millions of people who are preparing to move in with a sweetheart or already have, and who deserve accurate and useful information.

Most unmarried partners want not just to live together, but to stay together.

The future is full of unknowns, and every relationship—whether you're dating, cohabiting, or married—involves some degree of faith. But the more clear and realistic your expectations, the better it's likely to turn out. As William Hiebert, one of the founders of the field of premarital counseling, said, "There is a difference between shacking up and intentionally cohabiting. The more intentional people are, the better it works."[3] This chapter is designed to help you avoid utterly blind leaps of faith, so that you and your partner are as well-prepared as possible to plunge into living together. Even if you already share a home, you may benefit from exploring the topics raised here.

We'll start with three issues to consider before you rent the U-Haul:
1. Is the time right?
2. Are the reasons right?
3. Is the relationship right?

IS THE TIME RIGHT?

In order to calculate the right time to move in with your sweetie, take the number of weeks since your first date, multiply it by 3.14159, and then divide by your own age and add one year for each time you . . . just kidding. If only big relationship decisions were as simple as a mathematical formula!

In some ways deciding to live together is like making or accepting a marriage proposal. In either case, your chance of success increases if you make the decision slowly, seriously, and with great care. That's because moving in together is so easy to do—maybe too easy, given that moving out can involve expense, hassle, and heartache as intense as divorce. In fact, this "hassle factor" can lure some cohabitors into poor marriages, because getting married feels easier and more natural than moving out and starting the search for love and living space anew. Therapist and relationship educator Maya Kollman says, "When you move in with somebody, your unconscious mind starts to experience that person as part of your family."[4] Family connections are powerful, which is why the end of a living-together relationship can be so devastating.

When you live apart, it's simpler to take your time getting to know each other, negotiate what you need, and assess whether your relationship is truly ready to be upgraded to the next level of seriousness. You probably wouldn't buy a house without careful thought, and you shouldn't agree to share a kitchen and bedroom without the same kind of consideration. Double this advice if there are children involved, or if you're the impulsive type who falls passionately in love and feels *absolutely certain* about things that in retrospect weren't quite so clear. Enjoy the passion of new love, and savor the desire to spend every moment together—just delay living together for awhile. (As an added benefit, this will help your relationship's sexual spark last longer.) The best way to prevent a breakup down the road is to take your time making a careful decision in the first place.

▶ Practice Makes Perfect

Cohabitation is sometimes called "trial marriage." Why not have a trial cohabitation? Although this may not be an option for those who live with parents, children, or roommates, others can "practice" living together by spending a lot of time in each other's houses. An extended stay of a week or two is ideal. Keep in mind that vacationing together, even in your own homes, is different than living together. Don't be enticed by fantasies of spending long, lazy days in bed followed by heartfelt conversations while you prepare dinner elbow to elbow, looking adorable. Carry on your regular lives. Give yourselves a real feel for the pressure of the morning dash to school or work, the low energy I-just-want-to-crash-in-front-of-the-TV evening, and the negotiation over who will do the dishes.

Daren had the opportunity to try out living with his partner, Merav, before she left for a long trip. They'd started dating only a month earlier, and she had been trying to avoid spending money on rent in order to save money for traveling.

Merav was planning a trip to Israel for October and she was living with friends for the month of September. She decided to postpone her trip so we could get to know each other better before she left, but she wasn't enjoying her living situation. I said, "Why don't you move in with me for a few months until you leave?" and she did. She went to Israel in December. It was my first time living with someone, but there was no fear because I knew she was leaving in December.

Daren visited Merav in Israel, and when she returned they decided to continue living together. Seven years later, they're still together.

A trial cohabitation might go fabulously well, and lead you to plan for the real thing. It might crash and burn, leaving you with the conclusion that this wasn't the right relationship for you. Or you might learn that while you're passionate about each other, you're not so hot for the idea of sharing space 24/7. That's what Jacquie discovered. As she explains, their hearts were compatible, but their habits were not.

I take the wrapper off the soap and throw the wrapper away. But he likes to keep the wrapper. I have shoes galore, I love my shoes. This man takes his shoes off and throws them in the middle of the floor. He says, "If we lived together I would have to kill you in two days because you're always picking up my shoes. I know where my shoes are." But I say, "You can find them better in the box." Can you imagine these two people living together for the rest of their lives? We tried it for a month and it was no good. It was like eating ice cream when you know you have a lactose intolerance.

Jacquie's relationship with her partner survived because they agreed never to live together. She says that now, after not seeing him for four or five days, "When I do see him, it's like drinking a glass of cool water."

For people with children, trial cohabitation probably doesn't make sense. Children need stability, and asking them to give up or share their space is a very big deal. Instead of living together temporarily if a relationship looks serious, the transition to being a stepfamily should include having your partner spend a lot of time with you and your children, and maybe taking some trips together. Until the adults are certain they are ready to commit to being together long-term, they shouldn't uproot the kids or try to add an unmarried stepparent to their lives.

WHAT'S YOUR STYLE?

THERE ARE AT least six basic styles for moving in together, and some people fit into more than one category. If you're already cohabiting, do you recognize one of the beginnings below?

INSTANT COHABITORS: Here's the recipe: Take two people on their first date and send them home together afterwards. Add water, stir, and—*voila!*—Instant Cohabitors. One pair we know calls theirs the longest one-night stand in history—they're still together ten years, two kids, and one trip to Disney World later. But they got lucky. Appealing though the love-at-first-sight scenario may be when you're mutually intoxicated with each other's apparent perfection, the just-add-water approach isn't the wisest.

ACCIDENTAL COHABITORS: These people never *intended* to live together—it just sort of happened. "I don't think it really was a decision to live together on my part," Tori says. "After spending time with me he just never went back home, unless it was to pick up something." Instant and Accidental Cohabitors usually share certain characteristics: their relationships start off intense and passionate, the partners tend to make quick decisions, and one enjoys a significantly more desirable living situation.

ESCAPIST COHABITORS: These cohabitors start living together because they want to leave another living situation, not because of a conscious choice to share a home. Eager to escape their parents' abode, young people sometimes move in with a partner—or marry—for this reason. Evictions, divorces, and dysfunctional roommates like Melinda's can also lead to Escapist cohabitations. She says, "We were in college and my roommates were intolerable. I stayed over on my S.O.'s [significant other's] couch for a few nights, and he offered to let me stay longer. I did, ten years so far!"

EVOLVING COHABITORS: The slow, almost imperceptible accumulation of one partner's possessions at the other partner's house is the hallmark of Evolving Cohabitors. They usually have a hard time answering the question, "How long have you been living together?" because by the time the official moving day arrives, only a few crates of old paperbacks and the rusty exercycle remain to be moved. Cary, for instance, explains that "Mark's apartment was the first place I really felt at home, so I tended to stay here most nights. Moving in together was definitely a gradual experience. First my cat moved in, then some of my clothes, then some of my kitchen stuff, then my bike."

Similarly, Kirsten's partner, Tom, lived with her for a few summers before he moved in full-time, so the final transition didn't feel like a big change.

We never really talked about moving in together—it just sort of happened. Housing was expensive in Burlington, Vermont, where I lived, and Tom was originally only coming during the summers while he was in graduate school. Once he finished graduate school, he just moved in permanently. It didn't feel like a big deal, it just seemed like the most practical and nicest option.

SITUATIONAL COHABITORS: Situational cohabitations are launched by a combination of practical or logistical issues that may or may not relate directly to the partners' relationship. Saving money on rent is the most common, though certainly not the only way Situational Cohabitors get their start. One couple's cohabitation was launched when one partner moved into the other's house to recover from an operation, and never left.

Valerie and her partner, Rodrigo, represent another kind of Situational Cohabitors. Deciding to move across the country, they got so focused on the cross-country adventure that they forgot to think about what living together would be like once they unpacked.

About six months into our relationship I decided to move from New York City to California to set up residency for graduate school and to be closer to my best friend. I told Rodrigo that I would be moving and that I would love it if he came too, but I understood if he did not want to since he had lived almost his entire life in New York. He was elated to join me, and there was an assumption that we would live together when we moved to California. Since we were moving across the country and Rodrigo was moving out of his parents' homes for the first time, the fact that we were moving in together was somewhat obscured. We were not fully realistic about the challenges we would face.

DELIBERATE DECIDERS: Deliberate Deciders see cohabitation as a big move. They talk at length with each other, friends, and relatives to be sure they're making the right decision, and they aren't afraid to wait a while. Joan was an extreme example of this—most Deliberate Deciders don't need a decade to make up their minds!

We'd been together fourteen years before moving in together. I was tired of living alone and also increasingly aware of how much easier it would be to help each other if we lived together. I think we are closer now, and we both like living together. I think he's been a bit surprised by this. He was fifty-one when we moved in, and had never lived with a partner before.

Kate and her partner had a "natural" opportunity to move in together fairly early in their relationship, but being Deliberate Deciders, they wanted to do so only when the relationship felt like it was ready for that stage.

We talked about living together and then each of us asked some friends and family for advice. We both independently decided that we shouldn't move in together simply because of the convenience of a particular time, like his lease being up and my looking for a new place to live. So I moved in to an apartment with a roommate. We did not consider moving in again until both our leases were up a year later.

ARE THE REASONS RIGHT?

The specific reasons that you and your partner decide to move in together aren't overwhelmingly important. What is absolutely essential, though, is that you agree on those reasons. It would be a rude surprise to find out a year from now that your partner saw cohabitation as an unspoken engagement when you thought it would be a good way to save on rent and see how things unfolded. Likewise, if you're already browsing bridal magazines but your partner is too shell-shocked from a recent divorce to be able to consider matrimony, it's not a good time to sign a lease together.

Don't assume that you're on the same page as your partner if you've never had an explicit, heart-to-heart conversation about what living together means to each of you. One way to get started is to use the list on pages 20–21, which includes many of the reasons people want to live together, in no particular order. You may want to photocopy these pages so that you and your partner can fill them out separately and then compare notes.

▶ Tips for Effective Heart-to-Hearts

When you've each finished your list, it's time to talk. Here are some tips to maximize what you get out of your talk.

- *Make enough time.* Important conversations deserve plenty of time. One potential cohabitor, Peter, had the right idea: he initiated a discussion well in advance. Kate remembers, "Peter brought up the issue of living together several months before either of us had to make a decision about our living arrangements. We were on our way to a movie, and started getting into a fairly intense conversation about it, until the movie started. My advice is not to bring up such a conversation during movie previews!" Long car rides, quiet walks, and other situations where you're away from kids and ringing telephones are great times to have serious conversations.

- *Don't start talking about an important topic if one of you is in a bad mood.* You'll only end up frustrated with each other if you do (more about this on page 101).

- *Use "I statements."* The most important outcome for a conversation about moving in together is for each partner to end with a good sense of the other's thoughts and feelings. One way to stay focused is to use "I statements" as you talk, to keep you focused on sharing your own thoughts and feelings and the reasons behind them, instead of telling your partner what he should think or do. Statements like, "I wish we got to spend more time together," or, "I get scared when you say you never want to get married, because marriage is really important to me," help conversations move forward. On the other hand, "You should move out of your parents' house," or, "You must not love me if you don't want to live with me," are more likely to make the other person defensive and intensify any disagreement.

- *Use the Speaker-Listener Technique if you think the issue at hand might be difficult.* This method, which we'll describe in more detail on page 98, provides a very structured way for each person to take a turn talking while the other listens, and then to confirm the listener understood by paraphrasing what the speaker said. It's particularly valuable if you know from past experience that a given topic is a source of conflict. Living together is a big commitment, and it can provoke a lot of strong feelings.

- *Set a time limit.* Sometimes we find it helpful to designate how long we'll talk, like one hour, to make sure whatever important subject we're discussing doesn't exhaust us emotionally or take over an entire hike. At the end of the hour, we'll decide if we want to continue the conversation or pick it up at another time.

▶ *Have more than one conversation.* You don't need to tie up every conversational topic with a tidy bow. Some topics come into focus over several conversations, as you peel back the layers. If you need to end a talk without a resolution—because you run out of time or energy, you need to gather more information, or you want more time to think about it—it can help to agree on when you'll return to the topic.

NOT NOW, MAYBE NOT EVER

HAVE YOU SPENT enough time together to know that you'd be on a collision course if you spent more than a weekend in the same apartment? Is it time to break up? Maybe—but not necessarily. Over a million married couples live apart,[5] many quite happily, and there's no reason unmarrieds can't do the same thing. Ellen and Nicolas are delaying moving in together partly to make sure they don't "get too comfortable" too early in their relationship. Ellen says:

> Right now, seeing each other is still an event. I look forward to the evenings I get to see Nicolas. If he's coming over, I'll scurry around making sure my room is clean and checking that there's something for breakfast. He says he does the same thing. We both really like feeling that anticipation, and we're not sure what living together would do to that excitement.

Three years into their relationship, Danita and her partner are living apart and plan to continue that way for the time being. She says, "Because of my children, and because of my parents' adamant opposition, and because we both own homes, living together is not something that we're in a hurry to do. But down the road it would be nice to have a common household."

Children were also a factor in Alan and Skip's relationship when it began. At the time, twenty years ago, Skip was clear that she didn't want to co-parent Alan's young children. Since they lived within walking distance of each other, spending time together when the kids were with their mom wasn't a problem. They recently married, but realized that although the kids were grown they liked their separate homes too much to change things. Alan says:

> When we're together, we do everything together. And yet we both also need to do things by ourselves, like reading, without interrupting each other or one of us feeling abandoned. We spend about four nights a week together. In the middle of each month we set out our calendar for the next month. We

try to stay a few weeks ahead so that if we have individual things we want to do, we plan them in the evenings we won't be together. So basically we have a lot of dates, four nights a week of dates, and when we're together we spend our time doing joint things. Since we got married we started to practice being under the same roof but not doing things together, so our relationship continues to evolve. Who knows? In another five years we may be living together.

If it's hard for cohabitors to have their relationship taken seriously by friends and family members, it can be even harder for partners who live apart. As Sue says, "People assume our relationship is casual because we don't live together, but I don't feel it's casual at all. It's just the way we've chosen to be." Wendy's mother told her that she couldn't imagine why Wendy would want to stay in her own house even though she was in a long-term relationship with Dan. Then, ironically, as a widow in her eighties, Wendy's mother ended up doing the same thing. Wendy recalls:

I remember the discussion we had about living apart, and I was saying how happy I was having my own house and having this great relationship with Dan, who lived in his own house, and she said, "Well, I just can't imagine that." Then, within six months after my father died, a man from a few houses down the road came and knocked on her door. They started spending time together. He was cooking for her, and then he would snuggle with her at night. In one conversation with her, I asked her if they were going to get married. She said, "No, I like my own house," as though she invented the idea. She liked her house and he had his house, and they were just fine. She had her freedom.

For Jacquie, living apart from her partner is simply a matter of knowing her relationship works for her. Compared to her experience living with her husband before their divorce, she says a long-term relationship with two different addresses is perfect. To listen to her talk, you'd never guess she'd been with her partner for thirteen years:

I have everything I've ever wanted. I have joy, I have happiness, I have a partner who is exciting—even sitting here talking to you about him makes my mouth water. I know that he feels the same way. The two of us know what is good for us.

IS THE RELATIONSHIP RIGHT?

The decision to live together is one to take seriously, even though it may not come with a lifetime commitment. You don't want to carry your cactus collection up all those stairs to your honey's apartment, only to have to carry them back down again as soon as they've settled in. The emotional experience of breaking up could be

WHY I WANT TO LIVE TOGETHER

	NOT IMPORTANT		SOMEWHAT IMPORTANT		VERY IMPORTANT
To make sure we're compatible	1	2	3	4	5
To share living expenses	1	2	3	4	5
To take the next logical step in our relationship	1	2	3	4	5
To get to know each other better	1	2	3	4	5
To have a better sex life	1	2	3	4	5
To spend more time together	1	2	3	4	5
To save on rent or mortgage payments	1	2	3	4	5
To get away from my roommates	1	2	3	4	5
To take a step toward getting married	1	2	3	4	5
To have our own space	1	2	3	4	5
To move out of my parents' house	1	2	3	4	5
To get away from my ex	1	2	3	4	5
To live in my/your place, which is much nicer than yours/mine	1	2	3	4	5
To eat better—you're a good cook	1	2	3	4	5
To make a commitment to each other	1	2	3	4	5
To take care of each other	1	2	3	4	5
To be less lonely	1	2	3	4	5
To live in the same city	1	2	3	4	5
To see you in person rather than talk on the phone	1	2	3	4	5
To convince others to take our relationship more seriously	1	2	3	4	5
To build trust with each other	1	2	3	4	5

To get a better sense of what you do each day	1	2	3	4	5
To have children	1	2	3	4	5
To have someone to help me with my kids	1	2	3	4	5
To help you with your kids	1	2	3	4	5
To be able to afford to buy a house or condo	1	2	3	4	5
To save on phone bills and transportation costs to visit each other	1	2	3	4	5
To be closer emotionally	1	2	3	4	5
To have someone to talk to every day	1	2	3	4	5
To have someone to help me _____(fill in the blank)	1	2	3	4	5
To help you _____ (fill in the blank)	1	2	3	4	5
Because we have more fun when we're together	1	2	3	4	5
Because it's better than any of my other living options right now	1	2	3	4	5
Because we're already spending most of our time at each other's places anyway	1	2	3	4	5
Because we're already engaged	1	2	3	4	5
Because we'll probably get engaged soon	1	2	3	4	5
Because we'll be getting married soon	1	2	3	4	5
Because our wedding is still a long way off	1	2	3	4	5
Because we may never or cannot marry	1	2	3	4	5
Other reasons (write your own):					
_____	1	2	3	4	5
_____	1	2	3	4	5
_____	1	2	3	4	5

even pricklier. Take the advice of psychologist Nancy Saunders, who specializes in working with unmarried couples: "My recommendation is, postpone living together until you're 99 percent sure it's a good relationship. Don't move in together just to check it out—that's a mistake. Move in together *after* you've checked it out."[6]

Many relationships start off with a thrilling high, what some people call "New Relationship Energy." When you're glowing with New Relationship Energy you think of your partner all through the day, can't wait until you'll see her again, and feel the electricity crackling between you when you're together. It's exhilarating stuff. But it's also temporary. Because New Relationship Energy is *not* proof that you're meant to spend the rest of your lives together, it's wise to delay moving in together until those initial flames die down enough for you to see what's underneath. You can build an impressive fire with a few pieces of crumpled newspaper, enough to toast a marshmallow. But if your goal is to heat your house through the night, you'll need a more substantial fuel source.

Psychotherapist Elizabeth Morrison says, "If a person is contented with him or herself, and has an accepting attitude toward life's inevitable small irritations . . . they probably have what it takes to create a successful relationship."[7] Kollman puts kindness and compassion at the top of her list of qualities to seek in a potential partner.[8] When you're considering whether you should live together, think about the traits that bug you, too. What is your partner like when he's in a bad mood? How does she handle conflict and stress? How do you resolve disagreements? If you've never had a disagreement or a bad day together, then it's too soon to move in. There is no such thing as a relationship without bad days, and you don't want to be taken by surprise when the first one arrives.

Likewise, if you see any bigger "red flags," now is the time to address them. "Moving in will not solve problems; it will just make them more pronounced as you see one another each day," says Karen Blaisure, a marriage and family therapist who leads couples education programs.[9] If your partner has ever been violent toward you, living together is not going to prevent that from happening again. Similarly, moving in with a partner who has a drug, alcohol, or gambling addiction, or chronic money problems, is likely to make things worse. These issues can be enormously stressful, and if you're living under the same roof it can be easier to get entangled and harder to escape. Excessive jealousy can be a warning sign, too. Blaisure says, "Jealousy—wanting to know where you are all the time, trying to reduce your friendship circle, getting angry if you talk with someone—is *not* a sign of love, but of control and insecurity."[10] If you know or suspect that the person you love has a serious problem, you don't necessarily have to break up with her. But you should be sure she gets the help she needs and changes her behavior before you agree to live together.

Other less ominous warning signs still deserve attention. You can learn a lot from what your partner says about his past relationships and how they ended. "Never assume that it was the other person who was to blame for all the problems of a past relationship," says sex therapist and advice columnist Chris Fariello. "For example, if a partner says that he broke up with his last girlfriend because she was too needy, that may indicate that he is emotionally distant."[11] Has your partner gone through many relationships, and have they all ended in similar ways? Your own love might head in the same direction. Here, too, you don't have to call the whole thing off, but you'll want to feel confident that your partner sees a real difference in this relationship.

OTHER THINGS TO TALK ABOUT BEFORE YOU MOVE IN

The better you know each other, the better your chances of making a good decision about living together. Explore your expectations about issues like work, commitment, marriage, children, and other "big picture" topics. Leave room to change your own priorities, but don't expect to change your partner's mind. Take note of differences that feel important, spend more time digging deeper into that area, and think hard about whether your sun-worshipping soul is really willing to move in with someone who thrives in ice and snow. Listed below are ways to explore some of the common big issues. You might also enjoy the Reflecting Back exercise, on page 35, to stimulate thinking and conversation about your earliest experiences and beliefs about relationships.

▶ How Do You Picture Your Life?

There's a famous quote, "If you want to make God laugh, make plans." Anyone over the age of thirty—and many younger folks, too—will tell you their life isn't turning out precisely the way they had envisioned it. But there are still two good reasons to talk about your visions for your life. First, if you don't know what you want, it's pretty tough to get it. People who are clear about their goals are much more likely to attain them, despite life's curveballs. Second, learning about the dreams that are closest to your partner's heart will help you understand what really makes him tick. Maybe you'll realize you have wildly clashing visions of the future: one partner who'd like to live in a serene cottage in the woods, the other who envisions a bustling house full of friends and dogs in a lively city. Or maybe you'll realize that helping make your partner's dreams come true would make you happy, too.

You could start by talking about these topics:

▶ Work: What kind of work do you want to do? Is that different from your current job or educational path? When do you plan to retire, and what will you do then?

▶ Geography: Where would you like to live? Would you rather be in a city, the suburbs, or a rural area? Is it important to you to be either close to, or far from extended family?

▸ Dreams: What concrete things, large or small, would you like to experience or accomplish in your lifetime? These could be anything from sewing a quilt to making a pile of money to starting a summer program for neighborhood youth to climbing Mt. Rainier.

▶ Commitment

The word "commitment" buzzes incessantly around the heads of unmarried couples. We hear that we should make a commitment, that "he can't commit," that "she likes him but just isn't ready to make a commitment," and a dozen other variations on the theme. The truth is, commitment and marriage often go together, but they're not the same thing. Unmarried partners can be absolutely committed to each other but never tie the knot. And we all know of marriages that don't last long because commitment was lacking.

Although "committed" is sometimes used to signify "monogamous," those are really separate issues, since a monogamous relationship can be very short-lived. We define commitment as the intention to stay together for the long-term, even through difficult times, and to give a heartfelt, concerted effort to make the relationship last. Commitment isn't an on-off switch (on, you're committed; off, you're not), but something that grows and evolves. That's how Elise experiences it:

> *Feeling committed to this relationship grew slowly. I think not being married to Nate allowed our commitment to develop organically—it's hard for me to imagine getting married and being expected to feel more committed one day than I was the day before. Some specific things bumped my feeling of commitment to a higher level, like when I turned down a job in another city so I could stay with Nate. It also felt like a real achievement, and another level of commitment, when our relationship had lasted longer than my parents' entire marriage. And when I was emotionally dependent on him for a while through a family crisis, that changed things again. At that point I realized it was pretty hard to imagine* not *being with Nate.*

Partners can agree to a *process* of commitment, even if they don't commit to a specific *outcome*. For Dan, who was divorced decades ago, the quality of his relationship with Wendy is more important than its duration:

> *I feel extremely committed to Wendy, as much as I ever did in marriage. I've told her, my commitment isn't 'til death do us part, my commitment is to make our relationship work, to make it meaningful and viable. Not to hang in there no matter what. Now, to make it work requires hanging in there, but the real objective is to make it work.*

A NOT-QUITE-SCIENTIFIC LIST OF COHABITATION TYPES

MERGERS AND ACQUISITIONS COHABITATION

Between you, you have at least two houses, two cars, two attics, and two basements full of accumulated and treasured possessions. Moving in together requires selling real estate and extensive negotiation over every square inch of space.

CHIC COHABITATION

The biggest crises relate to whether your furniture will match, how quickly you can arrange for a landscaper, and whether you prefer shiitake or portobello mushrooms.

UPGRADE COHABITATION

You live with a roommate, bond over the challenges of dating, cry on each other's shoulders after a breakup, and share all your secrets. One day, unexpectedly, you find yourself in bed together. The next day, it happens again. You've upgraded from roommates to lovers.

CLANDESTINE COHABITATION

When your "friend" comes to visit for the night, he parks his car down the street, not in your driveway. Or, your "friend" is already living with you, but your mother thinks you're just roommates.

NEW TURF COHABITATION

Both partners move out of their old places (parents' house, bachelor pad, college dorm, ex's garage), and into a new place together.

WEEKEND COHABITATION

You live in Portland, Maine and you've fallen in love with someone who lives in Portland, Oregon. You write love letters, have cybersex, and spend passionate weekends together before flying home to go to work.

NEVER WOULD'VE PREDICTED IT COHABITATION

Because of your generation or religious beliefs, you never guessed you'd live with someone without being married, but it turns out to be the best option.

ENDLESS SLEEPOVER COHABITATION

You wouldn't say you're living together, but you spend all your time at each other's houses, and friends have started sending you mail together.

ACROSS-TOWN COHABITATION

You don't live at the same address, but your relationship has the kind of personal meaning and commitment most people expect from partners who share a living space.

STILL NOT MARRIED COHABITATION

You've been living together ten years or more.

When it comes to commitment, the most important thing is simply to have a sense of what the word means to each of you and how you feel about it in relation to each other. If there are major differences between you, you'll be wise to reconcile them before moving in together.

▶ Marriage

If you're just moving in together, marriage may feel like a subject for the future. In fact, not being sure about whether this is the person you want to marry is exactly why you want to live together. For same-sex couples and those who can't marry for legal or financial reasons, marriage may not feel like a relevant topic.

But for those who have the option to marry, it makes sense to understand your partner's general attitude toward marriage, particularly if you have your own strong feelings about the subject. Is your partner eagerly anticipating the day she'll share your last name, or does thinking about matrimony give her hives? What if the financial situation changed so marriage became an option? Even though we've all heard dozens of romantic stories of women being delighted by surprise wedding proposals, those proposals work best when they come *after* conversations confirming that yes, you're both seriously interested in moving toward marriage. Talking about it now can help you avoid the situation Laina encountered:

> *He was about to propose. He got on his knees in front of me, took my hand in his, and I went, "Oh, no, no please. If this is what I think it is, please stop right now." He did. He came back and he sat next to me on the couch. I'd only known him for about a month at that time. I said, "This is just way too fast. I hardly know you. I don't want to go there, and I'm not even sure that I'm going to get married at all. Let's get to know each other first."*

Mary's run-in with clashing expectations about marriage was even more painful:

> *Bobby and I were in the jewelry store together and he decided that I could pick out some rings. So I picked out some rings and I asked him, "Does this mean we're engaged?" He said, "Well, it just means you have rings."*

Even though it's probably not the time to be making decisions about marriage, it's not too early to find out whether your partner is eager to propose or dreading it, pining for a ring or horrified by the sight of a partner on one knee.

These conversations aren't necessarily easy. Marriage can be an uncomfortable topic if you see each other as potential—but not definite—marriage partners. Wendy says it took her partner a whole decade to be able to talk about it without coughing.

For the first ten or twelve years of our relationship when Dan would hear the word marriage he would cough. And he denied it. He said, "I don't do that," and I said, "You do, you [cough, cough]." So we were lying in bed one time talking. And the M word came up. And he started, "[cough, cough]." I said, "What were we just talking about?" And he said, "Oh my God, you're right."

If it feels awkward to talk about it so directly, you can still learn a lot by paying attention to what your partner says when related subjects come up naturally. If a topic like long-term relationships, cohabitation, marriage, or divorce is in the news, or a friend is getting married, initiate a casual conversation about what you each think about marriage, whether a couple should live together first, and for how long. Part of your task will be to separate your feelings about this relationship from your feelings about marriage in general, and to decipher how your partner feels. Are her hesitations really about marriage, or about this particular relationship? Does he intend to stay in the relationship for a lifetime, even if he has no intention of getting married?

If marriage is important to you, be clear about your expectations and time frames. Regardless of whether they move in together, some couples set a date six months or a year in the future. They agree that on that date they'll do another serious relationship assessment and discuss how they're feeling about marriage at that point. Having a date written on the kitchen calendar can take the pressure off for a while, so you can relax and enjoy the weeks and months together, without having to worry that the next Big Conversation will slip further and further away. You can agree in advance to go out to dinner or do something else fun on the date you set for your conversation. In the end, it doesn't matter what you decide. What does matter is that you agree about how you arrived at this mutual conclusion, and that you feel good about the decision. The way to be sure is to keep talking.

LIVING TOGETHER expert tip:

Find out if he really likes you to use his legs to warm your cold feet.

—Karen Blaisure[12]

▶ Children

In the United States, the majority of unmarried women's pregnancies are unintended.[13] If you have both sperm and egg between you, now is not the time to get sloppy on birth control. Talk now about what you would do if a pregnancy test came back positive. If you're not comfortable with your partner's answer, think long and hard about whether you're doing enough to keep that from happening. Think, too, about whether your partner is saying no children now, or no children ever. Regardless of your sexual orientation, the decision to have children might be a long way off. But it's good to find out sooner rather than later whether your partner envisions a childfree life or a brood of ten.

Likewise, if you or your partner live with children, cohabiting means moving in not just with each other, but with each other's kids. That's a reason to take the decision even more slowly. As Mark says, "I didn't employ a strategy for assimilating Cary into our family life, but I remember thinking, 'This is the way it should be: gentle, slow, and intentional.'" Chapter 9 talks more about deciding whether forming a stepfamily, married or unmarried, is what you want to do.

IF YOU'RE NOT A TALKER

NINE OUT OF ten advice columnists will tell you communication is the key to having a healthy relationship. But what if you're not a talker or your partner is someone of few words? How can you keep your relationship in shape?

Fortunately, talking isn't the only way to trade information, thoughts, and feelings. Some people write notes or letters to each other, or jot down their feelings in advance and then use what they've written as a way to get the conversation started. Others find that even if they exchange very few words, they can get a really clear sense of what their partner is thinking and feeling. (Slammed doors or warm embraces are pretty good clues.)

You and your partner may have different communication styles. Some people are verbally expressive, and can easily explain their emotions, while others find it harder. The degree of comfort with talking about difficult issues varies among ethnicities and cultures, too. Even if you have the same cultural background, your families' conversational styles could be so different that you feel like you come from different planets. George experienced two contrasting styles in his two marriages:

> My first wife grew up in a family where no one ever raised their voice, and so she and I never yelled at each other, even through our divorce. Unfortunately, lots of buried dissatisfactions never got discussed. My second wife was a yeller, with everything out in the open. Disagreements were clearly—and loudly—expressed, and then we moved on. It was hard for the kids from the first marriage when they were with us—they were traumatized by loud arguments—but I thought it was better to get things out in the open. As I look back, I'm not sure either style was ideal.

One way to overcome communication hurdles is to be conscious of conversational patterns that may have developed in the relationship without your even being aware of them. Karen Blaisure says that in her therapy practice, "Some couples who [have different styles] have told me that sometimes the more talkative person can try listening and breathing deeply when they really want to talk, because the other partner may just need more time to think, process, and figure out the words. The talkative one has probably been trained over time to fill in the silences, or perhaps the partners were attracted to one another because of this difference."[14] If you realize that differing communication styles are tripping you up, consider seeing a family mediator, reading some books on communication in relationships, or signing up for a relationship education program like those described on page 111. Many couples say they find these kinds of resources incredibly valuable. Seeking them out can be a sign of strength, not of inadequacy. With some new tools that you learn how to use together, your ability not only to speak for yourself, but also to hear what your partner is really saying, will take a quantum leap forward.

PREPARING FOR THE MOVE

You practiced, you talked, you deliberated, you reflected, and you've decided cohabitation is the right choice for you. Now what? Your next task is to outline your expectations for living together. As Chris Fariello says, "Unmet expectations typically lead to resentment,"[15] and that's what you're trying to avoid. By now you should know if you see eye to eye about some of life's bigger issues, but some of the questions remaining to be answered could still become grounds for serious battles (as anyone who's ever lived with a roommate can attest). Who will take out the trash? Does the partner moving in have the right to change the artwork? Will you split the bills evenly, or prorate them based on your incomes? Most importantly, who is responsible for cleaning up the cat's hairballs? Thinking through the nitty-gritty details in advance will spare you some battles. Expect to do some fine-tuning once you're actually situated in the same place, so you won't be caught off-guard the first time your partner says, "Why did you put the clean glasses facing up in the cupboard? They're supposed to go face down, so dust doesn't fall in." Jean says it took her a while to adjust to the fact that Pat makes decisions differently than she does.

It's not a bad thing, but I learned the hard way that Pat does not like to be spontaneous—he will research everything thoroughly, from what type of car is the safest and the best buy, to which travel company offers the best deals, to which long distance plan is the best choice. We have spreadsheets for almost every purchase we have ever made, and spreadsheets for lots of things we never bought because I got tired of waiting for the spreadsheet to be completed and decided we didn't need a new vacuum that badly! If I see something I like, on the other hand, I like to go ahead and buy it—I don't care if I got the best deal or if it was the best model. I have learned that tedious as his method can be, we are always satisfied with the things we buy his way, and I don't spend nearly as much time in the return lines.

Whether you're the "spreadsheet" type or the "looks good, I'll take it" type, minimize the surprises ahead by, yes, having another conversation.

When mediator Julia Weber helps partners write agreements before they move in together, she starts with a big piece of paper and asks, "What are some of the things that come up for you when you talk about moving in together, living together, and your life as a couple?" As they brainstorm, she takes notes.[17] You can do the same thing at your kitchen table. Once you've made a good list, start working your way down it, thinking about what you expect for each item, checking to see if your partner shares your expectations, and coming to some agreements. To give you a sense of how this is done, we'll address three of the most common topics: money, space, and housework.

▶ Money

Based on her experience counseling couples, Blaisure says, "The number one thing couples argue about pre- or post-marriage is money."[18] Rose says she and her partner have had to work out a system to survive the different ways they manage finances:

PUTTING ON THE BRAKES

IT CAN BE difficult to decide to delay moving in if your partner is enthusiastic about the idea. But staying put is probably the right move if you still have nagging concerns. As Kate points out, "The risks of moving in together too early seem much greater than waiting a bit longer than necessary to make sure you are ready for the step."

If putting on the brakes feels like the best move, trust your instincts. Most of the time you'll be able to change your mind at a later point if you decide you're ready to share an address. Although there are sometimes significant costs to living apart—rent, phone bills, commutes to visit each other—these add up to less than the costs of a cohabitation you come to regret. If you worry that your partner will be hurt by your decision, reassure him that you're moving slowly because you think the relationship has so much potential—if that's the case. If, in fact, the delay signals serious concerns about your future together, it's probably time to discuss them. If all goes well, the next time your leases are up for renewal you'll be ready to sign one together.

I always pay bills at the correct time to maximize interest on our checking accounts. He pays bills as they arrive because otherwise he would forget. Since I manage the household account and my own personal account, what he does is of no concern to me—though sometimes it's a source of amusement.

Knowing that good systems and clear expectations can save you financial headaches, some of the things to talk about should include:

- Are you a saver or a spender? A planner or a splurger?
- How was money handled in your family growing up? How does this affect the way you handle your own money?
- Do you know what your partner's salary is? If not, why not? If so, how do you feel about it? (Many experts say it's a good idea for partners to know each other's incomes, assets, debts, etc.)
- Will you divide household bills in half or allocate them in some other way?
- How will you make decisions about large and small purchases?
- Will you merge your finances, keep them separate, or some combination of those two systems? (See chapter 6 for more on this decision.)

▶ Space

It's a funny thing: before you move into them, rooms look so big and empty that you can't imagine how you'll ever fill all the closets. Once you move in, though, there's never enough space. It can be a challenge finding a home that meets your space needs, particularly if your newly formed family will be significantly larger than your old one. Janie points out that it can be valuable to make a conscious effort to have individual space and time:

In some ways, living with a partner is similar to living with any other roommate. However, when you live with someone you're in a relationship with, it's easier to dismiss or forget about your need for privacy. It's always much cheaper to just share one room, but depending on what other spaces you have available to you, it can be hard to escape the other person—or their music or TV show or phone conversation—when you need a break from them or just some quiet time.

Moving into one partner's place brings its own set of challenges. Ashton says having Bob move into the apartment where she was already living actually made things easier for her.

MOVING-IN expert tip:

If you've rented a large truck for the move, we highly recommend you (1) buy the extra insurance and (2) be very careful to make wide turns. The first tip comes in handy if you forget the second tip, as Marshall did when driving a twenty-two-foot rental truck during our last move.

I must confess that one reason living together works is because he moved into my space. Many of my rules were in place and a lot that would otherwise have to have been negotiated—what stuff goes on the walls, what work space is his and what is the kids'—got decided before I knew he was going to be living here. I think in Bob's head we won't really live together until the next place, which we will find, finance, and fix up together.

But having one partner move into the other's home isn't always so easy, as Marion and Bill discovered when he moved into her four-bedroom house:

We're in our fifties, so we had the challenge of combining of two households already brimming with a lifetime's accumulation of stuff. We needed to rent a storage space for a while for what couldn't be absorbed in my house. Even though our children have grown and moved out, we still had attics, garages, and basements full of favorite school projects, toys, camping gear, bunk beds, bikes, sleds, and holiday decorations, in addition to lawn mowers, picnic tables, garden tools. That precious popsicle-stick tower my son made in third grade finally had to go. The child himself, now in his late twenties, said, "A photo of it may do just as well, Mom." He was right, so we took a picture and said farewell to the original.

Beyond simply finding room for that weight-lifting equipment, space has meaning. One of the hardest things for Marion to handle was her partner's request to use her son's bedroom as a work space: "Even though my son is now almost thirty and on his own for many years, that room still felt like his room, his special place where he would return on a visit back home. Making the transition was not only a physical change, but also an emotional one for all involved."

Here are some questions to start your conversation about space:

- What do you like about the space in which you currently live? What do you dislike?
- What do you like about the way your partner keeps her space? What would you change if you could?
- Where are you on the organization scale that runs from "A place for everything and everything in its place" to "I can probably find it if I can remember where I last used it"?
- How do you imagine your living space will be different once you are living together?
- How will you make decisions about what goes where?

▶ Housework

There's no right or wrong way to divide housework, as long as the division feels fair to those carrying it out. Jeff says, "I usually do more of the 'guy' jobs, like taking out the garbage and cleaning out the gutters. Robyn does the grocery shopping, although I come along, and the cooking, although I try to help. Other things, like gardening and cleaning, we share equally." Mark and Cary take a different approach. As Mark explains:

It's good to start out by throwing away all preconceptions about gender roles. Once they're gone, you can either pick them back up or leave them on the curb. There should be no convention that forces a woman to cook and sew, and there should equally be no convention that gives her a head trip if she enjoys doing those things. I do the laundry 'cause it's easier for me to handle the back stairs with a load in my arms, and because I derive a morbid pleasure being in a basement that reminds me so much of an Edgar Allan Poe story. Cary does any plumbing work we need done because that's her thing—she can talk to you intelligently for ten minutes about the difference between an Allen wrench and a screwdriver. I clean the cat box with an ancient pair of chopsticks 'cause that's what my Japanese father did, and I can imagine that it's something that my Samurai ancestors were doing during the Meiji Era. Allocate chores according to personality quirks, and you're golden.

Cary sounds equally enthusiastic:

Mark changes the light bulbs because he's tall and I can't reach them. We're pretty equitable on other domestic duties. For a long time I did almost all of the cooking, mostly because I really enjoyed it. Lately however, since my schoolwork has kept me absurdly busy, Mark has pretty much taken over. Mark does a lot of the laundry because I find the basement incredibly creepy. I usually clean the toilet because my threshold for dirty bathrooms is lower, but Mark typically does the vacuuming. We seem to be pretty evenly spread on domestic duties.

Partners are amicable about their division of housework tend to agree that chores should be assigned based on preferences: the person who despises the chore least gets to do it. Second, they advise taking people's different cleanliness standards into account. As Cary explains, "People should be aware of the other person's tolerance for mess and dirt, and strive to keep the house at the level of the person with the lower threshold. If there's no agreement on that and a large difference between thresholds, then one person will end up doing a lot more work and more than likely become resentful." In our own kitchen, Dorian gets annoyed when the top of the stove gets covered with cooking spills, and can't believe that Marshall considers the kitchen clean when the stove is still covered in a layer of baked-on food. On the other hand, Marshall has a much lower threshold for the cleanliness of the kitchen floor, and is incredulous that Dorian doesn't see the crumbs. As long as Dorian scrubs the stovetop and Marshall sweeps and mops, we're happy.

Instead of assigning tasks to a person, Christopher D. and his partner assign housework time. "Sometimes, we both set a day or an hour or some chunk of time for us to both do housework and then we'll work on different projects in the house," he says, admitting, "It's often when company is coming."

Some housework questions to get you started:

- Where are you on the neatness scale that runs from "Horizontal surfaces should stay clear and empty" to "Piles, piles, everywhere"?
- Where are you on the cleanliness scale that runs from "Pillows that fall on the floor need to be washed" to "A little dirt never killed anyone"?
- What household tasks do you like the least, and which don't you mind as much? Are there any you enjoy?
- How different are your standards for neatness and cleanliness? What do you think your major differences will be over housework?
- How will you divide housework in a way that feels fair to both of you?

MOVING DAY—TIME TO CELEBRATE!

When moving in together happens after a wedding, it comes with celebration, new sheets and appliances, and sometimes even the groom carrying the bride over the threshold. When the same move takes place before or without a wedding, though, friends and family generally yawn (or in some circles, treat you to a lecture about the error of your ways). You may already own a good blender, but moving in together is nevertheless a rite of passage that deserves to be recognized. It's a new stage in your relationship, and it's time to celebrate! Relationship educator Kollman says, "I would love to see people do a ritual when they move in together that makes them conscious that it's going to get bumpy. I think of flying in an airplane, when they tell me that I'm going to hit some turbulent air. It's very important to think of that process as normal, natural, and supposed to happen. If you do, you won't freak out as much and think something is wrong with you or you partner."[19]

In Quebec, some say it's common for newlycohabs (maybe someday it'll have the same ring as newlyweds) to throw a party.[20] Even if you just send out for pizza after a day of carrying boxes, eat it by candlelight. Toast your decision and your future together. Let your friends and relatives know that your relationship has reached a new milestone. Living together will always have bumps along the way, but thanks to all the work you did in advance, you can feel confident you've gotten the best possible start.

REFLECTING BACK[21]

THE EXPERIENCES WE have in childhood and young adulthood can powerfully shape our views on issues like marriage, cohabitation, and divorce. This exercise invites you to reflect on some of those memories. Afterwards, sharing memories can bring you closer to your partner, help you understand each other better, and provide starting points for discussions about how these memories, thoughts, and feelings affect your relationship today.

Sit back, get comfortable, and, if you wish, close your eyes after each sentence or two to take a moment to remember and reflect. Or, you and your partner can take turns reading this section to each other, pausing for a moment after the questions. It works best to have one partner think through all the questions before trading places.

Realize that memories come in all types: vivid and hazy, joyous and painful. You can spend as much or as little time as you want thinking about each of these questions. Also, not everything listed below will apply to you. If it doesn't, feel free to skip over it or to think of a similar situation that does apply.

Think back to when you were a child. Think of the place where you lived and the neighborhood where you grew up. If you lived in more than one place, pick the one that stands out most to you. Remember what the faces of your parents, stepparents, or guardians looked like to you then. What do you remember about their relationship? How did they get along? Did they express affection and love for each other? If so, how? If not, why do you think they didn't? When they disagreed with each other, how did they resolve their conflicts? How did they communicate with each other? How do you feel about the decisions your parents have made in their relationships?

What values did your parents, stepparents, or guardians show you or teach you about family? About conflict? About love? How did they shape your thinking about these issues?

As a child, how did you feel about marriage? Weddings? Cohabitation? How about terms like commitment? 'Til death do us part? What did your parents or guardians teach you, if anything, about those terms? How did you feel about what they said? What did your siblings teach you about these ideas? Your grandparents? Other relatives?

As a child, did you imagine yourself getting married? What did you think the wedding would be like? Did you think about having a husband or wife? If you imagined yourself getting married, how old did you think you would be? Did you ever pretend to get married to a schoolmate? What was that like? Did you attend weddings as a child, teenager, or young adult? What stands out for you from those events? What did you think about things that the brides, grooms, clergy, or justices of the peace said as part of the ceremonies? How did you feel about the weddings overall? Has your opinion changed as you've gotten older?

What did you think about divorce when you were a child? If your parents divorced, what do you remember of your thoughts and feelings at the time? How do you feel about their divorce today? Does it influence your view of marriage? Whether your parents are divorced or not, how did you feel when you heard about divorce in the news, in school, or from your friends?

When you were young, did you attend a church, synagogue, mosque, or other religious institution? What were you taught about marriage, cohabitation, and divorce there? How did it make you feel? If you attend a church, synagogue, mosque, or other religious institution today, are the messages about marriage and cohabitation different, or the same? How so?

In school, did your teachers talk to you about marriage and relationships? If so, what did they say and how did you feel? Did you or anyone you know get married while they were still in high school? What was that like? Did you have a class where planning a wedding was a class assignment? If so, what was it like? If you went to college, were marriage and cohabitation discussed in any of your classes? If so, what was said and what did you think about it? Did anything change your perception of these subjects?

Have you been in a serious relationship before this one? If so, what was that like? Did you talk about, or make the decision to move in together, get engaged, get married? How did you feel about those decisions then, and how do you feel about them now? Is there anything you would do differently if you could do it over again? If you are divorced or experienced the breakup of a serious relationship, how do you feel about it today? Does it influence your view of cohabitation or marriage?

Think forward to the present. In your circle of friends, are most of them single or in relationships? Married or not? Have you attended any of their weddings or commitment ceremonies? Have you had in-depth discussions with them about cohabitation and marriage? How do your friends' words and actions affect your thinking?

What do your parents and relatives say to you today about cohabitation and marriage? Have their opinions changed since you were a child? How do you feel about what they are saying today?

Have you read any books or articles or seen any movies or television shows that affected your thinking about marriage and cohabitation? What struck you about them? Are there any books or movies that represent the kind of relationship you'd like to have? What appeals to you about these relationships? Are your expectations realistic?

What other things have shaped your views of marriage, cohabitation, and relationships?

What stands out for you the most as you think about all the memories you have just revisited?

TWO

"WHY AREN'T YOU MARRIED?"

Answers to the Question Everyone Asks

EVERYONE WANTS TO know why unmarried couples haven't tied the knot. Parents and grandparents perfect the art of hint-dropping. Journalists wonder why we "won't commit": everyone we talk to manages to pop the question. At the end of our research interviews, when we'd ask people in unmarried relationships what they'd like to see in a book on the subject, most said they wanted to know why *other* people weren't married. They wanted the opportunity to talk and hear about different people's choices in a nonjudgmental context.

Below are the ten most common reasons cohabitors aren't married. While many of us have multiple answers to the question, "Why aren't you married?", no one says *everything* on this list is true for them. The reasons closest to one person's heart may not apply to the next person at all.

REASON NUMBER ONE:
It's a Step Between Dating and Marriage

The most common reason people live with a partner is because it's the logical "next step." They are dating, in love, but not ready to marry. April, for instance, says that moving in together was the next step in keeping a relationship that's going well.

> *Recently we decided to move in together, but not yet [get] married . . . We want to be able to spend more time together, be closer, and do more together . . . I see this stage of our relationship as being transitionary, and once we have settled into our life together, we can work out affording a wedding and starting a family. We are in no rush. But we don't want to waste our lives being apart from each other, when we can be together right now.[1]*

Since most couples today live together before they marry, cohabitation has become a normal stage between dating and marriage. In fact, despite headlines about how the average marrying age has climbed, people are still forming live-in relationships around the same age they always have. Many are cohabitations first, before they become marriages.[2] In *A Walk Down the Aisle*, Kate Cohen likens modern cohabitation to "old European betrothal . . . an extended transition between the single and the married state."[3]

Figuring out if your partner is really, truly the person you want to marry makes sense—and it's even better if you figure it out *before* you get married. By far the most common reason couples move in together is to test their compatibility.[4] As authors and partners Johnette Duff and George Truitt put it, "No matter how many Spanish lessons you take, you have to live in the country to really speak the language."[5] Jenna, for instance, says that even though she and her partner dated for a year, it wasn't until they moved in together that she realized how they'd always been on their best behavior with each other. "I hadn't realized how much I'd only been showing him the good parts," she says. "We had a lot of emotion to work through that hadn't been there before." The experience of seeing the not-so-pretty parts of each other—going "to the really ugly places where we had to go, and then turning around back toward each other" and working through them—is what ultimately convinced her that their relationship was marriage material.

Both in their thirties, Marie and Chris moved into an artists' collective together. Marie loves Chris, and wants to be very sure of what she wants for the long-term before she makes any decisions about matrimony.

> *The jury's still out, because I feel like I'm still figuring out what I want to get, or what I need, from a lifetime relationship. I used to have ideals when I was younger that that relationship would be everything for me, but I learned a long time ago that that wasn't true. When I met Chris I really started to get into that process of thinking through what elements I need in a long-term partner. And I'm still doing it.*

For many unmarried couples, cohabiting is a way of slowing down the courtship process. With few exceptions, there's no time bomb that will explode if you haven't gotten married by some arbitrary date. And a little hand-wringing won't kill your future in-laws, either.

REASON NUMBER TWO:
The Time Isn't Right

A few decades ago, the general expectation was for young people to get married as soon as they graduated from high school or college. "Ring by spring" was the old saying for college women hoping for an engagement before graduation. Today, on the other hand, many people see their twenties as a time to get their first job, go to graduate or professional school, travel the world, or have some adventures before settling down. Even for those who have been in a relationship for years, marrying often isn't at the top of the agenda.

Weddings are also grander and more expensive than ever before—the average wedding costs nearly the amount the average American earns in a year.[6] Saving for a wedding—even a small one—can be a monumental task. Couples who want the celebration of their dreams often choose to delay marrying while they sock away money. A twenty-six-year-old woman says:

> We actually don't have anything against marriage, except that it's too expensive to have a wedding like we want to have. We are not from wealthy families who can help support the expenses, so we have been trying to save for a wedding we want.[7]

Her experience is increasingly common, and weddings aren't the only reason young people are saving up. Elizabeth and Joey, both nineteen, have been dating for five years and live with Joey's parents. Elizabeth says they want to marry, but only when they can afford an apartment of their own: "We both hold full time jobs, I also attend school, we pay rent, own a car, buy our own groceries and take care of each other financially and emotionally . . . We are looking to move out when we are more stable financially . . . We wish to marry someday when we're ready."[8]

Jodi and her partner, Chad, had been together for three years when we interviewed them. She said:

> He wants to get a house before we get married so that my credit doesn't affect his credit. I want time to plan and do an actual wedding if I'm going to do it. Otherwise, there's really no point, as far as I'm concerned. The bottom line to me is that the marriage is just a legal piece of paper. Your marriage is between you and

the person you're with. It doesn't have anything to do with that document. I'm as much married to Chad now as I will be the day I marry him, if I ever do.

A year later, we received a pleased e-mail from Jodi saying she and Chad had set a date for their wedding. Indeed, left alone for long enough, the majority of male-female couples who live together will eventually tie the knot (usually to choruses of "Finally!" and "It's about time!").[9] Making sure the time is right for *you*—not just for your parents and friends—increases the chance that your union will be a happy one.

REASON NUMBER THREE:
Not Becoming a Wife (or a Husband)

Conventional wisdom holds that men don't want to get married, and women do. We find the general trend is quite the opposite. It's *women*, not men, who more often want to delay marriage or choose not to marry at all. Most recent surveys of unmarried men and women find that men are significantly more interested in matrimony than women are.[10] Some women hesitate before signing up for an institution that didn't start out particularly female-friendly. There are those who still don't like to think about the days when women were traded like property from man to man. Among the Romans, for example, marriage vows were exchanged between the groom and the bride's father, while the bride herself stood silent, and in weddings in the early Middle Ages, the groom "pledged his good faith and stepped on the bride's foot, a simple but definitive demonstration of husbandhood."[11] Even today, in traditional Protestant ceremonies, the father of the bride "gives her away" to the groom.

In many cultures, marriage still places significant restrictions on women. That's one of the reasons it held little appeal for Teri:

> *For me, as a Chinese woman, marriage was never a very attractive option. It's not like the American stereotype of marriage where you are basically carted off by your knight in shining armor. In traditional Chinese families, when women are married they lose a lot of freedom, a lot of individuality and self-respect, because they are farmed out to their husband's household and they become the low man on the totem pole. In Chinese culture marriage is more of a losing who you are, kind of a sacrifice, giving up your family connections to take on someone else's.*

The loss of selfhood in order to take on the role of "wife" isn't limited to specific cultures. Wendy says that given her experience of how easy it was to find herself inadvertently transformed into the role overnight, she wants to avoid marrying again.

I remember my first little house with my new husband. After we got married and moved in, I went down to the kitchen in the morning and started to make break-fast for us. And he sat at the table reading the paper. And we never did that before, but now that we were married, and we were in a house, this is how you do it. So you play house. It was weird.

When that marriage didn't work out, Wendy decided that being in an unmar-ried relationship made it easier to avoid what journalist Dalma Heyn calls "mar-riage shock" (more about this on page 231). Eighteen years later, Wendy and her partner are still together and happily unmarried.

We remember a woman who attended one of the workshops we gave about alternatives to marriage. Everything about her was vibrant, and she told us how her boyfriend had initially liked how funny and outgoing she was. After she married him, though, she said she felt a great deal of pressure from him and from the outside world to change her personality. It might be OK for a girlfriend to wear bright sweaters and crack lots of jokes, people seemed to be saying, but a wife should dress appropriately, speak appropriately, and behave altogether dif-ferently. She struggled within the "wife" role, and eventually got divorced. While there are certainly women who can define being a wife in a way that works well for them, for others it just feels like a bad fit.

There are expectations of what it means to be "husband," too. Previously-married men don't raise the issue of the husband role as often, but a few men do say they're uncomfortable with assumptions about what husbands "ought to" do or be. Husbands, for example, are often expected to be the primary bread-winners, and to be able to fix the carburetor and patch that hole in the wall. Some men who want to share the housework equally—change diapers in the middle of the night, or even stay home with the kids—find it's easier to divide roles in a gender-neutral way in an unmarried relationship. Indeed, studies con-firm that both men and women with less traditional gender roles are more likely to live with an unmarried partner.[12]

While women once depended on husbands to clothe and feed them, today having a husband has become a choice. Laina makes more money than her part-ner, has her own money saved for retirement, and says that for her, marrying simply isn't necessary.

In this day and age when so many women can be financially independent, they don't need a man to be making money so they can be alive. That's my situation. I don't need my partner's income in order to live comfortably. I just don't see any reason for getting married.

People who work with victims of domestic violence, or who are themselves sur-vivors of abusive or controlling relationships, cite concerns about the freedom of married women. Some wives feel trapped in abusive situations, especially if their money or property belongs partly or entirely to their abusive husband. Research suggests women feel more control over their own lives if they're not married.[13] Now widowed, Betty says that being with her unmarried partner, Ken, makes her feel both safer and more independent than being married did.

> When I had a husband, he had to know where I was every minute of the day. He used to check the mileage on the car when he left in the morning, that was his tabs on me. It took me so long with Ken to realize that if I went out somewhere and I was going to be a little late, I didn't have to call him and give him this big explanation. He just let me be, and that was a whole new idea to me, because I had been someone's possession, I think, before that.

On the other hand, some lawyers say that female victims of domestic violence can benefit from the property protection that legal divorce provides. This is clearly an area where there are no easy answers.

In the last few decades, millions of husbands and wives have proved that it *is* possible to redefine those words for today's relationships. Wives can wear aprons if they want to, or they can don power suits, hiking gear, or sexy lingerie (or all three on different days of the week). Husbands can still be the primary breadwinner, or they can be painters whose wives pay the bills, or they can stay home and nurture babies. The arrangements are ultimately up to the people involved, whether they're married or not, but for some it's easier to avoid roles outside of the conventional expectations of matrimony.

BOUQUET TOSS FALLS FLAT WHEN WOMEN AREN'T CLAMORING TO BE WIVES

ONCE UPON A time, not so long ago, the tossing of the bride's bouquet was a popular wedding custom. Tradition said that the lucky woman who caught the bouquet would be the next one to marry, and single women would crowd around competitively for their chance to grab the flowers as they sailed through the air.

Times are changing. As wifehood has become less of a priority for many women, so has catching the bouquet. At one wedding we attended, single women were so reluctant to participate that the groom had to identify unattached women one by one and lead each into position. Once a group had been assembled, the band struck up an expectant chord, the guests turned to watch, the bride tossed her bouquet over her shoulder—and the crowd of women parted, avoiding the flowers' airborne trajectory so they fell on the floor, untouched. Not to be deterred, the bride made a second toss attempt. This time, the bouquet flew directly into one woman's arms, and she caught it.

Anecdotal evidence suggests the scene we witnessed isn't uncommon. One woman posted this on a bridal forum online:

> *I have had to suffer through way too many bouquet tosses, and have yet to see anyone try to catch the bouquet of [her] own free will! At the last wedding I went to, we all bribed one woman to take the fall. When the bride tossed the bouquet, ten women took one step back, and one woman stepped forward to catch it. When questioned afterwards, we all swore that we had fought tooth and nail to catch it. And our friend Nicole has ten favors to cash in.*[14]

Some brides today choose to forgo the tradition, but most proceed, despite sometimes unenthusiastic crowds of bouquet-catchers.[15] Either way, the custom's sagging popularity provides commentary on young women's eagerness—or lack thereof—to get hitched.

REASON NUMBER FOUR:
Divorce

Sometimes divorce feels like it's everywhere. Even people who haven't been divorced themselves usually have parents, children, relatives, or a close friend who has been. Divorce drains some of the romance from images of marriage. If close to half of marriages end in divorce, couples today figure they need to be doubly and triply careful. After all, the joke goes, the number one cause of divorce is marriage. One of the most common reasons people say they cohabit is to make sure their match is a good one before making a lifetime commitment.

The majority of cohabiting couples include at least one person who's been married previously,[16] and people who have been divorced may wisely be less likely to rush into getting married. Alan, for instance, was clearly in no hurry to marry Skip after having been divorced before—they're the couple who married eighteen years into their relationship. When he and Skip were considering whether they wanted to get married, he said:

Before I was married the first time, I felt a lot of pressure to be married. That's what I was supposed to do. I'd be successful as a person if I found a partner, got married. And now that I've been there and done that, it's not so important. I've done it, and I know it's an interesting thing to do, but I don't need it in order to complete myself.

Divorced decades ago, Joan says marrying again wouldn't even occur to her. "Ever since I got out of my marriage in 1978, getting married again has never been a thing that I have for one second considered as a possibility," she told us. "I would just as soon jump off a cliff."

Divorce affects more than the divorcing couple. Amy grew up witnessing a marriage that ended and an unmarried relationship that worked well:

> My parents split up when I was a kid. Later my father met another woman. They been together for twenty years and have never gotten married. I grew up in a context where it was not important to get married. I saw one marriage break up, and I saw two people who did not get married stay together for the rest of my life, and I think that drove home a point to me that marital status doesn't really matter.

Divorce can affect gay and lesbian couples as well, as Kurt and his partner have found. After nineteen years together, they have no plans to get married if or when same-sex marriage is legalized.

> Most of the people we have seen get married are divorced within a few years. Our relationship seems to keep going on and on, while everyone else keeps breaking up. So we are thinking, what is the use of a marriage, if they cannot stay together?

But divorce isn't necessarily the primary issue for all divorced people or children of divorce—many have also known plenty of people who had wonderful, lasting marriages. Indeed, most children with divorced parents do get married when they grow up. Most divorced people marry again.[17] Human beings are resilient, able to witness the end of an important relationship and still go on to have other long, fulfilling relationships or marriages in the future. Seeing or experiencing divorce may make us less naive, but that's not entirely a bad thing: if movies were our only source we'd think marriage was all about moonlit walks and kisses stolen after the kids are in bed. Seeing a variety of married and unmarried relationships shows that marriage isn't a magical cloak that ensures a good relationship; that unmarried partnerships can also be defined by love and commitment; and that many veterans of divorce go on to have happy, long-lasting marriages.

REASON NUMBER FIVE:
Staying Away from City Hall

Hidden behind the tall wedding cake and the flowers lies a legal contract. Government requirements specify who is allowed to get married, what it costs, what you have to do first (blood tests, paperwork, fees, etc.). Getting married automatically triggers a myriad of state and federal laws that give married couples

SEEKING ALTERNATIVES TO MARRIAGE: A LONG TRADITION

MODERN-DAY COUPLES who choose not to marry follow a long historical tradition. Notable examples include Heloise and Abelard in the Middle Ages, the nineteenth century "free love" movement, John Stuart Mill, and Emma Goldman.

Heloise and Abelard: Medieval Lovers

In the twelfth century, Heloise was passionate about her lover, the scholar Peter Abelard, and equally passionate about her disinterest in wedlock. She wrote to him, "God knows I never sought anything in you except yourself; I looked for no marriage bond, no marriage potion. . . . The name of *wife* may seem more sacred or more binding, but sweeter for me will always be the word *mistress*, or, if you will permit me, that of *concubine* or *whore*."[18] After Heloise gave birth to their child and Heloise's uncle found out about the relationship, the couple did marry in secret at Abelard's insistence. Heloise always maintained that she would have preferred to maintain an unmarried relationship. Their story ended tragically, with Heloise sent by her uncle to a convent, Abelard castrated, and the two continuing to exchange devoted letters until their deaths. Heloise and Abelard remain one of the best-known pairs of star-crossed lovers in history.

Abelard and Heloise

Free Lovers: Affection Trumps Legalities

The "free love" movement of the 1830s through the 1850s encompassed a broad range of activists and communities that critiqued marriage, some calling for the institution to be thrown out altogether. Many free lovers believed that love between men and women was purer if it was based on affection alone, separate from any legal or religious recognition. When free love advocates challenged their opponents to debate marriage, halls would overflow with raucous audiences. One 1840 debate between movement leaders and antagonists sold 5,000 tickets and looked more like a sports event than a political one, each side's fans loudly rooting for their position and jeering the other.[19]

Some free love leaders, like theologian John Humphrey Noyes, based their arguments in Christianity. Noyes wrote, "When the will of God is done on earth as it is in heaven, there will be no marriage. . . . In a holy community there is no more reason why sexual intercourse should be restrained by law, than why eating and drinking should be; and there is as little occasion for shame in the one case as in the other." Noyes formed a small community of like-minded people in Vermont, until he was charged with adultery in 1847 and fled to upstate New York to form the explicitly anti-marriage Oneida community.[20]

The founder of Francis Heights, a similar community west of Cleveland, called marriage "that abomination of abominations" and shut out anyone who believed in the institution. Modern Times, an 1850s community on what is now Long Island, also became a haven for people opposed to matrimony. The residents of Modern Times believed women became slaves in marriage, and many members advocated for women's independence so they wouldn't need to rely on husbands.

The free love movement was short-lived but popular: thousands of people moved to the radical communities around the country where they could put their ideas into daily practice. Their views of marriage also sparked public debate, as newspaper editors opened up columns for argument about marriage and lecturers traveled the country to present an anti-matrimony perspective to the masses.[21] The issue even captured the attention of John Stuart Mill, the English philosopher and economist known for his essay about political freedom, *On Liberty*.

John Stuart Mill and Harriet Taylor: Re-Writing the Marriage Contract

Mill's respect for freedom extended beyond his political views to his personal life. When he married, he tried to reshape the standard contract in which husbands automatically "owned" their wives. The author of *The Subjection of Women*, he commented that since women had no choice but to get married, and since husbands were allowed to mistreat their wives, becoming a wife was akin to becoming a slave. When he prepared to marry his beloved, Harriet Taylor, in 1851, he wrote a statement rejecting the legal powers he would acquire over her in marriage, concluding that Harriet "retains in all respects whatever the same absolute freedom of action and freedom of disposal of herself and of all that does or may at any time belong to her, as if no such marriage had taken place; and I absolutely disclaim and repudiate all pretension to have acquired any rights whatever by virtue of such marriage." The couple lived together, working on articles and books about women's rights, until she died of tuberculosis seven years later.[22]

Lillian Harman and Edwin Walker: No Legal Marriage Contract

The 1887 wedding ceremony of activists and writers Lillian Harman and Edwin Walker contained two speeches declaring their marriage to be a private contract, and "deny[ing] the right of society, in the form of church and state, to regulate it." They did not get a marriage license or have the ceremony performed by a judge, minister, or justice of the peace, and Lillian kept her own name. The day after the ceremony, they were arrested for failing to meet Kansas's marriage requirements. A jury sentenced them both to jail, Lillian for forty-five days and Edwin for seventy-five.[23]

Emma Goldman: "Marriage Is a Failure"

A century ago, activist Emma Goldman argued that marriage was a poor investment, especially for women. In her 1911 essay "Marriage and Love," excerpted below, she cites the 8 percent divorce rate as one of her items of proof. In comparison to today's rate of 40 percent or higher, 8 percent would be a figure many would celebrate!

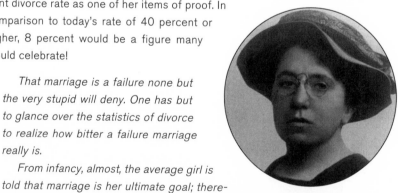

Emma Goldman

> *That marriage is a failure none but the very stupid will deny. One has but to glance over the statistics of divorce to realize how bitter a failure marriage really is.*
>
> *From infancy, almost, the average girl is told that marriage is her ultimate goal; therefore her training and education must be directed towards that end. Like the mute beast fattened for slaughter, she is prepared for that. Yet, strange to say, she is allowed to know*

much less about her function as wife and mother than the ordinary arti-
san of his trade. [After marrying] she learns soon enough that the
home, though not so large a prison as the factory, has more solid doors
and bars. It is not important whether the husband is a brute or a dar-
ling. What I wish to prove is that marriage guarantees woman a home
only by the grace of her husband. There she moves about in his home,
year after year until her aspect of life and human affairs becomes as
flat, narrow, and drab as her surroundings. Small wonder if she
becomes a nag, petty, quarrelsome, gossipy, unbearable, thus driving
the man from the house. She could not go, if she wanted to; there is
no place to go.

But the child, how is it to be protected, if not for marriage? After all,
is not that the most important consideration? The sham, the hypocrisy
of it! Marriage protecting the child, yet thousands of children destitute
and homeless. Marriage protecting the child, yet orphan asylums and
reformatories overcrowded, the Society for the Prevention of Cruelty to
Children keeping busy in rescuing the little victims from "loving" par-
ents, to place them under more loving care. Oh, the mockery of it!

Some day, some day men and women will rise, they will reach the
mountain peak, they will meet big and strong and free, ready to receive,
to partake, and to bask in the golden rays of love. If the world is ever
to give birth to true companionship and oneness, not marriage, but love
will be the parent.[24]

Fortunately, marriage has become a much friendlier institution for women
since Goldman's time and many of her claims no longer apply. Nonetheless,
her vision of "true companionship and oneness" ring true to many even today.

different rights and obligations than unmarried people. Legal experts point out that the marriage contract is the only contract most people sign without having had any opportunity to read or modify its terms.

For a variety of reasons, some people prefer to keep their personal relationships out of government records. Becky, whose unmarried relationship has now lasted twenty-one years and counting, says:

> *One of my reasons for not getting married is that I don't feel the state has a right to say who you can sleep with, who you can have a kid with, who you can live with, and who you can split up from! Of course, when I said that, my parents thought the main reason that I was doing this was so I could split up whenever I felt like it.*

Martha came to a similar conclusion:

> *The whole idea of making a contract with the state so that you have the right to have sex with somebody, and then when you want to stop having sex with them you have to pay a whole bunch of money, doesn't seem to be very smart.*

Some people are simply uncomfortable with the idea that the government has the right to decide who is allowed to marry and who is not. Jennifer says that the rules reveal a system that is arbitrary on some level. She's uncomfortable with the government's role in deciding which relationships "count" and which don't.

> *By engaging in this act you are basically saying that someone has the right to decide who can get married and who can't. I mean, technically, we could go into City Hall and ask for a marriage license, and they could say, "No, you can't have one." They could say, "Well, she's too short and he's too tall, and we want five-foot-five blond-haired, blue-eyed people, and we don't think you should get married." I mean, it doesn't happen that way, fortunately, but it says that they have the power to decide.*

Even if it seems preposterous to think that the clerk at the window would refuse to grant a license for such reasons, governments do have a long history of restricting who can get married. Before the civil war, slaves were not allowed to marry in slaveholding states. Until the late 1940s and 1950s, marriage between blacks and whites was illegal in the United States, and an Alabama law against interracial marriage was repealed only as recently as 2000.[25] According to marriage historian E.J. Graff, Prussian states did not allow disabled or blind people to marry at all, students could not marry before graduation, artisans could not marry before completing their apprenticeships, and peasants could not marry noblemen.[26] A similar list of people who are not allowed to marry exists today in the United States, including some prisoners, some mentally disabled people, and people with a same-sex partner.

REASON NUMBER SIX:
Finances

Getting married can definitely be worthwhile financially. In addition to receiving an average of over $7,000 worth of wedding gifts[27] and heirlooms, newlyweds can share a health insurance policy, usually worth several thousand dollars a year. Almost half of couples save money on their income taxes by marrying, and some employers give honeymooners extra paid vacation time. A few lucky couples get monetary rewards for tying the knot, like the couple whose parents offered them $20,000 toward buying a house if they would get married. (They did.) It is perfectly rational to consider a potential payoff in one's calculations!

But some people who would like to get married can't afford their vision of married life, which might involve an expensive celebration and the expense of children. Historically, marriage rates usually rise during eras of economic prosperity and drop in economic slumps.[28] Marshall's grandparents, for example, started dating in the Great Depression, but didn't marry until a few years later when his grandfather was able to get a steady job at the post office.

Many senior citizens and others with deceased spouses receive pensions and annuities that would cease if the survivor remarried. Often, the amount of money the surviving spouse receives each month makes up a significant portion of the total household income. For one in four unmarried senior women, Social Security is their only source of income.[29] Kathryn, age sixty-five, has been with her partner for twenty-one years, since the death of her husband. She explained to her adult daughter the reason they're not married: "'It's because of finances. I deserve your father's pension. I worked hard to get it. I earned it, and it's mine.' Money's kind of the final thing," she says. "You can't really argue with that." Combined with increasing cultural acceptance, this is a major factor behind growing numbers of unmarried partnerships between seniors.

Sherry and her partner each have children from previous marriages, and wish they could afford to marry.

> My previous husband was killed in a coal-mining accident, and the state compensates us for that loss with worker's compensation benefits. If I remarry, my children and I lose those benefits. They increase our income by about $24,000 a year. It's a big difference. Between the two of us we have six children—car insurance alone is unreal. Without those benefits, there's no way that we could live.

Finances are also a major issue for severely disabled people. Cheryl, for instance, is an able-bodied woman whose partner is a quadriplegic. His disability benefits pay for personal care assistants around the clock. If Cheryl married her partner, her income would be included in the calculations of benefits eligibility, and he would lose an estimated $1,525 a month and no longer be able to pay his assistants. Yet Cheryl can't afford to become his full-time caretaker—she has to work to support herself. She says that they didn't struggle with the decision; marriage simply isn't an option. According to Simi Litvak, Senior Researcher at the World Institute on Disability, such situations are quite common among people whose well-being depends on disability benefits.[30]

The "marriage tax penalty" has been the focus of much political attention (see Is There Really a Tax on Marriage?, page 149), since some couples' income taxes increase if they get married. A 1998 *USA Today* article featured a photo of Sharon Mallory and Darryl Pierce, a couple who decided not to get married after their accountant told them they would have to pay an additional $2,800 in taxes and forfeit a $900 refund.[31] Clarice and Ed, a couple in their sixties who have been unmarried to each other for twenty-one years, say their accountant had similar news: "We joke that when our accountants get together and say we should get married, we'll get married."

REASON NUMBER SEVEN:
Religious Aspects

Marriage and religion have a long and complex relationship. Although it is certainly possible to have a nonreligious wedding (at City Hall, or on a beach attended by a justice of the peace), many people feel that the institution of marriage is inextricably tied to religion. Libby Garland, a Senior Fellow at the National Jewish Center for Learning and Leadership, wrote, "I find [that all weddings], even secular ones filled with secular people, feel religious. It's as if weddings have absorbed all the leftover energy of jettisoned religious observances. Weddings are the high holidays of American culture."[32] The data shows that there is a connection between how religious people are and their choices related to marriage. On average, people who get married *without* ever living together are more enthusiastic churchgoers than those who cohabit, who tend to show up for services less frequently or not at all.[33]

Non-religious people, those who have had negative experiences with religious institutions, and those from traditions with less emphasis on marriage may feel less of a need to get married. Dave, for instance, says marriage has less of a draw for him because of religion's role (or lack thereof) in his life.

I'm not a religious person. I understand marriage can be non-religious, with a justice of the peace in your backyard if you want it to, but there's still a connection with a big church wedding and being in church, and I try to avoid churches as much as possible. There still feels like a fundamental connection between marriage and religion.

But people of faith grapple with the marriage decision, too. Chapter 3 explores this issue in more detail, including situations where religious faith is a source of pressure to marry, and how people have managed to remain faithful to their religion while being in an unmarried relationship. Amy struggles with the conflict between feminism and what she has been taught about Judaism, but she has decided that marriage is not for her:[34]

In the Jewish culture, being married and having children is very important. I feel a little guilty once in a while. But I find the way women are seen in Judaism as only mothers and wives offensive, and I do not want to have children. I am not going to be the good Jewish wife and mother.

Some religions have different words and definitions for marriagelike relationships, in which the legal part of marriage is an option, not a requirement. For Wiccans like Michaela, marriage is more of a multi-step process.

Wiccans have what's known as a handfasting ceremony, which is the equivalent to marriage but slightly different. Traditionally, in our belief system what happens is you get married for a year and a day, as sort of a trial period to see if you are sure this is what you want to do. After that year and a day, in its idealized form both parties would be able to say, "No, this isn't working," and walk away with no hard feelings. But then after that year and a day, if you decide, "Yes, this is the way we want to go, the way we want to live our lives. We are the people for each other forever," then you become handfasted.

In many ways like a marriage ceremony, the handfasting ceremony takes its name from the part of the ritual in which the couple's hands or arms are temporarily bound together with cord or ribbon to symbolize their bond. Although traditions vary, many Wiccan people believe that the couple can decide how long the handfasting will last. Some couples have a new ceremony each year (like a re-commitment ceremony); some make a commitment for five or ten years; some commit for a lifetime (like a traditional marriage ceremony); and some who believe in reincarnation make a commitment that will endure into all future lifetimes.

Why don't

melons get

married?

They cantaloupe

REASON NUMBER EIGHT:
Marriage Doesn't Represent the Relationship

Most people assume marriage to be a monogamous, lifelong sexual relationship between a man and a woman who live together and may have children. Of course there's room for negotiation: there are gay and lesbian couples who consider themselves to be married (even if they can't legally marry), married couples without children, group marriages (not legally recognized), and open marriages. How you actually live your life as a married person is limited only by your imagination, and possibly your state's laws. But the white picket fence image persists. For some people, that's reason enough to skip the marriage, or to delay long enough to establish patterns that work better for the relationship.

Choosing not to have children, not to be monogamous, or not to count on being together forever are a few common ways people alter the conventions.

▶ Childfree

Although childfree living is a more acceptable choice than it once was, many married couples still report that after getting hitched the pressure to marry is quickly replaced by pressure to procreate. In some cultures and times in history, marriages were only considered "real" or "consummated" once the couple had a child, so a couple without children wouldn't be considered married at all.[35]

Many people marry because they're eager to make babies or when a partner becomes pregnant, while others feel pressured to have kids only because they're married. That cultural link means that people who aren't on a parenting path may see no reason to sign a marriage certificate. Research confirms that the average unmarried couple wants fewer children than the average married pair.[36] As Laina said, "I knew that I didn't want to have children. And I just couldn't figure out why there was any good reason to get married if you weren't going to have children."

Many who are "finished" having children—as with most people in their fifties or older—don't see a need for matrimony. Nancy, for instance, has grown children from when she was married before, and has been in her current unmarried relationship for fourteen years. Now, at age fifty-nine, she says, "I suppose if I were a lot younger and we were going to have children, we'd probably get married." And younger people who make a conscious decision not to have children find that choice can relieve some of the marriage pressure they otherwise would have felt.

RESOURCES FOR CHILDFREE LIVING

THERE'S A THRIVING childfree community with websites, national and regional gatherings, listservs, and books. Here are some places to get started.

alt.support.childfree
> *An online discussion group.*

The Childfree-by-Choice Pages
www.childfree.net
> *Links, articles, and books about childfree life, and information about how to join the childfree e-mail discussion list.*

No Kidding
www.nokidding.net
> *A social club with regional chapters around the world.*

Pride and Joy: The Lives and Passions of Women Without Children,
> by Terri Casey

The Chosen Lives of Childfree Men by Patricia W. Lunneborg

Barren in the Promised Land, by Elaine Tyler May

► Monogamy-free

Monogamy is another central part of the marriage assumption (although only 16 percent of the 853 cultures on record urge adults to be monogamous, so we Westerners are in the minority on this one).[37] Wearing a wedding ring is usually assumed to mean not only, "I'm married," but also, "I will not have an intimate relationship with anyone except my spouse." Some couples, though, have made a mutual, conscious decision *not* to have their relationship be monogamous— those who have open relationships, multiple partners, or are polyamorous (honestly non-monogamous). Those who have chosen non-monogamy may feel that getting married would send exactly the opposite message. Michaela says she wouldn't feel the same freedom to create a relationship that works for her if she were married:

> *We have an open relationship in that we are totally 100 percent committed to each other, but at the same time we can feel free to see other people. I'm not an emotionally monogamous person. Not to be crass, but I have a low threshold of boredom when it comes to sexuality. This way, instead of jumping to a new relationship, I can see someone else and fulfill that aspect of me that is not being*

fulfilled, but still have my wonderful solid relationship back home. I think that if I were married I would feel obligated to be monogamous, regardless of my personal desires or what I think would be best for me emotionally, physically.

Sean is in a long-term four-person relationship with two women and another man. He could marry one of the women but not both of them, and he couldn't marry the man at all. He says that for him, marriage just doesn't make sense.

OK, I'm going to be living with three other people. And if I was married to one of them and not another one, I would feel like I was saying this person was the person I was bonded with in some permanent sense; these other people are here kind of for the moment. I prefer a level playing field. And since I can't marry all of them, the level playing field is to marry none of them.

Some people believe that just as few animal species form monogamous lifelong pairs,[38] humans are not evolutionarily "designed" to be monogamous. Others who choose open relationships think monogamy can be a great choice for many people, just not the best option for them.

RESOURCES FOR
NON-MONOGAMOUS RELATIONSHIPS

Loving More
www.lovemore.com
Box 4358
Boulder, CO 80306-4358
(303) 543-7540
    A polyamory organization that produces a magazine, holds conferences, and maintains an extensive website.

Alt.polyamory
www.polyamory.org
    This homepage for the newsgroup alt.polyamory provides lots of links and answers to frequently asked questions.

▶ Forever-free

"Forever" is a touchy subject for many people in unmarried relationships. Outsiders often assume that unmarried couples are less committed—if we really intended this love to last a lifetime, we would just buckle down and get married, right? In order to have our relationships taken seriously, long-term unmarrieds often find ourselves arguing that we are as stable and committed as any other relationship or family. And many of us are! There are plenty of unmarried relationships that have outlasted many marriages.

Many unmarried couples expect to stay together their whole lives, just as if they'd taken formal marriage vows. Some *have* made formal vows in ceremonies they designed. But some feel that no matter how wonderful the relationship, and how perfect things feel right now, they have to question the notion of a "forever" commitment. Not surprisingly, these people sometimes feel guilty admitting they really don't know if theirs is a forever relationship—after all, in our society anyone who can't promise forever is diagnosed with "commitmentphobia." Some emphasize that they can make promises only for the "foreseeable future," but that at least those promises will be entirely honest. Amy says:

> *Pledging to be together forever, I would feel like I was lying. It has nothing to do with not being committed to our relationship, it has to do with the fact that I have evolved as a person my whole life, and so has Mike. It is not impossible to think that there might be a time when we might evolve away from each other, although I hope that does not happen, and I hope we could do it together.*

For some people, the reluctance to promise forever comes from the personal experience of having made that kind of promise with great confidence in a relationship that later ended. Based on her past experience, for instance, Sue feels she can promise her partner that she'll always be a part of her life. But she doesn't feel it would be honest to promise their relationship won't change:

> *Whether our lives will work as sexual partners or lovers for the rest of our lives, I don't know. I guess I kind of doubt it. I've felt that way enough times and I'm no longer sexual with those women, to know that it's not likely. But I would certainly want her in my life. Most of the women I've been lovers with I have in my life in some capacity.*

Some who don't feel they can honestly commit to " 'til death do us part" choose instead to pledge to be together for five or ten years, and then renew for another five, and another. Married or not, all people in relationships have to contend with the uncertainties of the future, as Lyn points out:

> *I feel like the hard part is about really getting OK with the fact that we live our lives like we'll be together, but there's no guarantee. I think that's the hardest part for everybody, for people who choose to get married or don't, and for our parents about us not being married: wanting that guarantee. I feel like there is no guarantee. The guarantee is that we'll work really hard. The guarantee is that I really want what's best for you, and what's best for me, and I hope that's being together,*

but if it's not I still want what's best for each of us. I don't feel like very many people are comfortable with that. That's important to me, the truthfulness.

Many people dream of the security and familiarity of knowing precisely what marriage means. But if one or more of matrimony's many meanings doesn't fit your life, the institution may not feel like a good match. Alternately, you may find that taking the time to create your relationship's patterns *before* getting married allows you to maintain those patterns—even nontraditional ones—after the wedding.

REASON NUMBER NINE:
They Can't

Not everyone can get married.

If your partner happens to be the same sex as you, it is not currently legal for you to marry anywhere in the United States.[39] Not in Hawaii. Not in Vermont. Not in any other state. Vermont comes closest to granting equal marriage rights, with the civil union legislation it adopted in 2000. Same-sex couples who live anywhere in the country can travel to Vermont to get a civil union, which gives you the same legal rights and responsibilities that the state of Vermont grants married couples. Civil unions don't give same-sex couples federal marriage rights, and unlike marriage, which is "transferable," civil unions lose their legal meaning at the state border.

As of the 2000 Census, there were 1.2 million people living with a same-sex partner in this country[40]—and most demographers estimate the actual number is higher, since many gay, lesbian, and bisexual people may not feel safe telling the government that their same-sex "roommate" is actually a sweetheart.[41] Although not all people in same-sex relationships want to get married, many do. Since marriage brings so many legal rights and validation for a relationship, it is blatantly discriminatory to restrict marriage on the basis of the sex of one's partner. Some say that the purpose of marriage is for childbearing, but if that were true we would prevent senior citizen couples from marrying. Banning same-sex marriage doesn't stop gay, lesbian, bisexual, and transgender (GLBT) people from parenting, as they are doing in growing numbers, but it does leave their families without legal recognition or protection. Upholding marriage's "traditional" rules doesn't hold water, either, since cultures in other places and times—including the Christian church—have recognized same-sex couples as equivalent to different-sex ones.[42]

Legalizing same-sex marriage will only be a partial step toward recognition of contemporary families, but until it is done, couples like Brian and Raymond have the marriage decision made for them. Although at eighteen years, theirs is one of the longest-standing relationships they know (among both gay and heterosexual friends), it frustrates them that they're not legally considered each other's "family." One partner could be prevented from visiting the other in a hospital, they point out. They worry that when one of them dies, the surviving partner will be taxed on his inheritance, something married couples automatically avoid.

Same-sex couples are the largest group currently banned from marrying in this country, but they're not alone. Some prisoners and mentally disabled people are also prevented from marrying, and those who would face severe financial penalties often feel that tying the knot simply isn't available to them, either. Certain kinds of relatives are prevented from marrying each other (although experts say there's no genetic reason for these bans),[43] as are polygamous and polyamorous families. The community of unmarried people is remarkably diverse. It includes those who, like ourselves, are privileged enough to choose not to marry. But it also includes significant numbers of those whose unmarried status is not by choice.

Some couples who *could* get married choose not to do so because they're not comfortable taking advantage of a privilege that isn't available to all people. It's a sort of marriage boycott, with the hope that when large numbers of people stop participating, policymakers will start paying attention to the injustice. In our experience, people who choose not to marry for this reason often have close ties to the GLBT community or consider themselves part of this community. Janna's dad came out as gay after being married to her mom, and Janna's partner, Sebastian, has lots of gay male friends. Sebastian says he resents that marriage is a "straight privilege," and explains, "Not getting married amounts to a small protest against homophobia in our society. I feel like I've made this small token statement of support for my friends." Kirsten, a bisexual woman, was previously in a long-term relationship with a woman but is now partnered with a man. She finds the issue close to home, too.

After having been with a woman for five years, and understanding how deep homophobia is in our society, it makes me very uneasy to move ahead and get legally married when I know that gays and lesbians can't.

Some churches have also joined in support of equal marriage treatment for gay and lesbian couples. The congregation of Edgehill United Methodist Church in Nashville, Tennessee, for example, decided that until the parent United Methodist Church allows same-sex couples to get married, they would not allow their church to be used for any marriage. Suzanne, a heterosexual woman from the Edgehill congregation, was recently married in a friends' home and says she's proud of her church's decision. "It's time for us as straight people to put our money where our mouth is," she says. "That sacrifice is how we're going to change the world." At some other churches, like St. Peter's and St. Andrew's Episcopal Church in Providence, Rhode Island, the minister will conduct ceremonies for any couple but will not sign marriage licenses until she can sign them for both same-sex and different-sex couples.[44]

REASON NUMBER TEN:
No Compelling Reason

Questioners often have a hard time accepting the last reason on this list, though it's quite common. Many people can't find a good reason *to* get married, and until they do, they're leaving things alone. What Dave calls his "laundry list" of reasons not to get married ranges from a discomfort with the institution's religious underpinnings to its less-than-proud historical moments to the marriage tax penalty. He admits that none of these reasons is insurmountable, but says he hasn't seen any incentive to overcome them and feels life with Ulla and their two dogs in the house they bought together is just fine.

I've sometimes thought

of marrying, and then

I've thought again.

—Noel Coward

I'd say overall it's lack of compelling reason to be married. Nobody's ever convinced me that marriage has a purpose that outweighs the various things I think about why I wouldn't want to be married. The positive that I see about marriage is it's a way to communicate publicly, "This is the person I want to spend my life with." But I think we've done that without marriage.

Katharine Hepburn said that her career was so interesting she didn't have time to get married.[45] Like Hepburn, Becky says that at the time early in their relationship when she and her partner Mike might have been expected to get married, they were occupied with other things. "While our relationship was deeply wonderful to us, it was also somewhat matter-of-fact," she explains. "We were too busy with more important matters in life, like activism and having a child." And along the same lines, Annie says marriage seems beside the point: "Getting married feels like, I don't know, going to Hong Kong or something like that. It doesn't come up. It's not relevant to us exactly. It hasn't really been that big of an issue." And Jennifer says simply that getting married was never something they desired.

> It's never been on my list of things to do. I never thought, "Oh, when I grow up, I'll get married." I was like, "Well, I'll be a mom, and I'm going to have a career." It wasn't on that To Do list for goals in my life.

Most in this final group of unmarried people aren't personally opposed to getting married but find that it just doesn't matter much. It may be their partner who makes the decision one way or another. Mara and her partner, Angelo, have each been married previously for over three decades, and she thinks everyone should try marriage at least once. But at age sixty-five she's finished having children, and she admits that cohabitation's recent social acceptability influences her willingness to do it ("If it were a big disgraceful thing, I guess we would've gotten married.") She's been with Angelo for seven years and expects them to stay together the rest of their lives.

> If Angelo had come along and said, "Oh, I really want you to marry me, it's important," I would say fine! Whatever. I just don't feel strongly about it one way or the other. And it's fine for me not to be married.

While those of us who feel that not having a good reason is reason enough not to marry, it doesn't give curious outsiders the kind of juicy insight they're often seeking. People who don't marry for this (lack of a) reason like to turn the question around: "Why *should* I get married?" The questioner may have his or her own answer to that question, but one person's convincing reason to get married may not resonate with another. Elise still finds herself struggling to explain:

> When I tell people I haven't found a good reason to get married, they seem frustrated with my answer. That makes me feel like my answer was unsatisfactory, so I usually tell them some other reason why marriage doesn't appeal to me. Without exception, they latch on to the second reason I give, or keep poking around for the real, hidden reason, and forget that for me, the lack of a good reason is the most convincing reason why I don't want to get married.

The movies teach us that couples in love get married as soon as they possibly can, and diagnoses those who don't with serious commitment problems. The reality, of course, is less clear cut. Committed couples often have rational, honorable reasons for postponing marriage or not marrying at all. The very categories pitting "married" against "unmarried" are misleading, since most people spend various segments of their adult lives moving in and out of both categories. In this highly personal process, shifting factors and passing time can change people's decisions over the course of their lives. Chapter 10 explores the decision-making process.

THREE

WHEN OTHERS DISAGREE:

Surviving Pressure and Discrimination

WE WISH LIVING together were easy. We wish all parents welcomed the news of their child's cohabitation with cries of, "How wonderful, darling! I'll bring over a lasagna so you won't have to worry about dinner while you unpack." We wish friends threw celebratory bashes, ministers blessed the new level of love and commitment, wise neighbors shared their insights about getting through hard times, and landlords cheerfully added another name to the lease.

Unfortunately, that's not the world in which we live. While an unmarried couple moving to the block generally isn't worthy of backyard gossip anymore, it's not unusual for partners to run into snags along the way. For gay, lesbian, bisexual, and transgender (GLBT) people, homophobia is often a bigger problem than marital status discrimination, though the two are closely linked. This chapter offers insights on some common challenges from the outside, and suggests practical ways to deal with those who predict catastrophe for your relationship, those who nudge you down the aisle, and those who discriminate against you. Although we can't guarantee the naysayers will help load furniture into your U-Haul for the big move, if you're lucky they might give you a friendly wave as you pull away.

MOM ALWAYS KNOWS

HAVE YOU HEARD the joke about the cohabiting guy whose mother came to dinner? His mom had long been suspicious of the relationship between her son, John, and his roommate, Julie. When they had her over for dinner one night, John read his mother's mind, and volunteered, "I know what you must be thinking, Mom, but I assure you, Julie and I are just roommates."

About a week later, Julie came to John and said, "Ever since your mother came to dinner, I haven't been able to find the beautiful silver gravy ladle. You don't suppose she took it, do you?" John said, "Well, I doubt it, but I'll write her a letter just to be sure." So he sat down and wrote a letter:

"Dear Mother, I'm not saying you did take a gravy ladle from my house, and I'm not saying you did not take a gravy ladle from my house, but the fact remains that one has been missing ever since you were here for dinner. Love, John."

Several days later, John received a letter from his mother:

"Dear Son, I'm not saying that you do sleep with Julie, and I'm not saying that you do not sleep with Julie, but the fact remains that if she were sleeping in her own bed, she would have found the gravy ladle by now. Love, Mother."

PRESSURE NOT TO LIVE TOGETHER

There's no question acceptance of cohabitation has come a long way quickly. In a span of a few decades the act of sharing a home without sharing a marriage license has been transformed from scandalous to normal. Today it's something most people do before they marry. But despite how common it's become, living together still draws frowns, wrinkled brows, and even outright condemnation from some people. Nicole describes her parents as "rigid Catholics" and says they frequently tell her she's "living in sin." Her father warns her of eternal damnation, saying, "Your life on earth is so short, but eternity is so long."

Every holiday it's a nightmare filled with anxiety when we have to get together with my family, because my mother makes it so uncomfortable for the two of us. Even though we've been together for nine years, and I don't rely on her financially or anything, she makes it very, very uncomfortable. About six months ago it all came to a head. She said that I wasn't welcome at her house, so I don't go to her house anymore except at holidays.

This intense disapproval isn't because cohabiting partners store their tooth-brushes so close together, or because people believe that seeing your sweetheart's morning bedhead should be an experience reserved for married spouses. The real reason why there's opposition to unmarried people living together is this: cohab-itors have sex. Of course, *lots* of unmarried people have sex, whether they live with their lovers or not. At least 70 percent of first-time brides and 83 percent of first-time grooms are not virgins on their wedding day—the percentages are even higher for younger generations—revealing exactly how much unmarried love-making is going on.[1] Much of that sex involves far less love and commitment than is present in many cohabiting relationships. But the nose-wrinklers care about sex between cohabitors because there's no attempt to hide it, no polite, "We were just sitting here in the back room having a conversation. Really!" When romantically-involved unmarried people live together, everyone assumes they're having sex, and critics say they're flaunting it. That's where the arguments begin.

COHABITATION (BUT NOT SEX) BEFORE MARRIAGE

THEY'RE RIGHT: ALMOST all cohabitors have sex. According to the National Health and Social Life Survey, more than 99 percent of unmarried couples who live together had sex in the past year, and more than nine in ten do so least a few times a month.[2]

But it *is* possible to live together without having sex. Some friends form intimate, long-term, nonsexual partnerships, sometimes called "Boston marriages" or "platonic marriages," sharing a life and a home but not a bed. One such couple, a pair of straight women in their thirties, list each other as contacts on their emergency cards and eat dinner together. Another pair, also heterosexual, go to parties as a couple and spend holidays with each other's families.[3] In other relationships the space between room-mates and lovers is shaded with gray. Roommates move in together and later fall in love; lovers move in together and fall out but continue to live together. Without a genetic, marital, or sometimes even a sexual connection, people in relationships like these often lack the words to describe the significance of their bond.

Others—very much intimate partners—choose to have a period of self-enforced celibacy prior to their wedding. A couple who were clients of Princeton, New Jer-sey therapist Maya Kollman decided to have eight sex-free prenuptial months. They slept in separate bedrooms and did nothing more than kiss. It worked so well for them, Kollman has suggested the approach to other clients. "It heightens that feel-ing of passion and romantic desire," she says. "Their wedding night was extraordi-nary, as were the next few months."[4] By adding a fresh spark to their sex life, the transition from cohabiting to married had added meaning.

But what about couples who plan to be virgins on their wedding night, even though they live together? Skeptical, at first, that these couples existed, we started researching and quickly turned up several examples. Most people in this category hold very strong religious convictions and oppose sex before marriage, but have a practical reason to live together. Some need to share rent costs, for example, or are relocating across the country and don't want to rent two apartments with their wedding just around the corner. Since living together provides so much alluring private time together, it's one thing to plan to stay abstinent, and quite another to follow through. As one person advised another on an online messageboard, "The temptation [to have sex] will likely be almost unbearable."[5] Some couples find sticking to their commitment to abstinence easier if they're living with relatives or other roommates who informally act as chaperones.

If the prospect of abstinence until marriage appeals to you, here are four tips on making it work:

1. *Know how you'll define abstinence.* For some abstinent people, nearly anything is OK except intercourse. Others draw the line at touch below the waist. Some couples really like cuddling and spooning fully clothed ("two bodies curling around each other, fitting perfectly into each other's nooks and comfy places—like two spoons in a drawer")[6]. Make yours a mutual decision, so you'll be working toward a shared goal rather than negotiating every nuzzle and caress.

2. *Have separate bedrooms.* By living together, one couple is able to afford a three bedroom apartment. Each has his or her own bedroom and they're saving the third until after marriage. "It will be 'our' room at that time . . . until then it will be kind of sacred."[7]

3. *Set a wedding date, preferably not too far away.* Like a marathon runner pacing herself for the final few miles, it's easier to stay focused if you know exactly how much distance remains.

4. *Be realistic about what sex will be like the first time.* Anything that's off-limits for a while can come to seem more exciting, and possibly more important, than it really is. Sharing your lives and your home without being sexually intimate can compound the feeling that sex is a really, *really* big deal. Be realistic that whether the first time happens on your wedding night or before, only characters in romance novels are guaranteed instant fireworks.

THE ARGUMENTS

Whether you're already living together or just talking about it, odds are you've crossed paths with some of the common arguments against cohabitation. Maybe your relatives are the number one anti-cohabiting campaigners in your life, or perhaps you've encountered a sermon in church or read some disturbing statistics about living together in the newspaper. Whatever the source, almost every line of argument fits into one of these categories: Living in Sin Arguments, Pseudo-Scientific Arguments, or Mars and Venus Arguments. Each one emphasizes a different concern and warrants a different response. Below are explanations about the problems with each kind of argument, and tips for how to respond.

▶ Living in Sin Arguments:
The Moral View Against Cohabitation

These are the classic arguments, the meat and potatoes, of why you shouldn't live with your partner. You've probably heard, "Cohabitors are living in sin. It's wrong," or "The Bible says you shouldn't cohabit," or "People who shack up are undermining family values." Those are just the polite versions. At their most hostile, these sometimes bring dire warnings of hellfire and eternal doom.

Words like these can be deeply hurtful, particularly when respected people of faith aim them at people of their own religion. Some cohabitors feel forced to choose between their faith and their relationship, even when the relationship is a good one. Anita says:

> I have been in so much turmoil about my perplexing situation. I am forty-nine years old and engaged to a wonderful man, but because of my past divorce I will lose all my medical benefits if I marry. I love this man with all my heart. I want to marry by my Christian beliefs, but I have a heart problem and limited funds, so I cannot afford to lose my health insurance. We live together, and we are happy. But I am so torn. I pray all the time for God to love me and not scorn me for what I am doing. I would love to have His blessing upon us without the legal marriage, and to know that we will still go to heaven.

What makes a relationship holy . . . is how the two individuals within the relationship honor each other and themselves with their actions and words. Honesty, trust, constancy through difficult and easy times, and giving mutual support are far more the landmarks to commitment, love and intimacy than whether or not a union has religious or legal sanction.

—REVEREND COLETTA EICHENBERGER, ordained Disciples of Christ minister, Boonville, Missouri[8]

Jacquie says that the Bible's messages are the only things that trouble her about being in an unmarried relationship.

> According to the scriptures, I'm in trouble. The book of Deuteronomy says that my former husband is my husband until the day they throw dirt on me. In the church's eyes, we are wrong. In the African-American community, that is one of the biggest things that we struggle with.

Fortunately, there are many religious and ethical people who disagree with this moralistic view against cohabitation, and believe in supporting healthy, loving relationships regardless of marital status.

How to Respond to Living in Sin Arguments

▶ *Understand the Bible in today's context.* You might be surprised to realize that despite claims like, "Cohabitation is entirely contrary to God's law,"[9] there's nothing in the Judeo-Christian Bible that explicitly says cohabitation is wrong.[10] In fact, the Bible includes teachings about holy unmarried relationships that are valid alternatives to marriage (see page 120), and poems in the Song of Songs that celebrate an unmarried relationship.[11] Rabbi Arthur Waskow says of these, "I believe that the Song of Songs is our best guide from the ancient tradition as to how sexuality could express the joyful and pleasurable celebration of God."[12]

While parts of the Bible do address "fornication," or sex between unmarried people, many religious leaders and scholars believe that some Biblical teachings are no longer applicable to today's world. Of the many mores mentioned and permitted in the Bible, most faith traditions—liberal, mainstream, fundamentalist, and evangelical alike—now condemn "Biblical" behaviors such as polygamy, slavery, and the treatment of women as property. Reverend Jim Maynard of American Baptists Concerned says, "Most hold that the Bible is inspired by God but written in the words of humans. It contains human perspectives and prejudice that reflect that time and place in which it was written. What is normal for one day and time is not always applicable to others."[13] While the Bible can provide inspiration and guidance, many clergy agree that one need not interpret it literally to remain true to one's faith. It's the relationship between the two spouses (even legally unmarried ones) and God that ultimately matters, not the opinion of the minister or the cranky lady in the front pew.

Many Christian leaders have called for the church to stay focused on Jesus's message of love. For instance, in 2000 Dr. William Walsh, the Bishop of Killaloe in Ireland, publicly apologized for the Catholic Church's attitude towards cohabiting couples and said, "Christ did not condemn those who failed to meet the ideals of the church . . . We must not condemn. We must not question the nature of that love that may not meet with our ideals. We must celebrate family, and all that is possible in family; the love between married spouses and between parents and children; the love of the unmarried mother and unmarried father and their children, and the struggle that being an unmarried mother and father can be in our society."[14]

Help others respect your decision. If the person who accuses you of "living in sin" is close to home—a parent or relative, member of your faith community, or someone else with whom you'll have an ongoing relationship—you can work to help him better understand and respect your decision to live together. It helps to know exactly what concerns him. If the values underlying your relationship are his primary care, he may soften if he realizes you share his values of commitment, honesty, love, and integrity. It might help him to understand what your relationship means to you, how your shared values are central to your love, and why you aren't or can't be married. Witnessing you put these values into practice over a period of years can be the most powerful way to earn the respect of these doubters. Few would remain judgmental of Anita, the woman above with a heart problem, if they understood her situation and saw the Christian values woven into her daily life.

Other objectors' opposition to living together stems from a deeply held moral or religious belief that opposes all unmarried sex and rigidly upholds heterosexual marriage as the only acceptable form of family. A friendly conversation is unlikely to transform one of these types into someone who supports your relationship. It might be possible, though, to come to respect each other's points of view, mutually understand that you've made different choices, and agree to disagree. Marshall experienced this "hate the sin, love the sinner" approach firsthand:

> From Biblical times on, Judaism never decreed that you had to marry in order to have sex. Throughout the Jewish Scriptures, we read about consensual nonmarital relationships called *pilagshut*, or, literally, 'half marriage.' . . . This form of relationship was prevalent even among the holiest of people . . . They even had children within such nonmarital relationships, and . . . there was no stigma of illegitimacy—[it was] strictly kosher.
>
> —RABBI GERSHON WINKLER,
> San Juan Valley Hebrew Congregation, Durango, Colorado[15]

Before his death at age ninety-one, my grandfather regularly attended Sunday services at his southern Virginia Baptist retirement home. One of his preacher's favorite pastimes was rallying against those who "live in sin." Although our living together had never seemed to concern my grandfather before he moved to the retirement home, over time this preacher's message caused him to decide that he no longer wanted to see or talk to Dorian and me because of the sin he felt we were committing. His silent treatment lasted for months, and while it hurt us, we were fortunate to have support from the rest of my family. After lots of conversations with my parents, he eventually came around, reaching out to us with the compromise, "I don't hate you, I just hate what you're doing." We were glad to have several months of positive reconnections before he passed away.

It's not easy, and sometimes not even possible, to reach this point with every family member. But it can be worth trying.

▶ *Live the kind of "family values" that matter.* Pundits and politicians who lament "declining family values" are usually talking about a narrow view of family. In the real world, family ties aren't based on whether you're legally married, have children, or are heterosexual. Unmarried partners can be a family unit, and part of each other's extended families. Connect with each other's extended families by going to visit them (especially for important occasions like reunions, graduations, performances, and significant birthdays and anniversaries), spending holidays together, planning opportunities for each other's relatives to meet each other, signing greeting cards together, staying connected by phone and e-mail, and finding common interests or hobbies to explore with "in-laws" (some unmarried people jokingly call theirs "out-laws"). Joan said this kind of positive family relationship earned her and her male partner, Fran, a respectful tolerator, if not a supporter:

We are encouraged in our faith to accept and affirm all people. We have the example of Jesus's blessing and supporting the love and intimacy of people. I believe that people who are coupled, and have that bond recognized by their faith community, will be able to contribute to the benefit of all in a much more profound way. Because love is difficult, I hope that the church and the state would affirm all people who find wonderful, healthy, nurturing love.

—REVEREND T. MICHAEL ROCK,
Associate Minister, United Church of
Christ, Providence, Rhode Island[16]

Fran's dad is eighty-four and very opinionated. He's been a deacon in the Catholic Church. Considering how conventional and traditional his views are, it's amazed both of us that he has accepted me and accepted our relationship as well as he has. It's really been a pleasure. I think it's because he kind of likes me, and I like him. He's also very close to Fran, and I think it's really important to him to maintain Fran's love and goodwill and the closeness that they have. I think he would like it if Fran got married, but he doesn't make an issue of it.

The more your relationship fits into your family's culture, the easier it becomes for people to choose to forget about how you are different. Finding ways for each other's relatives to meet and connect is one of the most powerful ways we've found to strengthen ties. Dorian describes one method we've used:

Marshall and I each have sisters who are much younger than we are. When we were in college they'd sometimes visit us, so we decided to create an annual "Sister Convergence" weekend. Starting when the girls were six, seven, and eight, they'd come every spring with teddy bears and sleeping bags in tow, eat piles of peanut butter and jelly sandwiches, teach us the sing-song hand-clapping games they'd learned on the playground, make embroidery-thread friendship bracelets they'd sell to our housemates, and surprise us with stealth tickling attacks. The hiding of the peanut butter jar's top became part of the annual tradition; back home they'd talk to us on the phone, giggling with glee when they heard we'd finally discovered where they stowed it behind a sofa cushion or deep in a sock drawer. They grew up knowing each other and looking forward to their weekends together. Even though they're not related, I think they feel like each other's extended families.

▶ *Create your own family.* Unfortunately, connecting to extended family isn't an option for everyone. Many who have been rejected from or need to separate themselves from their family of origin find tremendous strength by forming an intentional family.[17] These kinds of families can include your partner, close friends, or other people who play a significant role in your life. You might choose to share holidays or important events with them, and see them as an place to turn for support during difficult times.

▶ *Find a supportive faith community.* If you're a religious person, you may not have to settle for a faith community that condemns your relationship. You can tell a lot about a given church's stance on diverse families by looking at its approach to gay and lesbian issues. Some denominations and many individual churches, synagogues, and clergy have affirmed their support for GLBT people, and these are more likely to welcome all kinds of nontraditional relationships. Unitarian Universalists, Quakers, Reform and Reconstructionist Jews, and the United Church of Christ are particularly known for welcoming all people, regardless of their sexual orientation or marital status.

It is possible to shape a sexual relationship between two unmarried people that is sacred and holy. It is the organized Jewish community that sins when it refuses to join in shaping the ethical and ceremonial forms that would make this more likely.

—RABBI ARTHUR WASKOW,
The Shalom Center, Philadelphia,
Pennsylvania[18]

▶ Pseudo-Scientific Arguments:
The "Scientific" View Against Cohabitation

In the 1980s and 1990s, when arguments based on morality ceased to pack the punch they once did, anti-cohabitation campaigners donned crisp white lab coats, retooling their messages for today's science-trusting public. The new arguments sound like, "Living together before marriage increases the risk of divorce," "Cohabitors are less committed to each other than married couples," and "Cohabiting couples experience more domestic violence than married ones." Gwen heard them from her mother:

I received a major backlash from both my parents in response to my choice to live with my boyfriend. My mother actually called and lectured to me extensively for forty minutes about the various kinds of research to substantiate her opinion that cohabiting relationships are very unhealthy.

Arguments like these can be confusing, since to many couples it makes intuitive sense to live together before tying the knot. The reality is, many of the statistics batted around in the media don't tell the whole story. It's not a coincidence the general public is becoming familiar with these semi-truths—some political groups have made them a central part of their anti-cohabitation campaigns. Yet most of the facts about cohabitation that are published in respected research journals and presented at academic conferences draw quite different conclusions.

How to Understand the Truth Behind Pseudo-Scientific Arguments

▶ *Understand the difference between "the average cohabitor" and your life.* You are not necessarily "average." With eleven million cohabitors in this country, it is nearly impossible to draw any meaningful conclusions about what we all have in common. Yet pseudo-scientific arguments do just that.

People live with a partner for incredibly varied reasons—if cohabitors were paint colors, we'd be a veritable rainbow. For sake of explanation, imagine that one kind of cohabitor, couples who live together as a step between dating and marriage, are red paint. Senior citizens who live together so they don't lose their pensions will be yellow paint, and unmarried couples of several decades' duration with no plans to marry are green. Low-income couples who would like to marry but want to be sure their future spouse can help them escape poverty are blue.

Anytime a researcher comes up with an average about cohabitors, she takes all the red, yellow, green, blue, and a bunch of other colors for all the other cohabitors, stirs them together, and comes up with a oh-so-serious, scientifically accurate shade of—you guessed it—brown. As everyone focuses on this average number that's been produced—the muddy brown color—they forget that this average is utterly meaningless when it comes to understanding the red cohabitors, the yellow ones, or any of the others.

Cohabiting types that exist in large numbers affect the color of the whole pool when it's averaged. So since poor people, whom we colored blue, cohabit at higher rates than middle or upper-class ones, the average brown color will always have a blue tint. That means that certain characteristics about poor people, like the fact that they tend to have more health problems and higher rates of depression will make the average for *all* cohabitors look more depressed and unhealthy. But those tendencies aren't necessarily true for other cohabitors in the pool. Average cohabiting couples who plan to marry or are considering marriage have characteristics very similar to married people.[19] Green cohabitors in very long-term relationships are statistically a small splash—their characteristics hardly show up in the average at all.

In short, because of the way some groups pull the average up or down, statistics about cohabitation often lead to distorted conclusions. Poor people who cohabit in large numbers make the average cohabitor income look low, but if you're making a good salary, that doesn't affect you. There are higher levels of alcoholism in the cohabitor population because people are less likely to marry partners with alcohol problems,[20] but that doesn't mean that living together will drive you to drink. The quality of your relationship—not any statistical average—determines whether your union will be strong.

▸ *Realize there is no evidence that cohabitation causes divorce.* It's true research finds that on average, cohabitors who later marry have a higher divorce rate than those who marry without living together first. But it's a misrepresentation to say that cohabitation *causes* divorce. Here's why. This research compares two groups of people, those who live together before they marry and those who don't. But people aren't randomly assigned to these different groups—they choose to live together or not because they're different kinds of people. Those who don't live together before marriage are a minority today, and they tend to be more conservative, with stronger religious beliefs and stronger opposition to divorce. Given this, it's no surprise that this group doesn't consider divorce an acceptable option. The difference between the two groups' divorce rates is likely attributable to the types of people in each group, not because cohabitation ruins relationships. As sociologist Judith Seltzer writes, "Claims that individuals who cohabit before marriage hurt their chances of a good marriage pay too little attention to this evidence."[21]

Given that many couples cohabit to test their compatibility before making a lifetime commitment to marriage, could cohabitation actually result in *lower* divorce rates? It's possible. The divorce rate has been falling slightly since its peak two decades ago.[22] During that same time period, the cohabitation rate has skyrocketed.[23] There's no way to know for certain how the changes in divorce and cohabitation affect each other—just because two things happen at the same time (correlation) doesn't prove that one caused the other (causation). Since some cohabitors live together to try out a relationship but then ultimately break up, it's likely these people successfully avoided a marriage that would have ended in divorce. Chances are good the divorce rate would be higher if not for cohabitation.[24]

Cohabitation opponents make a lot of noise about divorce statistics because divorce is such a common fear. When you look at all the facts, whether you divorce ultimately may not have much to do with whether you live together. If you never marry, you don't need to worry about divorce, though the end of a long-term relationship has the same emotional impact. Chapter 4 is about what you can do to keep your relationship strong.

▶ *Know that commitment and marriage are not the same thing.* As with most stereotypes, there's a grain of truth to the claim that cohabitors are less committed than married spouses. Dating couples are usually less committed than married ones. Since most people move through the stages from dating to living together to marriage, you'd expect average commitment levels to follow the same trends—lowest among dating couples, highest among married ones—and they do.[25]

Of course there are some cohabitors who have no commitment to each other, just as there are married couples who aren't very committed and soon get divorced. Other cohabitors' levels of commitment easily match the most loving, stable married pairs. Some have plans to marry and just haven't done so yet, while others stay together for decades without a marriage license. In all the murkiness of averages, there's no way to distinguish the couple who has owned a home together for thirty years from the couple who moved in together last week when one partner got evicted. Sure, scientists can come up with an average number to indicate commitment among cohabitors. But it won't tell you anything about your own relationship.

It's worth pondering how those scientists even come up with a number that equals commitment. It's a slippery concept to pin down using a survey—imagine trying to compare your commitment to your relationship to your friend's commitment to his using a numerical scale. One oft-cited study of cohabitors and married couples found a difference of 1.3 points on a twenty point scale of "commitment,"[26] and a finding that small isn't unusual. So the pundits are telling the truth when they say cohabitors on average aren't as committed as married people—but it sure isn't the whole truth.

The best way to win the argument over commitment is to prove your relationship can stand the test of time. As the years tick by and you weather some tough times, outsiders will realize you're in it for the long haul. Calling yours a "committed relationship" or describing yourselves as "life partners" can help people understand.

▶ *Understand the "accumulation factor."* Cohabitation opponents exaggerate every negative research conclusion about the subject while ignoring research that finds cohabitors are just like everyone else. One of the most alarming claims might be that cohabiting women are at higher risk of domestic violence than married ones. What's actually going on? First of all, there isn't much of a difference between married and cohabiting women on this characteristic. One British study that's often cited found that two percent of married women had experienced domestic assault in the previous year, compared with three percent of cohabiting women.[27] Nonetheless, since any amount of domestic violence is unacceptable, even a one-percent difference could be cause for concern.

A more recent study explores why that difference exists. It finds that if you track a group of new cohabitors over time, the ones with less violent relationships are more likely to marry. No surprise there. The couples still in the cohabitor pool after the nonviolent couples marry—the ones who "accumulate"—are probably using excellent judgement by deciding not to make a lifetime commitment to a dangerous partner. But they affect the average for the whole pool, and make it look as if cohabitors have more abusive relationships.[28] It's likely that a similar process clouds a great deal of the research that compares married to unmarried people.

Marriage isn't a shield that can protect anyone from abuse, and cohabitation isn't automatically a battleground. A nonviolent partner is unlikely to turn aggressive because you've cohabited too long. An abusive partner is unlikely to be transformed if you get married, and in fact, marrying could put you at greater risk. Marital status is a poor way to predict whether any particular relationship will be safe.

▶ Mars and Venus Arguments:
  The Gendered View Against Cohabitation

Mars and Venus Arguments assume that all men (from Mars) are looking for sex without responsibility, while all women (from Venus) are looking for husbands and babies soon after. Mars and Venus are believed to be in their own orbits, at risk for major problems when they interact or live together. Women are most often the targets of these kinds of arguments, but men aren't immune. Perhaps you've heard, "In cohabitation, men get to have sex without making a commitment," "Women are the ones who get hurt by living together," or, "He won't buy the cow if you give away the milk for free."

It's certainly possible to run into these kinds of problems if you and your partner haven't talked about what living together means to you. If one of you thinks it's a new level of commitment while the other thinks it's a way to split the rent check, you're headed for trouble. If one partner thinks you're practically

JOHNNY'S ROOM

The a cappella group The Bobs performs a song about a couple who's forced to sleep in separate beds when they go to visit her parents. Here's an excerpt:

We've been together for a month now
Why are they so uptight?
When they invited us to dinner
I didn't know it meant "spend the night"

I helped with dishes
Your mother told me all about when you were small
And then she said:

Before it gets too late I'll show you where
you'll sleep tonight
You'll share a room with Johnny
(Repeat)

I bumped my head getting into bed
In Johnny's lower bunk
I couldn't sleep, 'cause the little creep
Snored and his tennis shoes stunk
I listened to this fish tank
And the bubbles seemed to be saying to me:

Before it gets too late I'll show you where
you'll sleep tonight
You'll share a room with Johnny
(Repeat)

At two A.M. I couldn't help myself
I tiptoed down the hall to your door
But then your dad came out and said
"Where are you going?"
"I guess I lost my way to the bathroom"

Before it gets too late I'll show you where
you'll sleep tonight
You'll share a room with Johnny
(Repeat)

engaged while the other sees the setup as a roommate "with benefits," there's conflict ahead. But if you're on the same page because you've had a few of those capital letter Relationship Talks, you're unlikely to be taken by surprise, whatever your gender. Don't be surprised if Mars is the one dreaming of hearth and home, while Venus is hesitant to get tied down—gender roles aren't what they used to be. Sebastian gets a kick out of reminding people of this:

> My friends and acquaintances will say to me, "Oh, how long have you guys been together?" I'll say, "Almost eight years." They're in shock, and of course the next question is, "Why don't you get married?", as if they're asking, what's wrong with you? And of course they immediately assume that Janna wants to get married and I don't, because I want to go sow my wild oats, afraid of commitment, guy problem, or whatever. It's actually kind of fun to pop their bubble, to explain the decision that we've made together. I enjoy seeing them try to take that in.

Despite all the stereotypes, many more women have serious hesitations about marrying than men.[29] Among hundreds of couples we've talked to who have chosen not to tie the knot, it's nearly always the woman who feels strongly about not marrying. Women's preferences about marriage generally seem to "trump" their male partners, perhaps because they tend to have stronger feelings on the issue—if a woman wants to marry, she'll keep looking until she finds a man who consents. Stacey is a typical example:

> I've been with my partner for fifteen years and we've lived together ever since my pregnancy and the birth of our daughter, who is now ten. My father always wanted to know why we didn't get married. He pestered me about it, refusing to accept that I didn't wish to be married—after all, he thought, all women want to get married. One day he finally asked my partner straight out why he didn't marry me. When my partner said he was more than willing to get married, but that I was the one refusing, I think my father just gave up.

How to Respond to Mars and Venus Arguments

▶ *Point out that it's a lot easier to have sex without commitment if you're not living together.* If you're feeling bold, try, "We were making love long before we made the commitment to move in together." People who truly want sex without commitment don't cohabit—they just find a casual relationship or one-night stand. By comparison, most partners who move in together are already in an intimate, sexual relationship and want to *increase* their level of connection and commitment. We don't know anyone who decided to cohabit because they wanted sex without commitment. As Mark told us, "My girlfriend and I intend to marry but do not want to rush into it before we are truly ready. We decided to live together because we were spending all our time together, anyway—why rent two apartments when we could rent one? We saw living together as a commitment to each other."

▶ *Point out that humans are not cattle.* "Mom, I'm not a cow," ought to suffice. Many younger women have never even heard the warning that if they "give away the milk for free," their partner "won't buy the cow." The adage used to refer to women who "gave away" sex without holding out for marriage. The theory was that if the man could get sex without paying the price (marriage), he would never feel the need to say "I do." Women of older generations were probably surprised to read the recent discussion about the saying on the Alternatives to Marriage Project's online list:

> *Someone mentioned the old adage about the cow and men getting free milk. What is this supposed to mean? Isn't the woman getting "free milk," as well? After all, women do enjoy sex, too.*
> —*Jessica*

> *I've been saying that to my boyfriend for about fifteen years. I also told him that if he wanted to get married, he shouldn't have moved in with me. When I saw the phrase, I thought the woman was getting the free milk.*
> —*Tori*

Most women today recognize themselves as sexual beings with their own desires, who choose sexual relationships—or not—based on their own situation and values. It doesn't make sense to men today, either. More than eight in ten men have sex before they marry, yet by their late twenties most men make the trip to the altar, undeterred by all that "free milk."[30]

Gendered double standards still exist. Women are still expected to guard sex, are labeled "sluts" if they're perceived to be having too much sex, and are targeted for warnings about "ruining their reputations." Men, on the other hand, are told they need to guard their money. Guys hear that if they're not careful, while he's busy enjoying sex with his live-in lover, she will max out his credit cards and expect a stream of expensive gifts until she finds the next guy to run off with. The best way to prevent being taken advantage of is to understand your partner throughly—whatever your gender or what you want to protect. Know whether each of you is responsible with money, what sex means to each partner, and what your expectations are about commitment and monogamy. If you're clear about what living together means for you, it'll be much easier to calm the fears provoked by Mars and Venus alarmists.

PRESSURE TO GET MARRIED

Pressure to get married sprouts up everywhere, like weeds in a sunny patch of backyard garden. People experience pressure from family, friends, television pundits, religious institutions, the wedding industry, government, magazines, and even strangers on the street, usually without regard for whether marriage is actually in a given couple's best interest. It begins before we can remember, as Elise, a nurse, witnessed at a birth she assisted:

> *Minutes after the baby was born, the mom and dad were holding him and talking to him, the way parents usually do with new babies. And one of the things they told him about was who he might marry someday, and who he should not marry.* This baby was not even five minutes old, and his parents were already making plans for his wedding day.

Planning for an infant's marriage isn't so unusual. During a *bris*, the traditional Jewish circumcision ceremony, the whole community prays for the baby boy's marriage, which is expected to take place under a *chuppah*, the traditional Jewish marriage canopy. The following prayer is said twice, once by those attending the ceremony, and once by the *mohel* who performs the circumcision: "Even as he has been introduced into the covenant, so may he be introduced to the Torah, to the marriage canopy, and to a life of good deeds."

IF YOU'RE A single woman, chances are you've been asked the following three questions:

1. Why aren't you *married?*
2. Why *aren't* you married?

. . . and the very, very popular:

3. Why aren't *you* married?

(give or take another 999,999,997 more such questions).

—Karen Salmansohn in *Even God Is Single (So Stop Giving Me a Hard Time)*[31]

Alice recalls this conversation she had as a young child:

> *I remember some relatives of mine—I think it was my grandmother or my mother—had this necklace and they were showing it to me and saying, "This will go to you when you get married. Only when you get married, though." And I thought, "Why only when I'm getting married? Isn't anything else I do worth so much?"*

> **I think a single woman's biggest problem is coping with the people who are trying to marry her off!**
>
> —Helen Gurley Brown, former editor of *Cosmopolitan* and author of *Sex and the Single Girl*

Children grow up hearing, "Someday, when you're all grown up and married . . . " as if "grown up" and "married" always went hand-in-hand. Regardless of your age, gender, sexual orientation, or whether or not you're even in a relationship, "marriage madness" surrounds you. Kathy, forty-four, says she feels it constantly.

It's just there in the air that you're supposed to be married, and that there's something wrong with you because you're not. Every time you have to go somewhere and have people say, "Oh, is this your husband?", and you have to say, "No, it's not." Or every time you go on a vacation and have to check in and it's not your husband and there's this weirdness about it. And every time you have to go to your company picnic and introduce your unmarried spouse, and everyone else is married and you're not. I've even had some people say to me in a pretty direct way, "Living together was fine when you were twenty-one but you know, you're grown up now. You're supposed to settle down, get married, do the legal thing."

Even though Tracey is delighted with her unmarried relationship, people tell her to break up with her boyfriend:

There's a lot of pressure from my sisters, from girlfriends, and female family members. Women say, "Well, he won't marry you, so hey, go loose, girlfriend!" And I tell them, "That's not important to me," but they don't understand that. "Mm-mm, girl, if he won't marry you, you have the right to do this, that, and the other." It's a really big thing for a lot of people. "You've been together nine years, and what, you're not married? He ain't put no ring on your finger?"

Another woman writes:

As a young single woman in my mid-twenties I'm treated as if I'm a fruit. I'm considered "ripe" for marriage and frequently told that if I don't marry soon I'll lose the opportunity, I'll get old and wrinkly like a apple gone by, and just like rotten fruit, be left at the bottom of the relationship barrel. . . . Despite the fact that I'm studying medicine, still competing athletically . . . and in a happy, stable relationship, people continue to treat me as if I'm a failure. I recently won a wonderful award—the friend I called to tell about it didn't even address it. She only asked if I was still "single" (meaning unmarried) and when I said yes, she told me that everyone fails at something. I haven't called this "friend" since.[32]

Kim says, "Even my seven-year-old nephew asked me if I would ever get married, and didn't I want a baby like his little brother who was so cute? I told him he was worse than his grandmother."

The pressure can intensify over the years, particularly for different-sex couples who haven't married within the appropriate period of time (whatever *that* is). Some people subtly ask, "How are things going with Patty?" while others cut to the chase with "When are you getting married?" Jennifer and Phil get the sense that the questioners expect them to break up because they haven't had a wedding.

People say, [concerned tone] "So how's your relationship going? How are things with Phil?" And I feel like they wouldn't say that if we were married. There wouldn't be an assumption that things might not really be so good.
—Jennifer

Maybe you should ask them the same thing. [Same concerned tone] "So, how's your marriage going? You're not considering divorce, are you?"
—Phil

There are public expressions of joy when a couple announces their engagement, often accompanied by comments like, "It's about time!" and, "I don't know what took them so long!"

On the other hand, if there's no engagement announced, at some point people stop expecting it. Perhaps on some level they forget that the couple isn't married, and the partners' years of togetherness come to substitute for a marriage license. Perhaps the expectant attention shifts to newer couples. The time it takes people to think of long-term unmarried couples in their own lives demonstrates this point. After jogging their memories for a while, most remember some relative or family friend who has lived with a partner twenty-three years and never married. Although they may know this couple well, they don't think of them as the-ones-who-never-got-married, but rather as Joe and Sue, or Aunt Molly and Uncle Ivan, just as they do the married couples in their lives.

> At my sister's wedding, we counted thirty-two hints, nudges, insinuations, and direct questions, as in, "So, when are you two tying the knot?" and "Does this give you any ideas?" and "Taking notes?" and "I'm looking forward to the next one, if you know what I mean."
>
> **—Kate Cohen, *A Walk Down the Aisle: Notes on a Modern Wedding*[33]**

Of course, the intensity of the pressure is also affected by how public the couple is about their marital status. There aren't as many visual clues as there used to be. Sharing a last name or wearing wedding bands are options for married couples today, not requirements. Meanwhile, unmarried couples can choose to wear rings on their "wedding ring fingers" and take the same last names (see page 126). Because it's become less apparent who's married and who's not, many people assume that different-sex cohabiting couples are married. Our favorite example of this came soon after we appeared in a national television news segment about cohabitation. Marshall went into the local convenience store where we buy our Sunday newspaper, and the store owner greeted him with enthusiasm: "Hey, I saw you and your wife on TV the other night!" In his mind, if we bought *The New York Times* and the occasional pint of ice cream together, we were married—regardless of what he'd heard us say on the news.

To avoid some of the pressure to marry and the discrimination that unmarried couples face, some male-female couples choose to blend in and let people assume they're married. Betty and her partner, who has since passed away, didn't lie about their marital status, but they didn't correct people, either. "Anywhere we met new people, they would just assume we were married, and we never felt it was necessary to say, "Oh, but we aren't.""

Some prefer that only their families know the truth. For others, it's the reverse: they hold weddings to lead their families to believe they're legally married, but their friends know they're not. The good news is that attitudes about cohabitation are changing. As the stigma surrounding unmarried relationships decreases, more unmarried couples are comfortable being public about their status.

▶ How to Survive the Pressure

Unfortunately, there's no magical keystroke that will delete the "when are you getting married?" question from your cousins' memorybanks. Some strategies for surviving the pressure:

- *Be connected to supportive people.* Knowing that you have friends and relatives who respect your choices can give you the emotional strength you need to confront the world's "it's time to get married" chorus. Find someone who's experienced the same kind of pressure and doesn't mind listening to you vent. Some people say that joining one of several online groups for unmarried people reminds them they're not alone.
- *Help your pressurers understand.* Educating your father about the possibility that you could be fulfilled without a ring on your finger may be a challenge worth accepting. Don't assume that people in your life have a background in marital status etiquette. You might be the first person to point out to them how repeated questions about marriage can be disrespectful. If you're up for it, tell them the reasons why you've chosen to

delay marriage for a while, or why you're not planning to marry. 'Becca realized her parents weren't trying to exclude her partner:

For years I had assumed that my parents understood what was going on in my relationship and that any lapses in their treatment of Daniel were due either to their moral judgments against us or to their not being used to him yet. But I realized last summer that they were waiting for an explanation and, in the absence of one, they assumed he wasn't very important to me. Now that we've talked about it, there's still some contention about whether they'll accept him, but at least now they know that I feel he is a part of the family tree.

▶ *Let others know how you'd like to be treated.* Sometimes family or friends appear disapproving because they're uncertain what to do or say. What words should we use to describe her to our friends? Should we send him a birthday gift as we do to Judy's husband? Initiating a conversation about questions like these can help clear the air. Billy learned the hard way that his parents not only wanted to understand his relationship, they also wanted to know what to do with the information.

We had decided we were not going to get married, and we felt good about that. The next time we went home to my parents, I think it was Christmas. We were all sitting in the kitchen, and I don't know how it came up, or if I just blurted out the news about our decision not to marry. They didn't know what to say. My mother said, "I don't know what to do. Should we put champagne out?"

▶ *Be patient.* Most long-term unmarried couples say that after a while, the pressure to marry fades. When you and your partner have been together long enough, relatives may start treating you like all the other married folks in the family. This technique works best if you behave as they expect married people to behave. As the years have ticked by, Drew notices the pressure to marry subsiding.

TURNING THE TABLES

Debbie and her partner Jim have been together, unmarried, for seventeen years. They were tickled at an opportunity to turn the tables on her father when he visited:

When my dad came up to visit, his wife, Judy, was not yet his wife. I remember picking them up and taking them to our house, and Jim and I thought we'd play a trick on them. I was showing them around the house, and I said, "OK, Dad, here's the room you'll be sleeping in, and Judy, this'll be your bedroom over here." They both kind of looked at me, and then I just burst out laughing.

Our relationship is now ten years old. As we get ten years out, more and more people in our families are realizing that it would be kind of weird for us to decide to get married all of a sudden—though I think some of them still have the hope in the back of their heads.

▸ *Select some ingredients of marriage without baking the whole cake.* Would having a commitment ceremony help your dad feel like you're doing the right thing? Would choosing the same last name alleviate anxiety about your family's unity? Since marriage is a complex institution, it's possible to choose parts of it that might help reduce the pressure without getting legally married. For instance, Ulla and her partner went shopping together for a ring for her.

About a year ago Dave bought me a nice ring that looks like an engagement ring, and part of the reason I wanted the ring was because I wanted some kind of public sign that says, "This isn't just living together, this is something more than that. I wanted something I could look at and think of Dave during the day. It makes me feel more connected to him.

Chapter 10 further explores the idea of finding creative ways to incorporate aspects of marriage into your life.

▸ *Remove yourself from the discussion.* If everything else has failed, maybe it's time to withdraw from battle. You might let go of "winning" and just chuckle to yourself when your neighbor makes his millionth rude comment. You might tell your parents you'll no longer be discussing the issue with them, and then stick to your guns. For Teri, just accepting that her family will never embrace her unmarried relationship has helped.

My relatives don't approve of anything I do, but that's been the case since I was a child, so it's nothing new. My relatives are kind of conformist, so they don't really understand why anybody would want to rock the boat and do things in a way that attracts attention. Growing up with that, I've always known that whatever I do—whether it's the clothes I wear, the books I read, the friends I have—they're not going to approve. They never have, they never will. It doesn't matter anymore.

▸ *Get married!* For different-sex couples who were planning to marry eventually, pressure from the outside world is a perfectly legitimate reason to nudge the date a little closer. Lori's sister tied the knot to end the grilling by intrusive strangers and meddlesome relatives.

She said people would tell her directly, "Gee, why haven't you gotten married? You've been living with this guy for seven years. Get married. What's wrong with you? He must not be committed to you. He must not love you. If he won't marry you . . . . " She was very explicit about saying, "I got married because I wanted the acceptance of society." She said, "I was tired of not having that support and respect. I was tired of people looking down on me and thinking I was some kind of a slut because I wasn't married to this guy. I know I'm not. I know what my relationship with him is about. But I had to get married legally in order for other people to recognize what my relationship is all about."

Just don't make the mistake of marrying *only* because it will make everyone else so happy, as Jared did. In retrospect, he says his marriage didn't last because he agreed to it for the wrong reasons.

After we'd been together for about five years she ended up getting pregnant. All of a sudden when we started talking about marriage, her entire family totally approved of me and then everybody was behind us 100 percent. "Yeah, go, go!" They made me feel more like I was part of their family. So we got married.

Marriage will certainly put a quick end to the pressure to marry (only to be quickly replaced by the pressure to produce offspring). If this is the path you choose, be sure that it will not only please your partner and her family, but make you happy, too.

DISCRIMINATION: UNMARRIEDS NOT ALLOWED

Almost half of those we've surveyed in unmarried relationships say they've faced discrimination because they're not married. There seems to be a never-ending list of situations where these incidents take place:

I've had to pay $150 a month for the last twenty years for health insurance, because my partner's plan won't cover me unless we're married. Think about what it comes to when you add that up, $150 a month times twelve months times twenty years. That's the discrimination I am experiencing. I'm paying $1,500 a year in order not to be legally married. Getting married would give me $1,500 a year. I'd get that reward instantly.
—Kathy

We went to the bank to set up a savings account for our new baby and they wouldn't let us open a joint account that we could both put money into.
—Derek

The Peace Corps wouldn't take us. We wanted to go in the Peace Corps when we retired and they said, "Well, since you're not married, we couldn't assure you we'd send you to the same place."
—Kathyrn

Since I had done a lot of work with crime victims, I had always thought it would be interesting to be a probation officer, to see what I could do working with offenders to try to make them more responsible adults. So when I moved to Arizona, I applied for a state position. I passed the written test, and then I had to fill out a six page affidavit. It asked if I was a murderer, if I was a child molester, if I was an arsonist, and I went down the page, "No, no, no, no, no." I got to the very last page, and it asked me if I was "living in open and notorious cohabitation." And I thought, "Well, we pull the shades. What do they mean by that?" I looked it up and found out that cohabitation is illegal in Arizona; it's considered a sex offense.[34]

So I called and learned that indeed, they wouldn't let me interview for the job. I was just appalled, I can't begin to tell you. Even at that time, our relationship had lasted longer than a lot of marriages.

I ended up getting a job with Social Services as a child protective worker. When I was interviewing for it, I told the guy I was cohabiting. I said, "I feel obligated to tell you because I know that there is this statute on the books, and I don't want to hide anything." And he laughed and said, "Well, half the people in this room are cohabiting. That's not important to us." And I said, "Wait a minute. You're telling me that for child protection work in this state, I can cohabit, and yet to be a probation officer I can't? What's the logic in this?"
—Debbie

Stories about marital status discrimination are surprising in part because most of the time unmarried relationships are smooth sailing. The ease with which we create unmarried families deceives us, lulling us into forgetting that discrimination is still a reality. Family members are the source of some of the greatest pain: one woman contacted us because her sister wouldn't let her see her young niece and nephew, lest they be exposed to her unmarried relationship. Some of the biggest culprits for marital status discrimination—though by no means the only ones—are:

- adoption agencies
- banks and loan companies
- car rental companies
- data collectors (that rely on outdated marital status categories, erasing unmarried relationships)

- employers (in hiring, promotions, assignments, and benefits)
- hospitals
- landlords and housing managers (renting, buying, and student housing)
- immigration laws
- insurance companies (health, dental, car, tenants', homeowners')
- the military
- safety-net programs for poor people like Temporary Assistance for Needy Families and Medicaid
- tax laws (state and federal income tax, inheritance tax, tax on domestic partner benefits, etc.)

There are heartening examples of improvements underway. At many banks and thousands of workplaces, domestic partners are now treated exactly like married couples. Discrimination continues to be commonplace at other bank

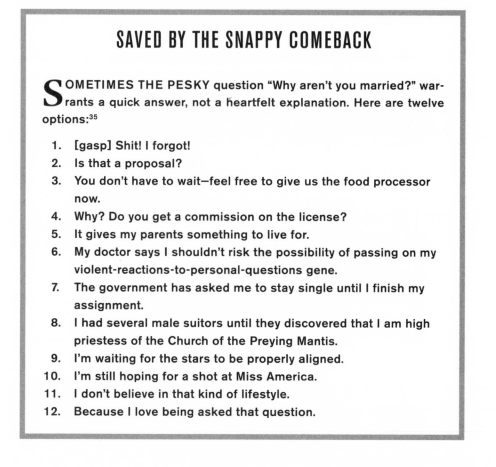

SAVED BY THE SNAPPY COMEBACK

SOMETIMES THE PESKY question "Why aren't you married?" warrants a quick answer, not a heartfelt explanation. Here are twelve options:[35]

1. [gasp] Shit! I forgot!
2. Is that a proposal?
3. You don't have to wait—feel free to give us the food processor now.
4. Why? Do you get a commission on the license?
5. It gives my parents something to live for.
6. My doctor says I shouldn't risk the possibility of passing on my violent-reactions-to-personal-questions gene.
7. The government has asked me to stay single until I finish my assignment.
8. I had several male suitors until they discovered that I am high priestess of the Church of the Preying Mantis.
9. I'm waiting for the stars to be properly aligned.
10. I'm still hoping for a shot at Miss America.
11. I don't believe in that kind of lifestyle.
12. Because I love being asked that question.

counters and employers, but the trend is to revise policies to recognize unmarried relationships. Voting with our collective wallets is a powerful way to encourage companies to treat us fairly in a competitive marketplace.

In other situations, the gradual change in social attitudes means that unmarried partners are less likely to be turned away by landlords, relatives, and emergency room nurses, even if discriminatory laws and policies remain on the books. While laws forbidding marital status discrimination in housing or hospitals would be great (and they exist in some places), they become less necessary as time passes and acceptance of our families increases. In adoption, attitudes seem to be moving in two directions simultaneously. It's easier now for single people and gay people to adopt a child than ever before, but there's also a backlash underway that's attempting to restrict eligibility to married couples (for more on adoption, see page 219).

In some areas, change comes at a snail's pace. The Immigration and Naturalization Service is unlikely to start treating domestic partners like spouses anytime soon, which severely limits the options for unmarried bi-national couples. Tax laws remain a bastion of tradition, so those lucky enough to receive domestic partner health benefits continue to be taxed on benefits their married equivalents get tax free. In the legal world, family is still usually defined by blood, marriage, or adoption. Progress is slow, but momentum is on our side.

▶ If It Happens to You: Responding to Discrimination

If you experience marital status discrimination, here are your options.

1. *Educate.* If the social worker seems reluctant to consider you as adoptive parents or your aunt excludes you from her dinner party, put on your consciousness-raising hat. Help her understand what your relationship means to you, why you're not marrying or haven't married yet, ways that you demonstrate your commitment, and what you have in common with married couples. Listen to her concerns, address what you can, and be willing to accept some areas of disagreement. The idea that a relationship can be stable, loving, and committed without marriage is a new one for some people, and they may simply need some time to mull it over.

2. *Come back later.* If you encounter a gatekeeper who is being unnecessarily difficult, you may be able to make a second approach with a new person. Teri finds this method effective when she runs into problems in a school setting. "Sometimes I just go away and come back later when somebody who's more reasonable is running the counter," she says. If there's an office you can try another day, or a customer service number you can call again, the new representative may have a different perspective.

3. *Take your business elsewhere.* Rather than fighting for your right to rent from a landlord who thinks cohabitation is sinful, find another apartment. (Do you really want to depend on this guy to fix your broken toilet promptly?) Rather than paying double for car insurance, shop around to find a company that will allow unmarried partners to share a policy—and write both companies letters to let them know how they gained or lost a customer. Dollars sometimes speak louder than discrimination complaints.

4. *Advocate for change.* Policies change because someone becomes the squeaky wheel. Domestic partner health benefits are a perfect example of this: most employers who add benefits do so because an employee, or a group of employees, asks for them. You may need to be that first employee. You can ask your local hospital to adopt a formal policy allowing people to designate their unmarried partners as "family," or ask your legislator to sponsor a bill that would repeal your state's law against cohabitation. Marital status discrimination is a vast expanse of fertile ground for social change activists. As Margaret Mead said, "Never doubt that a small group of thoughtful, committed citizens can change the world. Indeed, it is the only thing that ever has."

5. *Take legal action.* Couples who have filed discrimination complaints or sued for fair treatment have had mixed success. Some, like the couples in Alaska and California who sued their landlords, win court cases when judges agree that marital status discrimination is illegal.[36] But many others, like the heterosexual man who sued his employer for its same-sex-only domestic partner policy, lose their cases when judges say it's OK to privilege married couples.[37] Taking legal action can be risky: if you lose, the result could be the state-approved legalization of discrimination. Consult a lawyer or legal advocacy group, and consider carefully before choosing this course of action.

6. *Learn to live with it.* If Uncle Marvin won't budge, or you're tired of spending your evenings trying to organize for fair treatment at work, it may be time to let go. There are things you won't be able to change, and others that aren't worth your time. There's wisdom in the famous serenity prayer: "Grant me the serenity to accept the things I cannot change, courage to change the things I can, and wisdom to know the difference."

7. *Get engaged or married.* Uncle Marvin might be a bit happier with you if you had plans to marry eventually. While getting engaged won't miraculously resolve all kinds of pressure and discrimination, and isn't always an option, it can ease the burden for some. People may be more willing to make allowances for your choice to live together if they anticipate marriage being just around the corner. Some people, like Oprah Winfrey and her partner, Stedman Graham, make "engaged" a long-time status. They

got engaged in 1992 but still haven't walked down the aisle. If you're a binational couple where one partner can't stay in the country, and marriage is an option, you may have little choice in the matter. If you feel forced into marriage, use your "insider" status as a married person to fight to make marriage an option for everyone, but the only option for no one.

FOUR

IN IT FOR THE LONG HAUL:

Ten Tools for Staying Together

MOVING IN WAS the easy part. After you've unpacked the boxes, found a sunny window for the ivy plant, and lined up your CD racks side by side, you've succeeded in moving in. Staying together for the long-term, though, is an entirely different matter.

Now that you live under the same roof, you may discover your sweetheart's most annoying idiosyncracies, begin to interact with each other's families, even have some fights. Chapter 1 described how to lay a strong foundation for your relationship before you live together, so you don't sink into the mud as soon as you settle in. Once you have that solid foundation, your next task is to maintain your relationship so it will shelter you through the years ahead. Whether marriage is the ultimate goal or not, we assume you want your relationship to be healthy and fulfilling, and to last for a long time. This chapter provides ten tools to help you reach the goal of staying together, an assortment that includes a collection of expert recommendations and our personal favorites. Since each individual relationship is unique, there's no guarantee that every tool will be a good match for you. But if you add some of these to your relationship toolbox, you'll be even better prepared to do the maintenance that every long-term relationship needs.

FIRST TOOL:
Make a Commitment to Working for the Relationship

Ideally, you'll stay in your relationship because you want to, because being with your partner feels so good and right that it wouldn't occur to you to do anything *except* stay together. Most of the time that's how it will be, but every long-term relationship hits some stretches that require work to get yourselves back to the place where everything feels good and right. In order to stay together, you'll need a willingness to do that work, a strong internal sense of why it's important to you to be together for the long-term. Bill Hiebert, a marriage and family therapist, describes this concept as "loyalty to the relationship." He says, "Couples who believe they are in it for the long haul are going to try harder to work things out if problems arise than those who believe there's a back door through which they can escape. If you want your relationship to improve, don't unlock the back door and let it stand open—that's going to hamper your ability to succeed. Loyalty to the relationship makes the difference."[1]

If you don't feel like you already have this sense of loyalty, don't despair. As we discussed earlier when we talked about commitment, it's normal for relationship loyalty to develop over time. The passage of months and years, and life's normal ups and downs, are like fertile soil that encourage loyalty and commitment to grow. Sharon says sticking together through one of the hardest times of her life is part of what convinced her that she and her partner would make it:

> We had an awful year this year. We had a lot of tragedy in our life and a lot of financial things that went along with that. And we made it through the year. I think after we've been through this year then there shouldn't be any reason why we can't stay together the rest of our lives.

If you and your partner don't feel you have enough commitment yet, you can make an effort to develop more, or to identify the barriers that have kept you from developing it. The first step is to move both the idea and the threat of moving out a safe distance from you, and to keep it there even when you hit a rough stretch. It's hard to relax in a relationship where the potential for breakup is always hanging over your heads like a leaky roof. Janie and her partner have come to this conclusion:

> If we're having an argument about something that's not related to the fact that we're living together, we don't threaten to move out or worry about having to move out, because it's usually possible to resolve things without having to change your

living situation. The longer we live together, the easier this gets. The potential trauma of one partner suddenly moving out can make ordinary differences of opinion unnecessarily dramatic and scary.

If you hit a crisis big enough to shake the foundation of your relationship, it can be helpful to reassure your partner of your commitment as you express your feelings: "I'm *really* hurt (or angry or frustrated) right now, but I'm not leaving this relationship." Knowing that your future together isn't on the negotiation table, it can be easier to start the work of untangling the crisis. The threat of ending the relationship should be used only when circumstances are so extreme that separation is a real possibility, the way most married couples only talk about divorce as an absolute worst-case scenario. Some partners promise each other that if things got so bad that they were seriously considering ending the relationship, they would see a couples' counselor or therapist together, or take a relationship education course designed for couples in crisis. Even if you don't feel comfortable promising you'll be together forever, you can still agree on a certain minimum level of effort you'd make before throwing in the towel.

Some people never threaten to move out, but in the back of their minds they consider it whenever tension rises in the relationship. One of the best ways to address that is to realize that in relationships, as in the rest of life, there are lousy days and euphoric ones, good months and bad. Make a commitment to yourself and your partner that you're willing to tolerate some difficult times knowing that better ones are likely to return. Rose says she and her partner privately agreed on a "three years rule" that has kept them together unmarried to each other through thirty-five years of cross-country moves, career changes, and other challenges. The rule is simple: "If we are ever unhappy for as long as three years we might reconsider the relationship. We thought three years was reasonable for any crisis."

We came to a similar conclusion when we asked relatives and friends whose long marriages we respected to tell us about their relationship's hardest times. (This was a fascinating process—we highly recommend it.) We were surprised to hear how long their difficult periods had lasted, periods they said were lengthy and painful enough that they considered ending their marriages. The couples remembered one year, three years, one even said five years of conflict and frustration. Yet talking to them now, they seemed perfectly happy, pleased to be together. It was sobering to realize that *long* periods where the partners were decidedly dissatisfied with their relationships weren't the exception but the norm, at least among those to whom we spoke. Although neither of us were certain we could bear five years of a relationship that wasn't working, we did agree that our relationship was valuable enough to wait out a serious stretch of rough road.

Your internal commitment to staying together and working through problems over the long haul can be enhanced by the support of friends, family, and other important people in your life. Since most weddings are public events, couples who get married benefit from having their community witness their loyalty pledges. But long-term commitment doesn't require marriage. If you're not married for now or forever, you can make your commitment more public by talking to your family and friends about what your relationship means to you, or by having a commitment ceremony (more on this in chapter 8). When you're having difficulty, these supportive people can offer assistance or simply remind you why you want to make the relationship last.

SECOND TOOL:
Recognize Tribal Differences

A great deal of relationship stress arises from differences: one partner believes in doing something one way, the other a different way, and both feel passionately about it. Rather than arguing about which way is right, you're often better off trying to understand the origins of your differences. Often it's because the families and communities you came from, your "tribes," had different cultures. It's easy to imagine two tribes of nomads who encounter each other for the first time and are astounded or even offended by each other's clothes, customs, rituals, or language. A similar process happens every day in cohabitors' apartments and houses.

Let's say two modern people move in together and discover that when they go grocery shopping, one always buys store-brand food and whatever is on sale that week, while the other believes gourmet mushrooms and fine cheeses are among life's basic pleasures. They might each be horrified by the other's food and spending choices. The fine-cheese partner could assume his partner is cheap and unhealthy, with no sense of taste and no appreciation for high-quality food, while the store-brand partner assumes her mate is an overindulgent snob who carelessly spends more than they can afford. In fact, their different supermarket decisions may have what we're calling tribal origins. She may have grown up in a family where money was tight and where each member took pride in finding the best deals, while his family relished their culinary adventurousness, bonding as they cooked and savored each meal together. Recognizing that many differences are not based on different morals, values, or opinions, but rather different *tribes*, can save you a lot of arguing.

When we stumble on an area of disagreement, especially when we're puzzled by each other's differing reactions to the same situation, we've learned it often helps us to ask, "How did your tribe do this?" Dorian's parents went to drive-through car washes, while Marshall's were devoted believers that only the hand-sprayer kind of car wash could clean *underneath* the car. While Dorian's family occasionally liked to have "reading dinners," where each member would sit at the table, reading their own book or newspaper as they ate, in Marshall's family, dinnertime was an important time for family members to talk together, and bringing a book to the table would never have occurred to any of them. The first time we exchanged holiday gifts Dorian gave Marshall one wrapped box, while he deluged her with ten. Each of these differences created awkward moments and left us confused by each other's behavior—until we realized that each was one more example of our tribal differences.

Once you figure out that some disagreement you're having is a result of your tribal customs, you may still have to make a decision (will you wash the car at the drive-through place or the one with the hand-sprayer?). But now that you're not annoyed with what had earlier looked like your partner's poor judgment or character flaw, your approach to sorting out the issues may be entirely different.

The advantages of recognizing tribal differences aren't limited to cleaner cars, either. It can also help you get at the heart of some of the bigger issues in your relationship. Victoria realized that differing cultural backgrounds affected the way she and her partner resolved conflict:

> *Paul is English and very conflict-averse. I'm Italian and don't like conflict, either, but when it comes my way I deal with it noisily and at length. Paul tends to be passive, waiting for things to resolve themselves. Oddly enough, they frequently do. He talks about options ad nauseum, but tends not to try any of them. I'm more likely to discuss and try one solution after another.*

Whatever the source of friction in your relationship—money, sex, housework, parenting—you and your partner may be able to trace your differences back to your tribes. Your challenge then, is to agree on your own tribal customs, possibly mixing and matching from the best of both traditions.

▶ Spending Time with Your Partner's Tribe

Even if you create your own family customs, distinct from your families of origin, there's still the sticky issue of dealing with in-laws directly. If your family stresses your partner, it's your job to try to improve the relationship. This might mean standing up for your partner, as psychotherapist Maya Kollman suggests. She says to communicate, "This is my partner, and you may not like her, but you need to be decent, honest, and kind to her, because she is the person I love."[2] Or it might be as simple as playing translator, helping your partner understand why your parents do things the way they do. Pinpointing what was making Megan uncomfortable about visiting Glen's family led them to find ways to reduce the tension, as Megan explains:

We've mostly had fights related to family money. My family is middle class, Glen's is rich. I used to get stressed out and upset when we would go on expensive cruises and island vacations with his family over Christmas and other holidays. We couldn't afford these ourselves, and I felt almost guilty, like I was betraying my family and our more puritanical visits with each other. We've compromised over the years on this issue. For my part, I realize that we need to spend time with Glen's family and that some trip-taking is necessary to do this, since they don't spend their holidays at home. Together, we've agreed to forgo the more elaborate vacations and try as much as possible to visit for the more casual, closer-to-home trips. We try to spend equal time with both families, regardless of what they have planned for us to do. More recently, we've bought our own home and hope to entertain our families here.

Carmen felt uncomfortable at her partner's family events for a different reason: "When I met his family, I felt out of place and not accepted by them. They speak Spanish, and I speak Spanish, but it's different, because I am Puerto Rican and they are Colombian. I felt stupid when speaking to them, like I couldn't act like myself." Carmen shared her feelings with her partner, Alex, who talked to his mother about them. Alex's mother reassured Carmen that she was loved and accepted by the family, and that she thought Carmen was a good influence on her son. Carmen says the relationship between her and her partner's family is stronger and closer as a result.

For Brenda and Howard, both in their late sixties, the solution to surviving each others' family commitments was to realize they didn't need to attend every family event together. With a combined total of seven children from previous marriages, plus their children's spouses, partners, grandchildren, and other relatives, Brenda and Howard receive a steady stream of invitations to christenings, graduations, weddings, and other family events. They've learned that trying to attend every event as a couple not only fills their calendars, it also sometimes leaves one or both of them feeling resentful. By agreeing that the person whose family made the invitation—let's say Howard—should rate the importance of having Brenda attend this specific birthday party or dance recital (they use a zero to ten scale)—they've become efficient at making decisions that satisfy them both. Now, they're sure to attend together the events that are most important, but don't find themselves both attending a family barbecue out of a sense of loyalty, when one's absence wouldn't even be missed. Brenda says using the scale is a way of realizing they can't read each other's minds. "It's a clean way to ascertain where somebody is before we start any discussion," she says. "Sometimes the answer is a great relief."

THIRD TOOL:
Resolve Conflicts Like Pros

Tool number three is actually a collection of tools, like a good wrench set for conflict. Research suggests it's not the number or type of conflicts that lead some couples to break up while others' relationships sail along, but the way the partners interact when conflicts arise.[3] To put it another way, you can't control *whether* you have conflicts, but you can control *how* you deal with the conflicts that will inevitably happen.

Disagreements can even help a relationship grow stronger, as therapist Kollman has found from two decades of personal experience with her own partner. "My relationship with my partner is a very volatile, passionate relationship. In the past we would have thought all the conflicts were dysfunctional, but our view shifted when we realized the upsets and passion were not a bad thing, but rather an opportunity to learn more about ourselves and each other. It made the conflicts an exciting opportunity for growth," she says.[4] Psychologist and author John Gottman studies how couples argue in his "Love Lab" and then analyzes which ones are able to stay together long-term. He reports that while calmly talking out their conflicts works great for some couples, yelling at each other works just as well for others. "No one style is necessarily better than the other," he finds, *"as long as the style works for both people."*[5] If your style tends to be avoidance, or you're just not a talker, see page 28 for tips about finding ways to communicate what's important.

Whatever your style, you'll need a willingness to tackle the problems that come up. Some partners even promise each other to bring up problems as they arise instead of letting them fester. Christopher says this is a lot like keeping their car's windshield clean:

> *The windshield will keep getting crusted over with bugs and leaves and other things that stick onto it. If you never clean off your windshield, slowly but surely it'll reach the point where you can't see through it and you're going to crash. But if you keep cleaning off the windshield, you can see where you're going.*

Anne adds:

> *If you clean it right off, it's pretty easy, but if you let it bake on, it's going to be pretty hard to scrape off.*

It's the same way with relationships, they've found: it's much easier to take on small problems as they come up, rather than waiting until so many things have annoyed you that you're completely aggravated with each other.

We did some of our earliest flirting as part of a college group of trained mediators that helped to resolve campus roommate arguments and office disputes. From our earliest weeks of dating, we found that the same skills we used to help two fraternities resolve their differences also came in handy in our own disagreements. Mediation is a deceptively simple but surprisingly powerful process of resolving conflicts without violence, and without determining who is right or wrong. As mediators for others we would serve as neutral third parties who facilitated the process for the people in conflict. The goal was to come up with a solution everyone involved could live with.

You don't need a professional mediator every time one of you wants to go to the movies and the other wants to spend a quiet night at home together. It's possible to use the basic principles of mediation yourself. Here are the fundamentals:

1. *First and foremost, listen.* Conflicts usually start with at least one person feeling hurt, angry, frustrated, or any other powerfully negative emotion. At the beginning of a conflict partners usually need to express their emotions and feel like the other partner has heard and understood, even if she doesn't agree. When someone is bristling with fury, being grouchy, or crying, it's a natural impulse to interrupt, try to calm him down, defend oneself, or start problem-solving. It takes effort just to listen without doing any of those other things. This concept is at the heart of PREP, a widely used relationship education program (more on this later in the chapter). PREP teaches the "Speaker-Listener Technique" in which partners take turns talking and listening to each other's feelings about sensitive issues. When one person speaks, it's the other's job to listen, and then after the speaker is done to paraphrase back what he is saying, without responding or making editorial comments. Paraphrasing convinces the talker that he's been heard and understood, or gives him the opportunity to say, "No, that's not quite what I meant," and then clarify. When the speaker's first point is clear, the listener becomes the speaker and they trade roles.

   The advantage to the Speaker-Listener Technique is that it slows down the pace of the conversation, a valuable thing when emotions are running high. Instead of planning the counterpoint, which is what many people do in the middle of an argument, this approach forces you to pay attention to what the other person is actually saying.[6]

2. *Separate issues from feelings.* The early stage of resolving a conflict is a time for dealing with emotions. But it's essential to recognize the difference between feelings and issues. You can't mediate a feeling, only express it and give it time to change. You can, however, mediate issues, or concrete problems. For example, let's say Jerome and Sheila recently

moved in together, along with Jerome's expensive stereo system and Sheila's cat. One night, Sheila's cat decides to use Jerome's speakers as a scratching post, causing considerable damage. When they wake up the next morning and discover what happened, Jerome is livid. While ranting, cursing the cat, and letting time pass may help him calm down—addressing his initial feelings—it won't fix his speakers. The issues that need to be resolved are how the speakers will be replaced or repaired, how those expenses will be paid, and how to prevent something like this from happening again. Sheila might not have much luck starting a conversation about the cost of new speakers if she doesn't listen to Jerome fume a bit first. But once he's expressed his feelings and been heard, they're ready to move on to solutions.

Carmen and Alex make the transition from feelings to issues by having a "cooling off" period. "We really blow up at each other. We scream. We exchange words," Carmen says. "Then we stay away from each other for a half hour or so, and try to assess the situation and cool down. When we've calmed down, we'll talk."

3. *Stay outcome-oriented.* Usually one of the goals of resolving a conflict is to prevent the same issue from continuing to be a problem in the future. After you know how each of you is feeling and have a clear sense of what the issues are, it's time to shift to possible solutions. Once you've calmed down and put your heads together, you may hit upon a resolution neither of you had considered before. There's a classic story illustrating this, about two sisters fighting over the last orange in the fruit bowl. They argued bitterly over who was entitled to it, until they actually stopped to talk about why they wanted the orange. They found out that while one sister wanted to eat the orange, the other only wanted the orange peel as an ingredient for a cake she was making. Problem solved!

4. *Work toward creating a fair solution.* Julia Weber says that as a mediator, she sees people enter into conflict resolution with an imaginary middle line, and envision themselves giving up 50 percent of what they wanted and keeping the other 50 percent. Instead, Weber says, just as with the two sisters and the orange, probing deeper sometimes reveals that finding a fair solution may be more important than one that's perfectly equal. "We ask questions, get people to think more critically, and try to get to the underlying issue of why people think things should be done a certain way," Weber says. She cites housework as an example, "People choosing to live together might believe that evenly splitting up tasks related to maintaining a household might be 'fair,' but upon closer examination, they may discover that one person enjoys doing certain things more than the other or is better equipped to get things done in a way that

makes both people happy."[7] Kollman points out that fairness also requires accepting that you won't always get your needs met immediately. "Americans are a very entitled group of people. We can't tolerate waiting and have to have instant gratification," she says. "Part of living with another person is having the humility to recognize that you are not going to get what you want all the time."[8]

5. *Make peace with unsolvable problems.* Psychologist Daniel Wile writes, "When choosing a long-term partner . . . you will inevitably be choosing a particular set of unsolvable problems that you'll be grappling with for the next 10, 20, or 50 years."[9] Hiebert's experience counseling couples confirms this: the issues partners talk about when he meets with them for premarital counseling are often the same ones they're fighting about thirty years after the wedding.[10] Rather than feeling like failures for not being able to resolve every issue they disagree on, people in happy long-term relationships find ways to live with their differences. A disagreement might become the subject of good-natured joking, or one partner may agree to the other's wishes even though both know he's not happy about it. You might be able to agree to disagree, and leave a subject alone after you've gnawed on it together for years.

FOURTH TOOL:
Timing Matters

One of the best things about living together is that you have access to all the things you like about your partner—shoulder massages, good conversation, someone to reach that serving bowl on the high shelf—every day of the week. But one of the disadvantages to all that proximity is that the less fun parts of being in a relationship, like needing to resolve conflicts, can also creep in any time, any day. Although issues may arise with a sense of urgency to them, most are not emergencies that need to be resolved immediately. You can decide which conflicts need prompt attention, and which are better resolved at another time. You're in control of whether you bring up a topic after a stressful day of work or on a lazy Sunday afternoon, but you should not avoid imortant subjects by shelving them forever.

▶ Timing Conversations with a Calendar

Brenda and Howard set aside time once a week specifically for talking about issues they need to resolve. While some of the topics they discuss at these meetings are major disagreements, more often they're figuring out who's going to research having the roof repaired or run a daytime errand. Throughout the week, if one of them brings up a non-urgent problem or issue, they try to write a note about it on a piece of paper, and put the paper in a red folder they've designated for this purpose. Howard says, "I like to be able to think about things before I respond, and by having meetings I'm able to spend some time thinking about it in advance, do research, and come to the table more informed, not giving opinions off the top of my head." They both agree that they enjoy being able to relax and enjoy the week, knowing their concerns won't be forgotten.

▶ Timing Conversations Based on Moods

The trick isn't necessarily to put your important conversations on a regular schedule, but to have them when you're not already feeling tired, overloaded, or stressed about something unrelated to your partner. George Pransky, author of *The Relationship Handbook*, likens changing moods to an elevator in a building. "Every time a mood shifts, it brings a new perspective, a different view of reality. What we see and think right now differs from what we saw and thought a few minutes ago. If life is an elevator, moods are the floors we visit." Pransky numbers the floors from the lowest, "doom and gloom," up to the highest, "inspiration."[11] If you step off the elevator on the lower floors and try to solve a relationship conflict, the situation looks dank and dreary, full of cobwebs and mold. On the top floors, the sun is shining, the air is clear, and everything is neat and well-organized.

Everyone has times when their mood soars and other times when it seems stuck in the basement. When you're in your emotional basement, don't get off the elevator. Don't think you and your partner can look around the basement and clean it up, or start a conversation about the future of your relationship, while you both inhale the mold. Don't try to make decisions. Simply introducing a subject of disagreement in this emotional environment will depress you further, and you'll end up even more frustrated than you began. (Small children understand this intuitively, which is why they know not to bring up the subject of the crayon marks that got on the dresser when Mom is already grumpy about something else.) Rather, wait until your mood improves, which it nearly always will do on its own in time. Disagreements are much easier to resolve in the sunshine. Occasionally you'll encounter a relationship issue so huge and upsetting that you walk around with a stomachache, knowing you won't be in a better mood until you have some resolution. But even when you know you're heading in to untangle one of these monstrosities, there will still be variation in your moods. You'll be able to tell whether your elevator is as high as it's capable of getting given the circumstances, or whether you just need to cry now and talk later.

▶ Don't Generalize from the Mood of the Moment

Just as it's wise not to start important conversations when you're already irritable, it's also important not to blow a single cranky conversation out of proportion. Some of us tend to extrapolate from, "He's frustrated that I forgot to pick up the drycleaning," to, "He really doesn't like me very much." Or, "Didn't she seem a little aloof on the phone just now?" to, "She's probably getting ready to break up with me." Since whatever we're feeling *right now* seems so present, it can be easy to forget about all the other information we have from other months and years in the relationship. Realize that if you're both in a relationship for the long term, you don't need to check constantly to see if your partner still likes you, or consider each week whether you might be able to find someone better. Don't let one argument erase your memories of all that's good about your relationship. While paying attention to moods and attitudes is important, getting overly invested in any one moment in time can lead you to wildly misleading conclusions.

FIFTH TOOL:
Enlist the Help of Others

There's an American myth that people in relationships should resolve their problems on their own, at least until they reach the point that they're ready to seek the help of a divorce lawyer. Given that the perspective of someone outside the relationship can provide a source of fresh ideas, creative solutions, and thoughtful support, it's definitely time to alter this view. The social support that comes with marriage is part of what helps marriages stay together. There's value in being able to talk to your dad about his marriage, or hear a friend at church talk about how she and her husband resolved a similar tension last year. Some faith communities have even institutionalized this process by pairing newlyweds with long-married couples from the same church or synagogue.

Unmarried relationships often don't receive the same kind of social support, and too often when unmarried partners do seek help they get lectures about the fact that they're not married ("What did you expect, moving in together without a commitment?"), rather than help with their current problem. Therapist Maya Kollman says that finding supportive community, whether parents or friends, is a critical factor for relationship success. "I can't get over how important it is when people start having trouble. Couples who are able to withstand problems have a community that believes in the *relationship*, not just the individuals involved."[12] Below are several ways you can tap into the power of social and community support.

▶ Relationship Mentors

You probably know someone who has a really great relationship. You might think so because of how long a certain couple has been together, how affectionate they are, the challenges they've overcome together, the similarity to your own relationship, or some other combination of factors. It doesn't matter whether they are married or not, as long as they seem more experienced than you about the ways of long-term love.

Tell them how much you admire their relationship—most people are deeply touched to know that someone noticed. See if you can engage them in a conversation about what the relationship has been like from the inside and ask them how they got through differences and hard times. Any relationship that's lasted a fair length of time has had ups and downs, and it's possible you'll learn that this couple who looks so happy has struggled with issues that aren't apparent from the outside. You might find out that they're just recovering from a serious squabble and be able to learn from how they solved the problem.

You might want to formalize the relationship by asking the person or pair you've identified if you can call on them from time to time for some words of couple advice. Or, you don't have to use the word "mentor" at all, but just engage the people you respect in conversations about relationships. Johanna finds her mother to be a source of insight and support:

> *My mother and stepfather have been married for over twenty years. Sometimes I seek my mother's advice, because after years of conflict, she and my stepdad are really happy and very much in love now. Things were terribly rocky for their first ten or fifteen years together, but they made it through, somehow. If she and my stepdad can make it, I think, then any dedicated couple can.*

Doug says his experience in a Bible study group with married couples helped him tremendously after the experience of being divorced:

> *I was in a group with five couples who had been together long-term. They shared their struggles with the group, and we helped one another through the hard times and celebrated in the good times. I learned "at their feet" and witnessed commitment. Their role modeling was a gift to someone who had been divorced twice.*

▶ Therapists and Counselors

Too many people only consider seeing a therapist, counselor, or mediator when they're in crisis. But many who have worked with professionals say they can help at all stages of a relationship. Laura and Chet have been to therapy for several periods in their relationship and like knowing there's someone in the world who's "rooting for us as a couple." Laura says:

> There was no major crisis that precipitated our going into couple's therapy. We turned to therapy early on as a safe place where we could explore our relationship and make some important decisions about who we were as a couple and where we were headed.
>
> In the years since, we have returned to therapy over and over again to deal with issues as they've come up. When our daughter was born, our previously harmonious relationship was challenged. I'd become a stay-at-home mom after years of having a career, the baby screamed for hours every night, and Chet was trying to juggle new fatherhood and his career for the first time at age fifty-one. There was a lot we needed to deal with and therapy provided the space and perspective to sort it all out.
>
> We haven't seen our therapist for two years, but she has made it clear that her door is always open, whether for a one-session visit or an extended period. Because she knows us well, and has seen us at our best and our absolute worst, we can go in and get right down to the issues.

Some say developing a relationship with a good therapist, as Laura and Chet have, is similar to having an ongoing relationship with a doctor. When you visit the doctor for routine checkups, he gets to know you and can give advice on how to prevent major health problems. In the same way, a therapist who gets to know you as a couple can help you ward off future problems. Then, if real trouble strikes, you can get support from someone with whom you already have a trusting relationship, who knows your history and has a sense of how you approach problems.

Psychologist Nancy Saunders recommends therapy for helping make the adjustment to new life stages, especially if you find your relationship is having trouble adjusting to circumstances like job changes, new children in the household, kids leaving home, and a variety of other issues. She suggests the "three times rule" as a guide to knowing when you might benefit from working with a professional: "If you have the same fight more than three times, and you don't get to a deeper level of understanding, get help. Most people wait much too long."[13]

WILL YOU BE MY THERAPIST?

YOU'VE DECIDED YOU want to find a counselor. How do you begin?

First, collect the names of a handful of people in your area. You can get suggestions from your health insurance company, human resources department, community or professional organizations, clergy, physicians, school counselors, friends, or as a last resort, the phone book.

Call each of the people you're considering, knowing that you'll often get voice-mail because they are with a client or on the phone. Tell them your first name, say that you're considering setting up an initial consultation for couples counseling, and if your health insurance will be covering some or all of the cost of therapy, make sure they will accept your plan. Then, Elizabeth Morrison, a therapist herself, says, "Give [the therapist] a brief, simplified explanation of your problem, and ask, 'Do you think you can help us out, and how?' " At that point, Morrison says, the conversation is a job interview for the professional. The therapist will either provide you with some initial explanation of how she thinks she might address the problem, or equally valid, suggest it might be better for you to discuss your needs and her approach in more detail in person. "As they talk, take some notes," Morrison says, listing off what you might be scribbling down: " 'Sounds intelligent and empathetic.' 'Sounds like a total loser.' 'Sounds uptight and preoccupied.' What you're listening for are signs that they are hearing what you are saying. Maybe you like their sense of humor, or you like that they seem quick and clever, or that they seem thoughtful, considering what you're saying very carefully." You can also ask about things like training, degrees and certification, and experience working with clients in situations similar to yours. The most important factor is whether this person feels like someone you and your partner would respect and want to work with. If the match isn't a good one, all the credentials in the world are useless for meeting your needs.[14]

SIXTH TOOL:
Have Fun Together

Children and dating couples have this in common: they usually don't forget to have a good time. When you're dating but not living together, the time you spend together is usually focused on each other, doing things together you both like. Partners who move in together are often excited to expand the number of hours they can spend snuggling, renting old movies, or doing whatever it is that they enjoy. What often happens instead, though, is that the hours of life's drudgery expand, but the cuddling time does not. As advice columnist and sex therapist Chris Fariello says, "When we first meet another person we find ways to make time together. Once we live together there never seems to be enough time together."[15] Making time for the tastiest morsels of being in a relationship often requires a conscious effort, as Marion found after her partner moved in with her:

We try not to let the discussions about the nitty-gritty of sharing a household— what needs to go on the shopping list, or what shall we do about the broken vac-

uum cleaner—replace the more meaningful conversations we used to have before we moved in together.

Having fun isn't just frivolous, but part of an overall strategy that will help your relationship survive when the sky is looking gloomier. Some experts say that sharing positive times, doing kind things for each other, and saying things that make each other feel good is like depositing money into the relationship's bank account. Having a conflict or putting each other down withdraws money out of the account. Like any bank account, you'll run into trouble if you're withdrawing more than you're depositing.

The best way to make sure you have time for each other is to schedule it, the same way you do for other appointments. Sarit and David, who lived together for eight years before getting married, still go on dates:

> *Dates have always been an important part of our relationship. Both of us enjoy going out—to the movies, dinner, music, drinks—and we enjoy the ways in which thinking about our times out together as "dates" helps us feel special and focus on each other. When I was working full-time and going to school at night, and David was working ten to twelve hour days, we instituted a weekly "date-night" in the middle of the week. We knew that Wednesday nights were times set aside just for each other, and our dates ranged from cooking a special dinner at home with a bottle of wine to [going] dancing . . . More recently, our dates have included Sunday brunch and a drive exploring a new neighborhood.*

For Tracey R. and Jane S., occasional weekend getaways are the solution to surviving their busy two-career, two-child household and still enjoying time with each other. Tracey explains:

> *We can get bogged down with routine and lost to each other with all the competing demands of work, kids, and keeping up the house. To us it feels essential that we have some time away. There are two different ways we've done this. Sometimes we plan time away together, but other times one of us surprises the other with a weekend with all the plans in place, including the babysitter. It can feel like entering another world to get to wake up together and have coffee, to be back in touch with the simple pleasures that get lost. Also, on a regular day our only time alone is late at night, when we're often too tired to have sex. When we're away, we have the incredible freedom to have sex whenever we want!*

Dates don't have to involve leaving home; a "date night" could be an evening at home together where you don't pay bills or decide it's time to vacuum under the sofa cushions.

You can also integrate fun and affection into your usual routine. Walking the dog together can be a way to enjoy each other, or having a ritual of getting ice cream on hot summer nights. Maya and her partner have a tradition that each time she returns home from being away on business, they play rock'n'roll music and dance around the living room for fifteen minutes. "It's a little thing, it doesn't take much time, but it gets us in touch with each other emotionally," she says. Marion and her partner connect quietly on a daily basis, by setting aside a time each night just for the two of them:

We enjoy having a time for mediation and reflection before we go to bed each night. We light a candle and read an inspirational passage from a book, and then have a time of silence. It's a good way to connect and a peaceful way to end the day.

TEN WAYS TO HAVE FUN TOGETHER WITHOUT BREAKING THE BANK

ENJOYING LIFE TOGETHER doesn't always require a big commitment of time or money. Sometimes it's just a matter of finding little ways to connect with each other, either spontaneously or as a part of your regular routine. Here are ten ideas for spontaneous and not so spontaneous things you can do. Reading the list may spark ten more!

1. Know your partner's favorite sweet treat and bring it home. (But not if she's on a diet. At least not too often.)
2. Give your partner a spur-of-the-moment head, neck, or shoulder massage.
3. Randomly send your partner a note or e-mail with a loving (or sexy) message. Tell your partner how lucky your are to have him or her in your life.
4. Hug often. Hug with both arms. And both legs.
5. Read out loud to each other books, poems, or articles that interest you both.
6. Buy something risqué once in a while and put it to use.
7. Add little surprises to your partner's day: a love note in a lunch bag or on top of a pillow, a flower for no reason, a kiss or hug when it's not expected, a helping hand with the other's "regular" household task.
8. Make it a habit to thank each other regularly and express appreciation verbally, even for doing things you're expected to do, like making dinner or cleaning the toilet.
9. Have a weekend morning ritual: coffee in bed, or special food, or particular music.
10. When the music inspires you, dance together in the kitchen without worrying that you look silly and don't know what you're doing.

SEVENTH TOOL:
Understand How a Long-term Investment Pays Off

In the stock market, it's easy to get caught up in investing in whatever the hottest new industry is, in hopes of making millions overnight. Usually, though, it's the patient, long-term investors who reap the biggest returns. The relationship equivalent of hot stocks versus long-term investing is the difference between a passionate new love affair and a long-term relationship. New loves will often offer more excitement, and may seem to have more of a spark or a better connection than old ones. It's not realistic to compare them one-to-one, though, because any new lover can't stay new forever. The excitement and intensity of lovemaking is one of the things that is likely to change. Victoria says that in a long-term relationship:

> *It's true that the flames die down. But we don't think low libido is a reason to contemplate splitting up—sex is not the reason why we're together in the first place, just as sensible folks don't marry the most arousing person they know. We're friends who share values and interests, have some complimentary aptitudes and, by the way, find each other physically attractive.*

Part of making a long-term relationship last is recognizing its benefits as being distinctly different, and with luck, ultimately better, than the benefits of "trading it in" for a new relationship. Psychologist Nancy Saunders says:

> *For me, living together is very comfortable. You have the ease of a companion in your home. You have somebody there to get you medicine if you have a headache, somebody with whom you can process your day. Human beings who are in successful partnerships do better. They have comfort, stability, familiarity, all of which are of real value.*[16]

'Becca has found she prefers a relationship that starts warm and heats up, rather than one that starts hot and then cools. It's interesting to consider that in some cultures, this kind of "heating up" is exactly what most people aspire to in their relationships; but in the U.S., most people want and expect fireworks at the start. Eight years into her relationship with Daniel, 'Becca says:

> *When I've begun a relationship on a hormonal high, it's ended after six to twelve months. What is different about my relationship with Daniel is that we never had that hormonal high or New Relationship Energy or any other giddy feeling, at least not in a way that pervaded the relationship for more than a few hours at a*

stretch. I don't mean that we have a dreary relationship devoid of sexiness and sparkle. It's just that, instead of having all that in one dizzying gooey stage at the beginning, we've somehow managed to distribute it into a lot of little moments over a long time. Instead of going through stages, our relationship has been a smooth slope of gradually increasing commitment, intimacy, love, and happiness.

EIGHTH TOOL:
Let Go of "Shoulds" and
Focus on What Works for You

Television shows are awash with images of the perfect life and the perfect mate. Movies and romance novels are full of stunningly beautiful people who fall in love effortlessly; go on sweet, whimsical dates; know with absolute certainty that they are meant to spend the rest of their lives together; and have elaborate, perfect weddings. What's "normal," in many people's minds, is when a married couple who have never been divorced live with their two children in a nice, suburban house with a white-picket fence and a golden retriever in the backyard. Even though you know that most people's lives don't fit that cookie cutter image, it's easy to slip into thinking everyone else is "normal," and you happen to be the only one who is somehow different. To the contrary, so many of us are "different" in some way that different *is* normal.

On a recent Valentine's Day, Dorian found a card for Marshall that read:

Our relationship
may be different
from what others
think it should be . . .

but that doesn't really matter,

because we know it's right for us.

With you, I can always be me . . .
and that makes me love you even more.

Marshall liked the card, and we were both struck by how many people must have relationships that are "different from what others think it should be": at least enough to buy a lot of greeting cards.

What matters is not whether you're average, but whether you and your partner agree on what works for you. This is true not only for big decisions like whether to live together or get married, but also for many of life's details. The stories people tell throughout this chapter illustrate this point perfectly. Some might find it strange to see a therapist early in a relationship when there isn't any crisis, to dance to rock'n'roll upon returning from a business trip, or to discuss relationship issues in a weekly meeting with your partner. Yet each of these approaches has served at least one couple well—and probably many others—precisely because they don't worry about what others think and have the courage to find what works for them.

Elizabeth Morrison, a therapist who has counseled hundreds of people, says, "Take the issue of how much time to spend with your partner. You may be dying to spend every moment of the weekend with your partner, focused only on each other. Or one of you might see the weekend as a time for self-reflection at the fishing hole. What matters is whether both people agree. The same is true with sex: it's not how often a couple does it that matters, but whether both people feel OK about the frequency."[17]

You can't expect to agree on everything; earlier we discussed ways of finding workable solutions to areas where you have differing opinions. But the key is to give yourselves permission to do what's right for your situation, as Kelly writes:

> [My boyfriend and I] are in a committed relationship and plan to marry one day. But we will get married when the time is right for us and we feel that all of the pieces are in place. The reaction from others is unbelievable. . . . Every holiday since we moved in together (especially Christmas and my birthday), I am [bombarded] with questions immediately upon returning to work. I hear, "Did he give you a diamond?" "Where is that ring?" He gets the giving end of the questions, "Did you give her a ring?" . . . Since we are not engaged, our relationship is completely demeaned to a sexual convenience. . . . People have no clue that we are more committed to each other and our relationship than many people are to their marriages. I love my boyfriend and plan to marry him—on my own terms and in my own time.[18]

NINTH TOOL:
Take a Relationship Education Course

Relationship education is a promising new approach to helping people have great relationships. The goal of these classes is to give people skills to help them communicate better, resolve conflicts, fight fair, manage anger, and rekindle the spark between them. At the very least, they offer an opportunity to take some time away from the hassles of everyday life to spend with your partner focusing on each other and your relationship. At best, they can bring your relationship to a whole new level if you're already on solid ground, or bring it back from the brink if you're not. There are a wide variety of types of courses, most taught by therapists, trained relationship educators, or clergy. Some take place over a series of evenings, while others involve spending a weekend away at a retreat or conference center with the group's facilitator, your partner, and the other people attending the workshop.

Eleven years into their relationship, Skip and Alan attended one of these weekend workshops and describe it as a turning point for them. Skip says:

> It was absolutely—if not life-changing, then certainly relationship-changing. We came out of it with really concrete tools and ways of handling differences, and ways of understanding how childhood issues were impacting the current relationship. They took us through some exercises on commitment and intimacy. I think we reached a new level of commitment during that weekend. And the relationship really turned a corner at that point. It was good already, but it's just taken off since then.

Not all relationship education courses are an equally good fit for unmarried relationships. Avoid classes focused exclusively on marriage that either ignore or are openly skeptical about the value of cohabitation and other kinds of relationships. You can probably cope with changing the word "marriage" to "relationship" in your head, but that's different than finding yourself sitting through a lecture against living together.

Fortunately, screening for classes that welcome unmarried couples is easy to do. Contact the person leading the workshop, tell her you're thinking about signing up, and ask her to tell you more about the program. Besides learning more about the workshop in general, your goal in the conversation will be to assess three things. First, do they serve people in relationships like yours (cohabiting but not engaged, gay or lesbian, etc.)? Second, are the skills they teach applicable to your kind of relationship? And third, do you think the class's leaders want to see your relationship succeed, whether you get married or not?

If their classes are attended by lots of other people in your situation, that's a great sign. If not, that's not necessarily a reason to cross them off your list. It's possible you could be the first to realize that someone who's not married might benefit from a workshop marketed toward married couples. You should be able to get a sense of whether you'll feel comfortable by listening to the workshop leader talk about the program. If you don't get a sense of the program from this conversation, ask to speak to others who have completed the course.

TENTH TOOL:
Celebrate Your Time Together

Most unmarried couples are optimistic about the future of their relationships. They want to be together forever, though they're realistic that there's no guarantee. Because that guarantee doesn't exist—for unmarried or married couples—it's important to celebrate the milestones along the way. If you've been in your relationship awhile—whether it's one year, ten, or fifty—you can be proud. Each passing year together speaks to the strength of your relationship. Taking the time to celebrate your anniversary is a way to mark that passage of time, take pride in the years you've spent together, and anticipate many more.

Married couples usually celebrate their anniversaries based on the date of their wedding. But anniversaries can be a challenge for unmarried partners since it's hard to know what date to pick. Should your anniversary be the first time you met, your first date, the first time you spent a night together, or the day you moved in? What if your friendship developed so gradually that you're not sure whether your first date was the time you grabbed coffee together after work, or the night months later that you got all dressed up and went out on a Friday night?

Whatever date they pick, many unmarried partners celebrate their relationship the same way married couples do, with cards, flowers, and maybe dinner out. Others find their own ways to celebrate the years that have passed. Myra and her partner celebrate two anniversaries per year: "One marks our commitment ceremony that involved friends and family. The other one is our anniversary of entering the journey of being lovers together." Kurt and his partner celebrate their anniversary even more often:

> We've celebrated our anniversary monthly since we got together, nineteen years and three months ago. Every month. We celebrate with maybe a card or dinner or whatever. If things are tough we still say happy anniversary. The first ten years he kind of said, "Oh, not again," but he caught onto it himself now. It was my project initially: I'm one of these incurable romantics.

Debbie says that rather than exchanging cards, she and Jim would rather use their anniversary and birthdays as an excuse to have an adventure.

> We'll just go off to the desert, or take off for a weekend camping, or take the kayak out and do something. It's just a chance to get out together. When we lived up in Alaska we got a bunch of friends together and chartered a limousine and went to McDonald's for lunch. One year we'd always wanted to parachute, and so we did that for our experience. We've gone ballooning. It's just a time to kind of do something like that with our lives, to remember. That's much more enjoyable than giving gifts.

We also decided that we didn't want to give each other presents on our anniversary, since there are plenty of other holidays for gift exchanges. Instead, we opted to resurrect an element of our relationship that we'd lost since moving in together: letters. While our earliest months were filled with e-mail flirtation and rambling summer exchanges, these days most of our writing to each other takes the form of hurriedly composed e-mails deciding who's going to get the car's oil changed. Now, every year, each of us writes a one-page letter to the other, reflecting on the past year and sharing what we appreciate about each other and our relationship. We limit the length so there's no way one of us will "out-do" the other or feel badly for not writing enough. The experience has been a powerful one, serving not only to draw us closer, but also to mark each year we share.

QUALITY MATTERS

We believe the quality of any relationship is deeply important, far more important than people's legal marital status or any other detail of their identities. One of the great things about most relationship tools is that they are available to all people, regardless whether they are married. If a specific tool is particularly valuable to you, you can use it while you cohabit and later if you marry, and possibly in nonintimate situations like work or school, as well. The ten tools described in this chapter include some of our very favorites, both the ones we use on a daily basis and the ones we dig out of the bottom of the toolbox when crisis hits. You can choose the tools you need, and add some of your own along the way as you experience life together.

FIVE

"THIS IS MY— UM, UH . . . ":

Naming Each Other

NAMING YOUR PARTNER

IF AN OLD friend introduces you to her husband, most people make different assumptions about them than if she calls the man at her side her fiancé—or "sweetie"—or "special friend." The man is the same guy, and the way he stands alongside her is identical in each scenario, yet we read different information into the picture depending on the label our friend gives him.

The simple sentence, "This is my wife," (or husband) implies an enormous amount of information. It generally means that the relationship between these two people is:

1. serious
2. long-term
3. committed
4. sexual
5. monogamous
6. and involves living together

When it comes to making simple introductions, people in unmarried relationships in this country are at a major disadvantage. Unlike some other languages, American English simply doesn't have a word or set of words that are the non-married equivalents of husband and wife. As a result, unmarried people are on their own. Laina isn't the only one who finds this frustrating:

> I don't think there's a good word that describes the situation that we're in. "Lover" implies getting together on an occasional basis, and there's a little illicitness in there, like he's somebody you've got on the side, when you've got a primary partner elsewhere. That's not the case. He's not my husband: we're not married. He's not my fiancé: we're not planning on getting married. There's just no good word to describe us. Paramour? I don't know.

Most unmarried partners are like Kirsten, who has a word she uses most of the time, but also a collection of other possible terms she uses depending on the situation. She says, "I refer to Tom as my partner. Or sometimes my roommate. Or my sweetie. Or, love of my life."

Others find new ways to use words that already exist. Jewelle says, "Diane and I say we are engaged. But not to be married. It's a wonderful end in itself. It's an active verb, as in being connected, involved, attracted, and interacting."[1] Jeffrey prefers "co-pilot," explaining, "It conveys a sense of shared adventure, movement forward and a certain kind of healthy resilience."[2]

Finding a word that works—whether it's a word everyone knows or one you invent yourself—is an important part of having a relationship that works, since many linguists and anthropologists believe that language helps shape reality. Simply having a name for something validates it, making it real.[3] We find that the most frequent terms people use are partner (including life partner, domestic partner, and unmarried partner), boyfriend and girlfriend, significant other (or S.O.), the person's name without any descriptive word, friend, and husband or wife. Below, we'll talk about the advantages and disadvantages of some of these.

▶ Partner: The Most Common Choice

We usually use the word "partner" when we're talking to new people, and we find it's by far the most commonly used introduction word. We like the way partner implies equality, people working together and sharing life's joys and challenges. We think it describes our relationship pretty well.

We also like what "partner" *doesn't* reveal. Partner can be inclusive of both married and unmarried couples: married couples know they're included, for instance, when a brochure about prenatal health writes about, "the pregnant woman and her partner." Partner also doesn't indicate the gender of the person, so it can be used with ease by heterosexual as well as gay, lesbian, bisexual, and transgender (GLBT)

MULTIPLE CHOICE

ARE YOU IN the market for a better way to make introductions? Here are some words unmarried people use to describe their loved ones to other people:

beau

better half

boyfriend/girlfriend

bride

co-pilot

companion

family (sometimes used to introduce more than one person, like two partners or a partner and child)

fiancé/fiancée

friend

honey

housemate

husband/wife

life partner

love of my life

lover

main squeeze

man/woman/lady

manfriend/womanfriend

mate

name (just introduce the person by name without a descriptive word)

other half

O.T.L. (stands for Own True Love)

personal joke words (anti-husband/anti-wife, Frootloops, boy toy, semi-spousal unit, fish-wife/fishmonger, etc.)

paramour

partner

partner in crime

POSSLQ (pronounced POSS-ul-cue) (Persons of the Opposite Sex Sharing Living Quarters, formerly the way the Census counted cohabitors)

primary

roommate

significant other

sin-in

S.O. (stands for Significant Other)

special friend

spousal equivalent

spouse

sweetheart

sweetie

symbiant[4]

unmarried partner

wife-substitute/husband-substitute

people. Since partner is used by people who are married and not married, straight and gay, we like the way it de-emphasizes the significance of marital status, gender, and sexual orientation. Using it can be a subtle way to raise awareness about family diversity by making it harder for people to make assumptions.

But partner isn't right for everyone. A couple who belong to an organized dance group told us that in their community, people would assume the word "partner" meant dance partner, and wouldn't realize they were in a relationship. Lydia doesn't like the way "partner" is used as part of "domestic partner," which she says implies that the relationship is all work and no play. "Domestic partner makes it sounds like all we ever do is housework," she complains.

Some people think partner means business partner, which can result in the kind of confusion Jennifer ran into:

I was talking one time to a stockbroker on the phone and said "partner." He said, "You have a business?" I said, "No, partner, significant other," and he'd never heard that before. He didn't know what I was talking about. I said, "Well, boyfriend." So I think whether people understand it depends on the context.

Some heterosexuals don't feel comfortable using a word that's often applied to same-sex relationships, since people might assume they are gay or lesbian. But Ulla says that in her experience, it seems like the term is becoming more commonly accepted as time goes by. "I used to have more of a feeling that I would say "partner" and people would just be stunned by that word," she says. "It was almost like the conversation would stop as I said it, and they needed time to figure out what I meant." These days, she says, that happens less frequently.

Even though we use "partner" pretty consistently, there are times when it just doesn't work, as Dorian experienced:

I wasn't paying attention one day and I got pulled over for speeding. The police officer who approached my car in his mirrored sunglasses was incredibly intimidating. "License and registration!" he barked. I handed them over, momentarily forgetting that the car was registered in Marshall's name.
The officer looked over what I had handed him and noticed that the name on my license did not match the one on the car's registration. "Whose car is this?" he demanded.
"My partner's," I told him promptly.
"WHOSE?" he barked again.
"My boyfriend's, my boyfriend's," I squeaked, hoping this answer was more acceptable. I suppose it was, because shortly thereafter he sent me on my way with only a warning.

Not all unmarried couples can switch to a safer term like Dorian did. For a lesbian driver in the same situation, for instance, switching from the gender-free word "partner" to "girlfriend" runs the risk of making the situation worse.

▶ Girlfriend or Boyfriend: Another Popular Option

After "partner," we find that "girlfriend" and "boyfriend" are the most commonly used words. The biggest advantage they have is how widely they're understood, leading many to rely on them for simplicity's sake. Allen says that he doesn't think there's a good word to describe his relationship, but that "girlfriend" is the easiest approach. "If it's people that I don't know, I'll say, 'This is my girlfriend, Deborah.' It just gets the introductions out of the way. Everybody knows what that means."

One challenge to the girlfriend/boyfriend option is the fact that couples aren't expected to stay girlfriend and boyfriend for too long. Even kindergartners will tell you that after being boyfriend and girlfriend, you're supposed to get married. Among adults, the words can still suggest a temporary status with the potential to be transformed into husband and wife later. While couples who hope or plan to marry someday may find boyfriend and girlfriend are the best fit for them, others think the words sound too young. Tracey, who's twenty-nine, says:

> As I got older, I use "mate" more often than boyfriend. But sometimes I slip, and I'll just casually say, "Oh, yeah, my boyfriend." But I don't really like using that term for him, because it reminds me of high school.

Gay, lesbian, and bisexual people in same-sex relationships face a different set of issues. Kay and Sue usually introduce each other as "girlfriend." But when coming out[5] feels unsafe or uncomfortable, they'll use "friend" instead. Simply claiming a GLBT partner is risky in some situations. Introducing a life partner as a "friend" gives the relationship even less public legitimacy than introducing him or her as a "boyfriend" or "girlfriend," yet for some same-sex relationships this kind of self-protective invisibility is too often a regular part of life.

▶ Spouse, Husband, or Wife: Married Words for Some Unmarrieds

Some unmarried people like to use words like "spouse" or "husband" and "wife" for a variety of reasons:

▶ As we explore elsewhere in the book, some people have wedding ceremonies but don't get legally married. These people may consider themselves married in every sense except the legal one, and using "husband" and "wife" is a standard part of being married. Be careful, though. If you're a male-female couple in one of the thirteen states that recognize common-law marriage, publicly calling yourselves husband and wife can transform your relationship into a legal marriage without so much as an "I do." (For more on how this works, see page 147.)

▶ They like the fact that these terms signify the seriousness of the relationship and help others understand that their commitment is more like marriage than dating. Clarice, who has been unmarried to her partner Ed for over two decades, worked as an insurance agent when it was still uncommon for women to be agents. Some work-related events were for the agents and their wives, so her employer created a word that validated her relationship as being equal to the married employees.

My boss called Ed my spice. "Bring your spouses and your spices." Ed was my spice. I had a good time with the people in the office, and they respected my relationship with Ed. They knew we weren't married, but he was always invited and expected to come along to the dinners and weekends and trips. He was expected just like the wives were expected.

▶ They believe that these words should not be used exclusively by those in legal marriages, and use them as a process of "reclaiming." One unmarried woman explained that she chooses to use "wife" even though she is troubled by the sexism in the word's history. By using a traditional word in a non-traditional relationship, she wants to be part of redefining it, altering its historical meaning. Chris, who's gay, enjoys the way using "spouse" challenges people's assumptions in a similar way. He says, "If I'm in a store or something, or a more formal kind of situation, I sometimes use the word spouse. They always think it's a woman. Then I correct them—that's part of the fun."

MOM, I'D LIKE YOU TO MEET MY *PILEGESH*

NOT ALL LANGUAGES are as ill-equipped for unmarried couples as English. The Hebrew word *pilagshut* literally means half-marriage. Biblical *pilagshut* relationships allowed an unmarried man and woman to live together in a committed sexual relationship and determine their own obligations, rather than having policies imposed on them by society or religion. The relationships, which were assumed to include more equality and freedom than marriages, could be considered as holy as formal marriages, and the children of *pilegesh* were considered as "legitimate" as the children of married couples. In Israel today, the partners in an unmarried relationship are called *ben zug* or *bat zug*.[6]

In Spanish, the word *marido* has a wider range of meanings than the commonly used word for husband, *esposo. Marido* is used for "husband," but also for "common-law husband" and "live-in boyfriend." It's what Carmen calls her partner, Alex:

Alex's family is Colombian and my family is Puerto Rican. Instead of say-ing esposo, *which means husband, I say* marido. Marido *sounds like husband but is more like live-in boyfriend. In English, I say this is my boyfriend even though we've been together for six years. It sounds better in Spanish.*

In Quebec, the terms for married spouses and unmarried partners have become more interchangeable, with some couples choosing the word they'll use based more on age than marital status. Younger unmarried partners usually refer to each other as *chum* (slang for boyfriend, borrowed from the English word "chum") or *blonde* (slang for girlfriend), but sometimes continue to do so after they get married. Older couples and those with more money tend to refer to each other as *conjoint* or *marie* (spouse), whether they're married or not. Unmarried cohabitation has become so common and accepted in the Canadian province that some married women now refer to their husbands as *mon chum* instead of the word for husband.[7]

In 1999 France adopted a legal structure that gives benefits to registered unmarried couples (both same-sex and different-sex), called *Pacte Civil de Solidarité* (Civil Solidarity Pact) and nicknamed PACS. According to news reports, the law inad-vertently created the new verb *se pacser,* or "to pact."[8] Unmarried French couples now have a commonly understood term for their relationships.

But Sweden takes the gold in the international name-the-unmarried-partners con-test. Those clever Swedes take the verb *bo,* to live, and tack it onto other words, cre-ating *sambo,* a partner you live with; *säerbo,* one you don't live with; and *helgbo,* a sweetheart you live with only on the weekends. Some Swedes even create other words like *kombo,* a partner you don't have sex with, or *faxbo,* a partner you fax.[9]

English has a lot of catching up to do.

WHICH BOX TO CHECK?

American society seems stuck using marital status categories that were invented in another era. Many of us no longer fit into the either-or categories "single" ver-sus "married." Legally, you may not be able to check off the "married" box, but if you've been in a decade-long live-in relationship you probably don't feel sin-gle, either. As Anne says, "I feel like it's lying when articles describe us as a 'hus-band and wife team,' but I also feel like I'm lying when I write on the IRS form that I'm single."

Sometimes these outdated categories lead others to make inaccurate assump-tions about our lives. Many women say that each year at their gynecological

LOST IN THE CHECKBOXES

BECAUSE OF STIGMA, cohabitors and gay couples are consistently under-counted, even when there's an "unmarried partner" checkbox available. Some long-term couples start claiming to be married, while same-sex and different-sex cohabitors who are particularly concerned about public disapproval call themselves single. Because of people's reluctance to categorize their relationship accurately, studies in other countries have found the actual number of different-sex cohabitors to be 18 to 50 per-cent higher than census findings, even in countries where cohabitation is widely accepted.[10] Studies examining the 2000 Census suggest that it may have under-counted the number of same-sex couples by 15 to 23 percent.[11]

exams, they are asked about their marital status. Kari, for example, has been in a monogamous relationship with her partner for seven years and says their decision not to get married is a final one.

I was at the gynecologist's the other day, and I was checking in, and they were looking at my chart—not the nurse, not the doctor, but the people at reception—and one of them asked, "Are you still single?" The way she said it seemed to be passing judgment on me. They should ask, "Are you in a monog-amous relationship?" I don't like the way they ask about marital status. It makes me feel really uncomfortable, and a little angry.

Another couple we talked to, Myra and Wolfsong, say simply check off the "married" box. Myra's explanation is simple: "I'm not single." Wolfsong said this is easy to do, since "they never ask for a copy of a marriage license. I've never heard of the IRS saying to anybody, 'Oh, you're not legally married.' " (We don't recommend that you follow their lead—at least until you check with a lawyer to be sure you're not committing fraud or inadvertently creating a com-mon-law marriage.) Sarah has a different approach to questions about marital sta-tus: "I always write in, 'NONE.' No one has ever asked me about it but they should, don't you think?"

Another possibility is to check multiple boxes—an attempt to get back at the people who design the forms by confusing their neat systems—or create a new category. This can be a great opportunity for small acts of activism, though the risk is that whoever finally has to put the information into a computer database will count you incorrectly or not at all. Kirsten chose to take the chance when she was applying for insurance: "They said, 'What's your marital status?' and I said, 'Domestic partnership,' which put it back in their court." Dorian fre-quently does something similar: instead of checking off married or single she creates a new box and checks "partnered." On the rare occasion that she encoun-ters forms that already include a partnered checkbox, she always writes, "Thanks!" in the margin.

Doctors and others who ask about marital status on standardized forms may need to re-think what information they are trying to collect. As Kari suggests above, a patient's sexual behavior might be relevant to the health care her gynecologist provides, but asking about marital status isn't an accurate way to find out whether a given patient is sexually active. Similarly, some adoption agencies that want to welcome unmarried applicants have changed their forms so that they don't start with lines for "husband" and "wife."

In 1990 for the first time the United States Census first asked people whether the other adult in their home was a "roommate" or a "partner." Any two people could check either box, regardless of their genders. The data the Census gathered allowed those of us who live with unmarried partners to be counted more accurately than ever. Previously, analysts could only estimate the number of unmarried partners based on the number of "People of the Opposite Sex Sharing Living Quarters" (POSSLQ). It doesn't take a demography degree to see the reason these estimates left a bit to be desired, since unrelated opposite-sex adults who live together aren't always intimate partners, and the way the POSSLQ was defined also missed some couples who really *were* partners.[13] It's a perfect example of how you can't get a good answer if you don't ask the right question.

Although the Census is updating its categories, many sociologists and others who study relationships and families are still comparing "married" to "single" people. Studies like these may find that married people are more likely to eat salsa or breed poodles, but they don't reveal whether it's *marriage* or simply being in a long-term relationship that creates the result. When researchers do consider cohabiting partners as a separate group, they often find that the biggest differences emerge between people who have partners and those who don't, rather than between "married" and "single." It's heartening to see that increasing numbers of researchers and data sets are taking unmarried relationships into account, allowing the findings of the future to better capture the reality of contemporary families.

WHAT SHOULD OTHER PEOPLE CALL YOU?

Once you and your sweetie have figured out what to call each other and what box to check, the language game isn't over. After a wedding, people usually start referring to each other with new names like daughter-in-law, son-in-law, mother-in-law, father-in-law, stepbrother, stepsister, stepmother, stepfather, aunt, uncle, niece, nephew, and the list goes on. Without marriage as a marker, even the best-intentioned relatives often have a hard time knowing how to define the relationship. Just as the people within the relationship need to find words that they feel good about, relatives may need to find terms that work for them. Janna has watched her partner's family struggle with the issue:

THERE'S NOTHING THAT I WOULD NOT DO
IF YOU WOULD BE MY POSSLQ

RADIO AND TELEVISION news anchor Charles Osgood wrote a parody of the sixteenth-century Christopher Marlowe poem, "The Passionate Shepherd to His Love." Osgood's 1981 version, updated for a different century, proves that even Census jargon can be poetic.

POSSLQ[12]

Come live with me and be my love,
And we will some new pleasures prove
Of golden sands and crystal brooks
With silken lines and silver hooks.

There's nothing that I wouldn't do
If you would be my POSSLQ.
You live with me, and I with you,
And you will be my POSSLQ.
I'll be your friend and so much more;
That's what a POSSLQ is for.

And everything we will confess;
Yes, even to the IRS.
Someday, on what we both may earn,
Perhaps we'll file a joint return.
You'll share my pad, my taxes joint.
You'll share my life—up to a point!
And that you'll be so glad to do so,
Because you'll be my POSSLQ.

Come live with me and be my love,
And share the pain and pleasure of
The blessed continuity,
Official POSSLQuity.
And I will whisper in your ear
That word you love so much to hear.
And love will stay forever new,
If you will be my POSSLQ.

They don't know how to introduce me to people. They always say, "Well, our potentially future daughter-in-law—uh, well, she's already part of the family." They don't really know how to—there's no box to put me in. I'm not the daughter-in-law. I'm not just the girlfriend. "Sebastian's sweetie" is what they call me.

Some friends and relatives may be delighted to hear you say you won't be offended if they use the language of marriage to describe your relationship. Most long-term unmarried partners don't mind being called son-in-law or daughter-in-law since it sums up the relationship quickly and easily. Many unmarried couples consider each other's parents their in-laws, too. Anne says that solving the language challenge for her mom reduced the stress enormously. "My mother's main problem about us not being married was what she should call Christopher," she told us. "As soon as I said, 'Well, you can call him my husband,' she felt a lot better."

Sometimes unmarried partners find that the birth or adoption of a child solves the language problem. Lyn's mother-in-law (the mother of her unmarried partner) had trouble deciding how to introduce her at a family reunion. Since Lyn and her partner had a baby, the mother-in-law's grandchild, the mother-in-law has started simply to introduce Lyn as "Jordan's mother." That's OK with Lyn, who says this approach "simplifies it for her. She doesn't have to explain. When she says, 'This is Jordan's mother,' the other person can make whatever assumptions they want about what our relationship could be."

Since most people in unmarried relationships haven't had a public ceremony to introduce new terminology, you can't expect each other's relatives to read your minds about what you want them to call you. After all, three years into a relationship, some people are still dating and sorting out their compatibility, while others have made a lifetime commitment and settled into long-term patterns. Great Aunt Matilda has no way of knowing how important this relationship is unless you tell her (and her old etiquette book probably doesn't cover it, either).

Don't be afraid to bring up the subject. You can wait until there's a natural opportunity or make it an "I have something I wanted to talk with you about" moment. Let your friends and family know what this relationship means to you. Tell them how you introduce each other, and give them some options. Of course, you may encounter resistance, but you may also be relieving their awkwardness at not knowing how to describe the situation.

▶ When People Call You the Wrong Thing

Most unmarried people have heard someone call their partner by a word that isn't on their own list of acceptable terms. It frustrates Nick:

It does occasionally become annoying, the habit people have of making that assumption. "Oh, is that your wife?" "Go ask your wife!" I say, "I don't have a wife! She's not my wife!" And then there's that explaining that you have to do. It's kind of annoying.

While some people, like Nick, have a policy of correcting people who make incorrect assumptions, others let the mistakes slide, or decide on a case-by-case basis. Certain situations seem to increase the likelihood that people will assume you're married. When we were exploring home-buying recently, we were amused by the number of realtors and housing inspectors who referred to us as husband and wife, even though we consistently introduced each other as partners. Parenthood is similar: many simply assume that the child's father is the husband of the child's mother.[14] Telemarketers are notoriously clueless; Betty says, "We used to laugh that I was "Mrs. his name" when it suited the telemarketers and other times he was "Mr. my name." But of course, having different last names can have its advantages, as Arthur found out as a child of unmarried parents:

> *Every couple of months we'd get a call for Mrs. [my father's last name]. I remember a lot of times I would be the one to answer the phone, and we'd know that that was a phone banker or telemarketer, and we'd just say, "There's no one here by that name." That was quite convenient.*

There's probably no reason to correct a telemarketer. To a close family member, on the other hand, it might be important to explain what you'd rather be called and why. Some people, like the friend Lyn describes, just need a gentle reminder.

> *One friend constantly refers to my partner as my husband, to the point where I finally said to her, "You know we're not married, right?" She said, "Oh, did I call him your husband again?"*

SMITH, JONES, JITH, OR SMONES: CONSIDERING LAST NAMES

MOST UNMARRIED PEOPLE are perfectly happy having different last names. But for some who can't get married, being able to have matching surnames feels like an inaccessible dream. Others, like Kierstin and Scott Bridger, want to share a name as a form of unity, even though they don't want to marry. Kierstin explains that they chose a new name to adopt because "We wanted to have a partnership and make sort of a statement that we were together and committed [with out being] a married couple. Marriage language is so often like, 'We're one.' We never felt like we completed each other . . . but that we made each other stronger."[15]

If having the same last name appeals to you, the process may be easier than you think. It's perfectly legal to change your name as long as you're not doing so for fraudulent reasons (to escape paying taxes, for example) and as long as your new name won't confuse people, invade someone else's privacy, or incite violence. A woman can take a man's name, a man can take a woman's, both partners can combine or hyphenate their names, or you can come up with a brand-new surname. Before taking the same last name, check to find out if you live in a state that recognizes common-law marriage (page 147). If it does, the fact that you had the same surname could be used to claim that you intended to be married. Assuming that's not your intention, follow the advice in that section on how to make sure you remain legally unmarried to each other.

In most states there are two routes to taking a new name. The first is simply to start using your new name consistently in every part of your life: at work, in social situations, and on forms you fill out. You'll also need to contact the appropriate offices to request that your name be changed on your bank account, driver's license, Social Security card, and other documents and identification cards. Most have a simple name change form, and for others you'll have to write an official declaration that you are changing your name.

The other option is to change your name in court, by going through a straightforward process that includes filling out a form and attending a routine hearing. This method gives you an official name change court order on a piece of paper, which can make it easier to get your name changed on other documents.[16] However you do it, there's no reason John Smith and Mary Jones can't become John and Mary Smones (or Jith, or Smith, or Jones) if that's what they want.

ISN'T THERE A SOLUTION?

Getting others to call you what you want to be called may be one of the most difficult parts of living in an unmarried relationship, because it requires a shift in the way people think about relationships. Cultural change is always a slow process. We can each make our own decisions about how to introduce our partners, and we can all work to change laws and update forms that exclude our lives from their checkboxes. Unmarried people are certainly not the only "minority" group to struggle with these issues: African-Americans, Native Americans, gays and lesbians, disabled people, and countless other groups continue to grapple with convincing society to call them by the names they choose. Even within any community, there are disagreements, yet naming is crucially important.

Perhaps one or several of the words currently being used to describe unmarried relationships will emerge as the leader. Perhaps someone will invent a new word that will catch on. Or perhaps unmarried people need to choose a word we like and advocate for its use. We argue that "partner" should take this honor, since most people already understand it, and since it captures the equality and inclusiveness that is important to many unmarrieds. The way to get around people mistakenly thinking we mean business partner, or assuming only gay people use the word, is simply for more people in intimate relationships to use it. If enough straight people and married couples use "partner"—in addition to all the others who already do—soon business partners will be the ones who have to be sure to say *"business* partner" to clarify what they mean.

Or, we could all just decide to stop taking ourselves so seriously. Debbie and Jim experienced fifteen minutes of fame after they spoke up about some discrimination they experienced because they weren't married. Debbie says:

> *We were on the Today Show several years ago, and they asked us if we have words to use when we introduce each other. I think we kind of shook our heads and said, "Well, not really." And then I said, "I just call him Frootloops." I still get jokes from people who say, "How could you call him that on national TV?"*

History gives cause for hope. Until around 1980, the term "domestic partner" didn't exist.[17] No one knew what an "S.O." was. Introducing someone as your "spousal equivalent" wasn't an option. Language is alive and ever-changing, and the vocabulary of unmarried people has come a long way in a short time. Each person who makes an effort to use words that affirm their unmarried relationship—even when it's awkward to do so—takes a small step toward awareness and acceptance.

SIX

IN THE EYES OF THE LAW:

Legal and Financial Protections

MANY UNMARRIED PARTNERS have a vague sense that they are vulnerable without the legal and financial protections that married couples take for granted. The good news is that most, though not all, of the important protections are also available to people in unmarried relationships. There's only one catch: if you want these benefits, you're going to have to work for them. You may need to think things through a little more carefully, have some honest conversations, fill out some forms, and write up a contract or two, but it's worth the effort. Nick has changed employers a few times and finds that legal marital status issues come each time he has to fill out the new employee forms:

> *When you get a new job, you have to go in through Human Resources and fill out all the insurance information, and disability, and everything else. There's a best route, a best set of answers if you're married, and there's a best set of answers if you're single. But as an unmarried couple, every time we go through it we have to get together and go through all their policies in minute detail to figure out what's going to work best for us. It just takes a little more time.*

Skipping the extra planning and paperwork could come back to bite you, particularly if you plan to stay together unmarried for a considerable length of time, or if one of you has sizeable assets. Dave, who owns a house with his partner of four years, says, "We've talked a lot about doing our wills and estate planning. We have good intentions of putting it all into writing at some point. We just haven't gotten around to it." Procrastination certainly isn't unusual, since the legal complexities can seem daunting. Also, doing the paperwork requires thinking about things most of us prefer to avoid: breaking up, dying, or having our partner die. Luckily, the steps to protecting yourself and your partner are easier than you might think.

We've done our best to focus on the most common and important issues, check our facts, and translate the legalese. But we're not lawyers, and legal and financial issues are far too complex to answer every question in a single chapter. We highly recommend working with an attorney to prepare the documents you'll need, investing in one of the excellent do-it-yourself legal guides listed at the end of this chapter, or both.[1] You'll also find legal information on the following subjects in other chapters:

- Discrimination on the basis of marital status: Chapter 3
- Taking your partner's last name, or both partners adopting a new name: Chapter 5
- Domestic partner health benefits: Chapter 7
- Having children and parenting: Chapter 9

THE LEGALITY OF LIVING TOGETHER

In most places you won't run into legal problems simply by moving in together. In some states where archaic sex laws are still on the books, though, it's technically illegal for an unmarried man and woman to live together.[2] If you discover that cohabitation is illegal where you're living, there's no reason to rush to close the blinds. For the most part these statutes aren't enforced: police don't knock on doors doing marriage license spot-checks. But anti-cohabitation laws still have teeth, and have the potential to make life difficult if you happen to find yourself involved with the courts for another reason, like a custody issue, property dispute, or unrelated crime. In these cases, judges and prosecutors can increase fines or hand down stiffer sentences based on your additional measure of "criminality."

For example, in Virginia in 2000, a young animal rights activist threw a tofu cream pie at an official who was advocating meat-eating at a nutrition conference. When her probation officer found out she was living with her fiancé, which is illegal under Virginia state law, she was told she'd have to either get married or move out (Virginia may be for lovers, but apparently not if they're living together).[3] Similarly, in 1998 a New Mexico judge humiliated an accused man by threatening to hold him in jail rather than release him on bond. The threat of harsher punishment was because the man and his partner, who was pregnant with his child, lived together, violating state law. (Three years later, New Mexico repealed its anti-cohabitation law.)[4] As long as you're not tossing tofu pies or winding up in jail for other reasons, though, laws against cohabitation are unlikely to cause you any problems.

▶ Renting a Place Together

Most landlords won't ask about your marital status, and you don't need to advertise it. But even if you're living in a place where cohabitation is legal, it's possible you could run into marital status discrimination when you're trying to find a place to rent, like we did (see page 6). Some cities and counties prohibit this kind of discrimination in rental housing, though in other places it's perfectly legal. Even in states with housing statutes prohibiting discrimination on the basis of marital status, the laws often apply either to married or to single people, not to unmarried couples. Only California, Massachusetts, Michigan, and New Jersey have nondiscrimination laws that have been found to protect unmarried couples. Some condo associations and planned communities (like retirement communities) also try to prohibit unmarried couples, though you may be able to win over those decisionmakers with your manners and charm.

If you know or suspect that someone won't rent to you because you're not married, you can call the local housing authorities, human rights commission, or city attorney to find out if you have any protections under city or state ordinances. If so, they can advise you on how to fight the discrimination. On the other hand, imagining all the ways a disapproving landlord can make your life miserable (postponing repairs, being stingy with heat or air conditioning, raising rents, etc.) may convince you to find housing in a place you'll feel more welcome.

MORALITY ON THE MAILBOX

A MARYLAND COUPLE found their way into a column in *The Washington Post* in 1999 when their landlord refused to let them put both their names on their mailbox. A vice president at the rental company told them that cohabitation was illegal in their county (Montgomery), and that the company couldn't condone unmarried couples living together. A lawyer they contacted confirmed that the law did, indeed, exist, but said, "the last time it was enforced, Abraham Lincoln was probably president." The couple planned to press charges, arguing that the policy was in conflict with renters' rights laws, since it might prevent one partner from receiving all of his or her mail.[5]

UNMARRIEDS ARE FAMILIES, TOO

BILLIE JO AND MARK, both full-time college students in Florida, chose to attend a school because they were excited about the new family housing complex for students it was opening. At the time, they had been cohabiting for six years and had two young daughters. When they applied to move into the family housing, though, they were told that their family wasn't eligible because they weren't married. Billie Jo was stunned that rather than helping a young, struggling couple and their kids find affordable housing together—the original goal of the new complex—the university would discriminate against them. She pointed out that not only was hers a stable mom, dad, and kids family, but that she and Mark were students the school could be proud of. Both were members of the national honor society Phi Theta Kappa, and she was president of the student government and head of the campus volunteer organization.

After some arguing with administrators, Billie Jo and Mark were able to convince the university to consider their relationship a common-law marriage, since they had previously lived in South Carolina, which recognizes such marriages.[6] The solution got them the housing , but also converted them into a legally married couple. (We'll explain common-law marriage later in this chapter.) And unfortunately, it won't help the next unmarried couple who comes along, since it did nothing to confront the underlying discrimination.

▶ Buying a House Together

You've been living together for a few years now, you're feeling confident about your future together, and you want to invest in a home of your own. Congratulations!

Although buying a house or condo isn't a simple process, your marital status shouldn't make it much more difficult. You're less likely to encounter discrimination when buying than when renting (though if you do, in most states there's not much you can do about it). Sharon and her partner have had lots of experience buying houses together:

> We had a sit-down conversation about how our plans for the future would fit together. We decided that we would buy a house and renovate it and sell it, and then buy another house, renovate that and sell it, and then buy a third house that we would actually live in awhile. Then maybe after that point that we would have kids, and probably get married. We worked out a four- or five-year plan. We're coming to the conclusion of our plan: We just bought our third house, and we're living in it.
>
> When we go through the mortgage process for each of our houses, having different last names makes it a little bit more difficult. They want to know what our

relationship is, and how financially stable we both are, rather than treating us as one entity, like a married couple. But they were OK with it. We stayed with the same mortgage person each time, and after the first house he was more comfortable with the fact that we were in a committed relationship and weren't going to cause financial problems.

Most loan officers care more about your income, debt, and credit history than your marital status, sexual orientation, or family structure. Since it's always a good idea to shop around for a loan, in the unlikely event that a bank or mortgage company gives you a hard time because you're not married, it's easy enough to cross it off your list.

Once you've identified a house and had your offer accepted, give some careful thought to how you want ownership to be listed on the final paperwork. There are at least three different ways you can "take title" on the house, and your decision can have lasting implications in terms of future estate planning or separation. The first option is to list one partner as the sole owner. That works perfectly if the house really does belong to only one partner, but not so well if you're doing it for financial reasons (so that one partner can take the tax deductions, for example). In that situation, the partner who is not listed on the deed is extremely vulnerable: If the owner partner dies without a will, the non-owner might not inherit his own house, and the owner partner could sell the house without giving any profits to the non-owner.

If you want to own the house together, you can take title either as "joint tenants" or as "tenants in common." Joint tenants are equal owners of the property, and if one dies his or her share passes automatically to the other, regardless of what the will says (this is called "right of survivorship"). It's only an option if both or all partners own an equal share of the house (fifty-fifty for couples, three shares of 33.3 percent for a group of three, etc.). That doesn't mean the partners have to contribute equal amounts of money to the house purchase, though. If one partner doesn't have enough savings to pay half the down payment, his partner can loan him the difference, both partners can sign a property ownership agreement and a separate promissory note, and he can repay the loan over time. If you take title as tenants in common, on the other hand, you can own the house in unequal percentages, but if one partner dies her share goes to whomever she names in her will, not automatically to the other tenant in common (though she can leave her share to her partner in her will).

Whatever you decide, buying real estate together is too big an investment to make without drawing up a written contract. Your agreement should specify how you are taking title of the property, what percentage each partner owns, what each person agrees to contribute to the down payment and mortgage payments, and what will happen if your relationship ends.

YOU BUY THE CEREAL, I'LL BUY THE MILK: FINANCES FOR UNMARRIED PARTNERS

When they first move in together, most partners keep their finances separate.[7] There are a myriad of fair ways to divide and share expenses. You can split every joint expense fifty-fifty or base the division on the ratio of incomes; track every penny or only expenses over a certain size; even up money you owe each other daily, monthly, or rarely (if you keep a running list of money owed back and forth); and transfer money between you in cash, check, or electronically.

> We transfer money between our bank accounts online. I got tired of writing IOUs on the refrigerator.
> —Melaina

> We keep track on paper of joint expenses and who paid them. Then we divide them in ratio to our incomes. If expenses get out of balance, the person who owes will pay a few more joint expenses to even things out.
> —Alan

> We put everything we buy on our own credit cards, and then at the end of the month we mark on the bills which purchases were individual and which were joint. At the end of each month one of us writes the other a check for whatever we owe. We split the utility bills—we each write a check and mail both checks.
> —Paula

> When I was working full-time, we used to split bills and whenever it was an odd amount, my girlfriend always "gave me the penny." In other words, if the bill was for $30.99, her check was for $15.50 so that mine only had to be for $15.49. It was a gesture of love and generosity. Now that I work part-time, she pays the big bills like the mortgage, and I pay the little bills like the utilities and phone. It works for us.
> —Flynn

It's a good idea to keep your money and credit separate at least for a while, especially if the relationship is still young. It removes one area for potential conflict, grants you some time to iron out incompatibilities between financial systems and values, and prevents you from being held responsible for your partner's old debts. If you agree to keep money and property separate, at least for now, be sure to take the same approach with credit cards and debt. Opening a joint bank account, signing up for a joint credit card, or co-signing a loan—all of which unmarried partners can do quite easily—make each partner responsible for the entire amount owed on that account. Even if you weren't aware of your partner's crazy shopping spree while you were out of town, if the bill doesn't get paid, your credit rating will suffer. Before mingling credit, you should have a lot of trust in your relationship, and clearly define for what purposes you'll use the account or credit card.

Some couples, married or not, find that permanently keeping their money separate works well for them. Becky and Mike, together twenty-one years and counting, are one such couple:

We keep our finances separate. We have a common banking account but the way we record deposits and expenses, it's clear who's put in what.
—*Mike*

Essentially, we pay money into the household account to pay for the house, the food, everything that we pay for our son, and any other expenses that we consider joint. And we each have our own money that we spend on clothes and things that are separate, that we haven't agreed to buy jointly. The lines have gotten slightly fuzzier over the years, but it's still basically separate.
—*Becky*

The longer you're together, though, the less you may feel it's necessary to keep everything separate. That's what Colin is finding:

Over time, keeping track of who paid for what gets much more difficult, and we care less and less. As long as the money's there, and the rent gets paid, there's not much to complain about.

Nate and Elise feel the same way. "Our income goes into a joint bank account and we pay our bills with money from that account," Nate says. You might feel like a "what's mine is yours, what's yours is mine" financial system is a way of taking your commitment to the next level. Regardless of the pooling system you come up with, you should write down your intentions (see the section on cohabitation agreements later in this chapter). Not only is this important protection in case your relationship doesn't last the rest of your life, but it can be a valuable source of clarification when questions arise. Halfway through a long discussion about a financial question once, we realized it might be addressed in the agreement we'd written and signed years earlier. Indeed, when we pulled the agreement out of our file cabinet, not only was the question answered, but the reasoning behind it struck us both as particularly logical and fair. We were sold all over again on the value of writing down what we decided about finances.

Keep in mind that paying for something and owning it are not necessarily the same thing. If one partner buys a car, for example, but you wish to consider it jointly owned, you can list both names on the title—just pay attention since this can legally be considered a taxable gift. For smaller (but still sizeable) purchases that don't come with titles, such as a set of pots or a computer, you can write a short agreement about the individual item that specifies the percentage share each partner owns, regardless of who paid for it originally.

RIG THE SAFETY NETS

To line up the most basic protections for you and your sweetheart, there are four documents you'd be smart to prepare:

1. A cohabitation agreement
2. A health care proxy
3. A durable power of attorney for financial management
4. A will

Whether you're just moving in or you've been living together for decades, it's never too early or too late to make sure you're protected. Significant life events and relationship markers like moving in together, buying a house, having children, or experiencing serious illness should remind you to think about legal issues.

SHOULD WE GET OUR DOCUMENTS NOTARIZED?

NOTARIZING IS A simple process in which a person called a "notary public" certifies that you are who you are, and that your signature isn't forged. While it's generally not a requirement (except for real estate documents in some states), it never hurts to get important legal documents notarized. For instance, if one partner died, a notarized agreement could reduce the questions about the authenticity of his signature. You can find notaries for free or a small fee at many banks, real estate offices, and law offices.

DO WE NEED A LAWYER?

FOR SITUATIONS THAT aren't particularly complicated, you might consider using a self-help legal guide to help you set up what you need. That can work out fine, and there are some great resources available. But be sure to consider what's at stake. If the costs of a mistake seem high, it may be worth it to hire a lawyer to make sure everything is done properly. In most places it's possible to get a basic will and the other key documents described here for a few hundred dollars per person. Hiring a lawyer becomes particularly important if you have a lot of assets at stake, if you're adopting a child or fighting for child visitation or custody, or if your situation is otherwise complex. For less complicated situations, some lawyers will agree to look over documents you've drafted yourself, which can save you some hourly fees.

There are other reasons to consider hiring a lawyer, too. If a hospital threatens to ignore your input when your partner has a medical crisis, your lawyer can fax over a copy of your health care proxy, and it's more likely to be taken seriously. If your partner were killed and your wills destroyed in a housefire, your lawyer would have the wills on file and could help you establish your rights. And of course, there's power in simply being able to say, "I'm going to call my lawyer."

If you do decide to hire a lawyer, be sure he is experienced with the law regarding unmarried relationships. Friends are the best source of recommendations, but you can also find family lawyers through the referral services of local bar associations, group legal plans offered by some employers and consumer groups, legal clinics (sometimes through law schools), the phone book, or online. Even if you're heterosexual, lawyers who specialize in gay and lesbian family law are often particularly savvy about unmarried issues, since they're familiar with the needs of families that can't rely on marriage's legal protections. Most of them are happy to work with non-gay clients, and you can look for listings in local gay and lesbian publications, referral lines, or groups. It may take a bit of research to find a lawyer whose experience, personality, and fees are a good fit. Don't be afraid to be assertive, ask lots of questions (you may need to pay for an initial consultation), and trust your intuition to ensure a good match.

▶ Cohabitation Agreements

The idea of writing an agreement with your partner may strike you as utterly unromantic. You're in love! Things are going well! Communication is great! Exactly. That's why this is the time to write a cohabitation agreement. Having an agreement in writing can increase your commitment, help you settle into living together, and help you remember the details of that financial conversation you had last year. Bettykay and her partner made writing an agreement part of celebrating the deepening of their relationship.

We had read a legal guide for unmarried couples. On our first year anniversary, we wrote up a contract about our living together and about the fact that I was supporting him, and what would happen if we broke up, and we signed that. It was a commitment of sorts, although we didn't publicize it among our friends or anything. We didn't make a big deal about it.

Regardless of whether cohabitation agreements are called living together contracts, domestic partner agreements, relationship contracts, or other similar terms, these are basically property agreements. They clarify how you handle joint expenses and deal with property ownership while you're together. And since unmarried partners can't always rely on divorce courts to help them divide things fairly if their relationship ends, these agreements can provide protection and guidance about how your finances and property would be divided if you part someday. Unpleasant as it may seem, it's a million times more pleasant to discuss, when you're in a good mood, who's responsible for a given bill or who gets the dog, than later, when you might be frustrated or angry. If you take your time, the process of crafting a good document is likely to help you understand each other better. Janie says putting their understandings in writing has helped her and her partner feel confident about their future together.

Some people think having an agreement sounds cold and pessimistic, but we both like the feeling of assurance that it gives us. I think that creating something that helps avoid conflict in the future is actually optimistic.

Rather than rushing through the agreement process, use the opportunity to go deep together. Have as many conversations as you need to talk honestly about money, property, and all the personal history and emotions that go along with those loaded subjects. Find out why she feels strongly about having her own checking account, or what it means to him to have his name on the mortgage.
Creating a contract is most important:

- if you expect to stay together without getting married for the long term ("the foreseeable future" can be a helpful way to think about it)
- if you plan to (or already have) made a major financial investment together, such as a house or car
- if one partner is moving into a house that the other owns
- if one partner moves across the country, leaves her job, or otherwise changes her life in a drastic way for the relationship
- if one partner supports the other financially

- if one or both of you has significant financial assets
- if you are parenting a child together.[8]

Most states will enforce property contracts between unmarried couples. Both written and oral contracts between partners are OK in most places (Illinois is an exception—you'll need to get legal help if you live there), but writing it down is definitely the smart way to go. More states recognize written contracts, and when your agreement is in writing you avoid the problems that could arise if later your memories differ on the details (or the existence) of your oral contract.

The best reason to write a cohabitation agreement, though, is not for the courts: in fact, your goal should be to avoid winding up in court. If you ever decide to go your separate ways, you can use your agreement, written when you were feeling calm, loving, and levelheaded, for guidance to divide your assets fairly. It's also sensible to agree in your contract to use mediation if conflicts arise over the agreement itself. It's significantly cheaper and faster to use a mediator than to engage in a court battle, and you're a lot more likely to leave with a solution you both feel good about.

There's more to writing a good agreement than we can include in this section, but you can find lots of advice and sample agreements online, in books, and from attorneys (see the Resources at the end of this chapter). In general:

> ## HOW TO FIND A MEDIATOR
>
> **M**EDIATORS HELP PEOPLE resolve conflicts without having to go to court, by working to create "win-win" solutions that feel fair to everyone involved in the disagreement. You may be able to find a local agency that offers mediation by looking in the phone book under "Mediation Services," getting mediator recommendations from people you know, or locating one from one of these online directories.
>
> Association for Conflict Resolution
> (referral list compiled by the Academy of Family Mediators),
> www.acresolution.org
>
> Mediate.com, www.mediate.com

- Your agreement should be written in clear language that you both understand, not in legal mumbo-jumbo.
- The most important things for your agreement to include are money and property—these are the subjects courts in most states will enforce. This is not a place to record who is responsible for cleaning the stove, or to specify what percentage of diapers each of you agrees to change.
- Agreements should never mention sex or even acknowledge that the partners in the agreement are having sex. That can invalidate the whole agreement by making it appear to be a form of prostitution.

A SAMPLE AGREEMENT

SELF-HELP LEGAL guides can be a good way for unmarried couples with relatively simple, straightforward situations to protect themselves legally without spending a lot of money. This agreement, for a couple who want to share their property, is one of many samples in *Living Together: A Legal Guide for Unmarried Couples.* This may or may not be the property ownership system that works best for you; many couples wait awhile before choosing to become legally and financially intertwined, and might prefer to construct their agreement from other samples designed to keep property separate. When one partner will move a long distance to live together, or when a couple plans a major purchase like a house or car, they'll need special language. If the sample below more or less fits your situation, you can easily modify it by deleting sections or adding language of your own.

Agreement to Share Property

Beth Spencer and **_Rich Portman_** agree as follows:

1. This contract sets forth our rights and obligations toward each other. We intend to abide by them in a spirit of cooperation and good faith.

2. All earned income received by either of us after the date of this contract and all property purchased with this income belongs in equal shares to both of us with the following exceptions:

3. All real or personal property earned or accumulated by either of us prior to the date of this agreement (except jointly owned property listed in Attachment B of this agreement), including all future income this property produces, is the separate property of the person who earned or accumulated it and cannot be transferred to the other person except in writing. Attached to this agreement in the form of Attachments A, Separately Owned Property, and B, Jointly Owned Property, are lists of the major items of property each of us owns separately and each of us owns jointly as of the date of this agreement.

4. Should either of us receive real or personal property by gift or inheritance, that property, including all future income it produces, belongs absolutely to the person receiving the gift or inheritance and cannot be transferred to the other except in writing.

5. In the event we separate, all jointly owned property shall be divided equally.

6. Any dispute arising out of this contract shall be mediated by a third person mutually acceptable to both of us. The mediator's role shall be to help us arrive at our solution, not to impose one on us. If good-faith efforts to arrive at our own solution to all issues in dispute with the help of a mediator prove to be fruitless, either of us may make a written request to the other that the dispute be arbitrated. If such a request is made, our dispute will be submitted to arbitration under the rules of the American Arbitration Association, and one arbitrator shall hear our dispute. The decision of the arbitrator shall be binding on us and shall be enforceable in any court which has jurisdiction over the controversy.

7. This agreement represents our complete understanding regarding our living together and replaces any and all prior agreements, written or oral. It can be amended, but only in writing, and must be signed by both of us.

8. If a court finds any portion of this contract to be illegal or otherwise unenforceable, the remainder of the contract is still in full force and effect.

Beth Spencer
_____
Signature

September 15, 200x
_____

Rich Portman
_____
Signature

September 15, 200x
_____

▶ Health Care Proxies

Medical emergencies can be a nightmare for people in unmarried relationships, since without a health care proxy (also called a durable power of attorney for health care or a durable power of attorney for medical care) your relatives, not your partner, have the right to make decisions about your health care. Having a health care proxy gives the designated person (your partner or someone else you choose) the authority to make health care decisions if you are too severely ill or injured to do so.

The good news is that health care proxies are so easy to make that you can take care of this in a matter of minutes. The forms vary from state to state, but they're available from local hospitals and doctor's offices, or from the Partnership for Caring. Once you've filled it out, make copies to keep in your files and your partner's files and to give to your doctors and anyone else who might be involved in your health care. Tell your relatives and close friends that you have them, so that in case of an emergency you won't need to waste time arguing about who has the right to make decisions.

Since it can be cumbersome to carry your health care proxy everywhere you go, this is a document your lawyer can keep on file and fax as needed. In addition to filling out your state's form, you can also make yourself a wallet-size card like the one at right. This isn't the format hospitals are used to seeing, though, so it may be less likely to be accepted.

A health care proxy is a powerful document if one of you is in a coma, but it may also be helpful if you're both conscious. If a grouchy hospital nurse tries to bar an unmarried partner from visiting and refuses to give you information reserved under hospital policy for "family members," you should pull out your health care proxy, challenge the nurse, and call your lawyer if necessary.

When you're filling out your health care proxy, it's also wise to make a living will (called a health care directive or medical directive in some places). In addition to spelling out whether you want life-prolonging measures to be provided or withheld if you become unable to communicate, these can specify what kind of medical care you want. The living will can serve as a guideline for your partner (or whomever you designate as your health care proxy) and doctor if they need to make difficult decisions about your care. The necessary forms are available in the same places as health care proxies.

WHERE TO FIND YOUR STATE'S FORMS

THE PARTNERSHIP FOR Caring lets you download each state's forms for health care proxies (medical power of attorney) and living wills for free.

www.partnershipforcaring.org
800-989-9455

► Durable Power of Attorney for Financial Management

This gives the designated person (your partner or someone else you trust) the authority to manage your property and finances if you become unable to do so. The person you designate would be the one to pay your bills, deposit your checks, and collect your benefits for you. The forms to set this up are fairly simple, but requirements vary from state to state. You can learn more about how to prepare this document from some of the books and websites included in the Resources section of this chapter.

HEALTH PROXY CARD

I HAVE DESIGNATED a Health Care Proxy that designates my domestic partner, Lataya Mitchell, as my Health Care Agent. Copies of my Health Care Proxy have been placed in my personal files and given to Lataya, my doctors, and my parents.

Terry McMasters   10/14/00

► Wills and Estate Planning

Most of us are pretty good at pretending we're going to live forever. But it's a downright risky endeavor *not* to have a will if you and your beloved aren't married. If you die without a will, your partner will inherit none of your belongings or assets. Instead, your legal "next of kin"—probably your children, parents, or other relatives—will inherit everything you own, from personal papers and pets to houses and savings. One of Marshall's family members suffered because her partner had no will:

> *Sterling and Ann lived in a mobile home on a shady plot off a country road, choosing not to marry because of pension benefits Ann received from her deceased husband. After ten years together, Sterling died suddenly of a heart attack. Because he had no will and because courts don't recognize unmarried partners as family members, Ann wasn't entitled to receive anything from his estate. The court divided the estate equally among twelve of his relatives, eleven of whom he had not seen in decades. At my grandmother's urging, the relatives agreed to redivide the money to give Ann a thirteenth share, but because the home was in Sterling's name, Ann was forced out.*

Even if your family and your partner are on good terms now, it's not unheard of for relatives to "pull rank" after they lose a loved one and shut out a long-time partner. Betty experienced this when her partner died without a will:

The whole time we were together, his daughter didn't come around much. But after he was gone, she wanted me out of her life. She didn't want anything to do with me. It was a very sudden death, and I think that just made it harder. I was grieving, and then she came to my house the day after the funeral and took everything she considered her dad's. I was so devastated at that time that I didn't stand up to her like maybe I should have.

In addition to inheritance problems, if your partner is not the biological parent of your child and has not legally adopted her, he may have no rights to visitation or custody, even if he has been acting as her parent for years. In a will, however, you can designate a legal guardian to care for your children if you die. Making a will is part of being responsible to your partner, even if you're young and healthy. If you have minor children or sizeable assets, the stakes are even higher.

Wills can be multipurpose documents. Among their potential functions are indicating to whom you leave your money and property when you die, recommending a guardian for your minor children, naming an executor (the person who will go through your drawers, find your old love letters, and be in charge of distributing your property), forgiving debts, disinheriting people, and specifying your funeral arrangements. A will is the only way to ensure these wishes will be respected.

A few key points to keep in mind:

- In order to make sure it's valid, date and sign your will, and get the signatures of three witnesses. These people don't need to read the will, but they do have to watch you sign it.
- You can change your will as many times as you like. At the very least you should review it if you marry, divorce, give birth to or adopt children, move to a new state, win the lottery, or otherwise get more money or property than you used to own.
- If your will includes important sections you think might upset people (for instance, if you're naming a guardian for your child who is not a relative), it can be to your advantage to give your family a "heads up" about these decisions. If they are surprised or disagree, it's much easier to explain your thinking now than to leave your partner facing a court battle after your death.
- Someone should know where your will is. If you keep it locked someplace, make sure your executor—the first person who will need to find it—has a key.

Wills can be simple and straightforward; most people can write an effective will without the expense of a lawyer. However, different states have their own requirements, so read up on the local guidelines to be safe. There are lots of good books, websites, and lawyers that will lead you through the process of preparing a basic will (see the Resources section at the end of this chapter).

Avoiding Probate

People with substantial assets may want to take additional steps to avoid probate, the costly and time-intensive court process of reading your will, assessing your assets, paying your debts and taxes, and distributing your property. This can be important if, for instance, you died and your partner needed timely access to your bank account in order to be able to pay the mortgage. Some of the most common ways to avoid probate are revocable living trusts, payable-on-death accounts, joint tenancy, life insurance or investments with named beneficiaries, and gifts given while you are living (just look into gift tax laws before giving away large amounts of money or property). Rose and her partner are pleased with the documents they've prepared, both as part of their estate planning and also for basic legal protections. She says, "We have a living trust to get around the inability to inherit unlimited amounts from each other, a durable power of attorney to deal with medical decisions should one of us become incapacitated, wills, and so forth. These were easily prepared and not expensive."

The Truth About Estate Taxes

Federal estate taxes are a concern for only two percent of the population, those with significant assets.[9] The taxes only apply to estates worth $1 million or more, and that cutoff is set to increase through 2010, so they'll affect even fewer people. In addition to the feds, thirteen states also tax estates (Connecticut, Indiana, Iowa, Kentucky, Louisiana, Maryland, Nebraska, New Hampshire, New Jersey, Ohio, Oklahoma, Pennsylvania, and Tennessee).[10] This is one area where married couples are at a major advantage, since everything left to a spouse is exempt from federal and state estate taxes.

If your assets are substantial enough that estate taxes are a concern, there aren't too many ways around this unmarried penalty. You may be able to reduce your tax liability by giving away gifts (up to $11,000 per person per year) or life insurance, or by creating an AB trust, or life estate trust, so the property legally belongs to the trust rather than to your beneficiary.

RENT CARS, SAVE MONEY

A FEW YEARS ago we rented a car from Avis for a trip that involved a lot of driving. The car was reserved in Marshall's name, and the employees at the rental counter told him that if Dorian were his wife, she could be a "second driver" at no additional cost. But because we weren't married, they said, we would have to pay an additional fee per day if Dorian wanted to be able to drive the car. We decided to have Marshall be the sole driver for the trip.

When we returned home, Marshall stiff and bleary-eyed from all that driving, we wrote a letter to the company president to complain about their marital status discrimination. The response surprised us: it said that Avis has a domestic partner policy. Under the policy, a "mate, life companion, significant other, or live-in" of any gender could be a second driver at no additional cost, just like a spouse.[11] We were delighted with the policy, but less than impressed with its implementation. Perhaps, we thought, the clerks at rental counters need to be informed that it exists.

At this time Avis is the only major car rental company that allows both partners and spouses to be second drivers for free (if you find others, let us know!).[12] We've put their policy to the test, and found that although often we're the ones informing Avis desk clerks of their own company's policy, if we're assertive enough they eventually confirm that we're right. Hertz is the second-friendliest: if both people are AAA members, any second driver is free, regardless of the relationship.[13]

Some other companies charge you for a second driver regardless of who that person is—spouse, partner, friend, stranger, at least they're consistent—while others discriminate against unmarried couples by charging them extra, sometimes double the cost that married couples have to pay. Even if it's tempting to save money by telling a car rental company you're married, if you got into an accident and your fraud was discovered, you'd have an expensive problem on your hands. Lying is not a good solution.

It's worth asking about the policy for second drivers when you reserve a rental car, encouraging companies to treat domestic partners and spouses equally, and letting them know if you take your business to a company that does. With all the unmarried car renters out there, Avis's forward-thinking policy may not stand alone for long.

SEVEN YEARS TO COMMON-LAW MARRIAGE[14]
AND OTHER MYTHS

Quiz: Common-law marriage is most similar to:

a.   *Santa Claus*

b.   *The tooth fairy*

c.   *A dandelion weed*

d.   *A blue moon*

Answer: d, a blue moon.[15]

Unlike the tooth fairy, common-law marriage does exist. But it's a rare creature, and it doesn't just hatch all by itself after the proverbial seven-year incubation period. Yes, yes, we know you've heard that after a couple lives together for seven years, they became common-law spouses. We'd heard it, too. In fact, the highly unscientific poll we took of thirty-seven people waiting at a bus stop in Illinois found that 100 percent of people who wait at bus stops in Illinois believe this same seven-years-to-common-law-marriage myth. They're all wrong.

Here's the truth. The idea of common-law marriage emerged in medieval England, because clerics and justices who officiated at marriages couldn't always travel to rural locations where some couples lived. In that case, the couple could establish a marriage "by common law."

In the U.S. today, only thirteen states currently recognize common-law marriage. Those states are Alabama, Colorado, Washington, D.C., New Hampshire (for inheritance purposes only), Iowa, Kansas, Montana, Oklahoma, Pennsylvania, Rhode Island, South Carolina, Texas, and Utah. Three other states are in the "phase-out" stage, only recognizing common-law marriages that were created years ago (formed in Georgia before January 1997, in Idaho before January 1996, or in Ohio before October 1991).

If you live in one of the thirty-five states that does *not* recognize common-law marriage, you can live together for seven years and seven more and then another seven and you still won't be common law spouses. There is one teensy exception to this, and that's if you travel together to one of the thirteen states that does recognize common-law marriage, hold yourself out as married and establish various kinds of proof there, and then come back to your own state. That could work because all states agree to recognize marriages formed in other states. But those are murky legal waters, and we wouldn't advise exploring them.

If you live in one of the states that *does* recognize common-law marriage, and you want to get married, the smart approach is to get married the same way everyone else does. Trying to form a common-law marriage isn't wise, because it's extremely difficult to know if your marriage is legitimate. If you live in a common law state and you're not ready to be married, don't tell your insurance company that you are. Common-law marriages are as legal and binding as regular ones, and all the laws that apply to married couples also apply to common-law marriages. Common law couples who later decide they want to break up have to get an official, legal divorce, even though they may never have had an official, legal wedding.

Most people don't give common-law marriage much thought until they're considering the matter in past tense, either wishing they had one or hoping they didn't. For example, if an unmarried partner dies suddenly without a will, the surviving partner sometimes researches common-law marriage to find out if he can claim they had a common-law marriage, so that he can inherit the deceased partner's estate. In situations like that, courts consider many factors, trying to determine if the couple truly demonstrated that they had intended to be married. No state requires a specific length of time for which you have to live together to form a common-law marriage, only that it be "significant." What matters is whether you *acted* like you were married when you were in public. If you told people you were married, referred to each other as "my wife" or "my husband," used the same last name, filed joint tax returns, and did other things married people do, you may have formed a common-law marriage. Like "regular" marriage, only different-sex couples can get common-law married.

If, on the other hand, you live in a common law state but *don't* want to be common law married, just be sure you never "hold yourself out as married." No matter how long you live together, you won't become a common law spouse unless you act like one. If you want to be extra sure—and especially if you do certain things that could make you appear to be married, like sharing bank accounts—write a simple document that you and your partner both sign clearly stating that although you are living together, you have no intention of entering any form of marriage.

The bottom line is: if you don't want to be married, don't form a common-law marriage. In particular, don't attempt to form a common-law marriage because you want some specific perk or benefit available only to married people. Despite its deceptive simplicity, common-law marriage is real marriage. You should take the decision to form one as seriously as you'd consider any other marriage proposal, and end it properly, by getting a divorce, if the relationship ends.

INCOME TAX

▶ Is There Really a Tax on Marriage?

Recently, there's been a lot of news coverage of the "marriage tax penalty," and politicians are eager to show they support families by rewarding married people. As a recent article asked, "What lawmaker isn't pro-marriage?"[16] Most people are confused by the commotion, though. As Billy said, "Some people say that you get a tax break if you're married, and some people say married couples get hammered by taxes. I don't know which one is right."

So, does getting married actually raise your taxes? The answer is, it depends. Essentially, whether a couple is penalized or rewarded for being married is based on how their household makes money. The current U.S. tax system was devised to reward the June and Ward Cleaver-style married couple where one spouse works and the other doesn't. If this is your situation—one partner earns 70 percent or more of the total household income—it's to your advantage (taxwise, at least) to get married.

However, when both partners work, which is the norm today, they end up paying more in total income taxes than they would if they were unmarried. On average, two-income married couples pay $1,400 more on their federal income taxes than they would if they hadn't tied the knot—some pay even more.[17] About 42 percent of married couples fall into this category, and experience the marriage tax.[18]

We don't see any logical reason to base how much anyone owes Uncle Sam on the status of his or her ring finger. Unfortunately, tweaking the tax system in an attempt to reduce the marriage tax will never result in a perfect solution. In TaxLand, whenever you help one group, you penalize another. The last sixty years of tax code reforms have shown that as long as marital status affects taxes, some group or another is going to be angered by the inequity. In the 1960s, for instance, the War Widows of America were outraged by the "singles tax" that punished them just because they didn't have husbands anymore, so the laws were changed to be kinder to people without spouses. As political commentator Ellen Goodman observes, "We have to decide who to discriminate against."[19] For the time being, the pendulum seems to be swinging in the direction of discriminating against the unmarried.

Recent laws will reduce the "marriage penalty" gradually between 2005 and 2009, but won't eliminate it entirely. Only time will tell what Congress will decide next.

► Some Reasons Unmarried Couples
Can Thank the IRS

▶ One of you may be eligible to file as "head of household" to get you into a better tax bracket.

▶ If you and your partner are in different tax brackets, you may be able to plan your income, expenses, charitable contributions, and other deductions so that you can pay less in taxes. The trick is to direct less of the household's tax-deductible expenses to the person in the lower tax bracket, while directing more of the tax-deductible expenses to the person in the higher tax bracket (to reduce the total amount on which she pays taxes). Consider the example of Kayla and Chris, who both work full-time. Kayla has taxable income of $60,000 a year, so she's taxed at 27.5 percent, while Chris has taxable income of $15,000, so he's taxed at 15 percent. Kayla and Chris own their home together, but they decide that Kayla will make the mortgage payments and pay the real estate taxes, $6,000 per year, since her income is so much higher. Then Kayla takes the itemized deductions on these taxes and mortgage interest. This way, they save $1,650 in taxes ($6,000 x .275). If they had split the payments, Kayla would only save $825, half as much, and Chris would get nothing, since his income is too low to justify itemizing his deductions. If they wish, they can agree that Chris will pay other bills during the year, so that the finances of their home are fair within their broader agreements about money.

▶ If you support your partner or her child, you may be able to claim one or both of them as dependents. This only works if one partner isn't working or isn't making much, and if you meet all the criteria set by the IRS. (It's easy to get the list of criteria from the IRS or from any accountant.) It's OK for either you or your partner to claim her child, but switching this back and forth from year to year will attract attention. A change is fine, but in general you should be consistent.

THINGS YOU JUST CAN'T GET AROUND

We like to focus on all the ways in which unmarried partners can protect themselves legally, if they're willing to make the effort. But there are also some legal and financial protections that are the unmarried equivalent of booking a vacation on Mars: for the time being, they simply aren't available. Access to those protections is one of the reasons many gay and lesbian people are eager to win the right to marry. Knowing exactly what's at risk—and not at risk—can help you think more realistically about the legal implications of not being married. Below we've listed the most common things that are legally off-limits if you don't have a marriage license. This list is *not* all-inclusive, but many of the federal laws affected by marital status not listed below affect only specific subgroups like federal employees, military personnel, or farmers.[20]

- ◗ *Social Security.* Unmarried partners can't get dependents' or survivors' benefits through their partner (these days, most people qualify for their own Social Security benefits, and that's not affected by marital status). This can hurt a partner who spent many years not employed (for example, as an at-home mom), because if her partner dies, she cannot receive the Social Security benefits that would be paid to a spouse. If you already receive Social Security benefits, living with a partner won't cause you to lose your benefits.
- ◗ *Retirement accounts.* There are many different kinds of retirement accounts, and most allow you to name whomever you wish as your beneficiary. However, a minority will not allow you to name a partner.
- ◗ *The right not to testify against your spouse in court, or to prevent your spouse from testifying against you.* There's no equivalent set of rights protecting you from testifying against your partner (or your mother or your child, for that matter).
- ◗ *Immigration.* Based on the principle of keeping families together, U.S. immigration law allows citizens and permanent residents to "sponsor" a spouse to be allowed to live and work in the country permanently. But since unmarried partners aren't legally recognized as families, they don't have this option.
- ◗ *Estate taxes.* Unmarried partners can't get a marital tax deduction. This can make a significant financial difference if your estate is worth more than $1 million (don't forget to consider your home's appreciated value), but it still affects a very small percentage of people. Good estate planning can help you get around the problem.
- ◗ *Survivors' benefits and wrongful death lawsuits.* Unmarried partners are generally not eligible for compensation if a partner dies, and they can't sue for wrongful death as spouses can.

It's reassuring to know that with a little work, and with only a few exceptions, unmarried partners needn't be left in the legal shadows. In fact, some couples like the freedom they have to define their legal relationship themselves, taking on certain "marital" rights or responsibilities and avoiding others. Other countries around the world have made significant strides toward ensuring protections for unmarried relationships and families, and although the United States has fallen behind the times, there's no reason it can't catch up. The existence of several states' domestic partnership and reciprocal beneficiaries laws are proof that it is possible to pass laws that recognize caregiving relationships beyond marriages, and even beyond sexual relationships. Slowly, laws and policies are changing to treat more families fairly, and the last chapter of this book will discuss how you can help lawmakers wake up to the realities of relationships today.

LEGAL AND FINANCIAL RESOURCES

American Bar Association
www.abanet.org
The "General Public Resources" section of their site provides information about hiring a lawyer, as well as a lawyer referral service through local bar associations.

Human Rights Campaign: FamilyNet
www.hrc.org/familynet
FamilyNet's Legal Center, which focuses on the needs of GLBT people, contains articles and downloadable sample forms for domestic partner (cohabitation) agreements, durable power of attorney for finances, health care proxy, hospital visitation authorization, wills, and living wills. Much of the information applies to both same-sex and different-sex couples.

Nolo
www.nolo.com
Click on the "Marriage and Living Together" section of this website to find answers to frequently asked questions, a few sample agreements and forms, and Auntie Nolo's irreverent advice on legal questions. Nolo publishes *Living Together: A Legal Guide for Unmarried Couples*, the best do-it-yourself legal guide we've seen on the subject. It includes sample contracts and blank forms for a wide variety of situations.

SEVEN

EQUAL PAY FOR EQUAL WORK:

Domestic Partner Health Benefits

A NEW ERA IS dawning. Increasingly, workplace health benefits policies are being made available to employees' domestic partners and their partners' children, not only their spouses and children. Given the price of health insurance—and the fact that health care itself is even more costly—it's a change unmarried partners should celebrate.

Whether or not one has health insurance can make a big difference in the quality of care a person receives. Derek's relative has two children who have different biological fathers and different insurance statuses:

> *One of the fathers is in the military and so that child has insurance, while the other one doesn't. There have been several occasions where the two children have been taken into the hospital, both with basically the same symptoms, close in time to each other. The level of care is phenomenally different for the uninsured child as compared to the insured child.*

There's something profoundly odd about the current system of providing access to health care through one's job (or one's spouse or parent), as if there were some reason that people with full-time jobs needed or deserved health insurance more than people without full-time jobs. A logical system would make quality health care a right of all people, not just those who meet certain employment, sexual orientation, or marital status criteria. Indeed, the U.S. is the only industrialized country that does not guarantee access to health care for all its citizens.[1] But in the absence of that system, domestic partner benefits can make health care more accessible for unmarried people and their children.

Because this issue is in a state of flux in the human resources world, employers vary widely in terms of their policies regarding domestic partners. Some offer full benefits to their employees' partners, others are considering adding benefits, and still others are just becoming familiar with the term. Since most companies don't yet offer the benefits, there's a great need and lots of opportunities to convince employers of their importance.

HEALTH CARE SHOULDN'T BE LINKED TO RELATIONSHIP STATUS

IF YOU AGREE that domestic partner benefits aren't enough, here's one way to join the national movement for health care for all:

The Universal Health Care Action Network
2800 Euclid Avenue, Suite 520
Cleveland, OH 44115-2418
(216) 241-8422
www.uhcan.org

THE THEORY BEHIND DOMESTIC PARTNER BENEFITS

Employers aren't required by law to pay a penny more than the minimum wage, but many do. In fact, many employers offer much more than the minimums required by law—in the form of salaries well above the minimum wage, 401(k) plans, life insurance, sick leave, tuition subsidies, on-site child care, health insurance, and other goodies—because it increases the likelihood of hiring and keeping talented employees. It makes sense that if an employee's family is well cared for, the employee will be happier, more productive, and less likely to leave the company for another offer.

It's a nice theory, but it hinges on who is considered the employee's family. The narrow definition that most employers use—people who are related by blood, marriage, or adoption—excludes a growing portion of employees' families. According to a *Newsweek* poll, three-quarters of Americans now say "family" is "a group of people who love and care for each other," a much broader definition.[2] Many experts now say family should be defined based on emotional and financial dependency and interdependency.

In 1982 the *Village Voice* newspaper was the first to officially recognize the family diversity of its workforce by offering health benefits to the domestic partners—both same-sex and different-sex—of its employees. The company already had an unofficial policy of covering employees' unmarried different-sex partners, and a gay and lesbian employee union group successfully argued that their partners should receive equal benefits.[3] Since that time, similar policies have been adopted elsewhere with surprising speed. While this chapter focuses on making "hard benefits" like health and dental insurance available to domestic partners and their children, many employers also allow domestic partners to take advantage of "soft benefits" like bereavement leave, university library access, or family housing.

INCREASE IN THE NUMBER OF EMPLOYERS OFFERING DOMESTIC PARTNER BENEFITS, 1980s TO 2001[4]

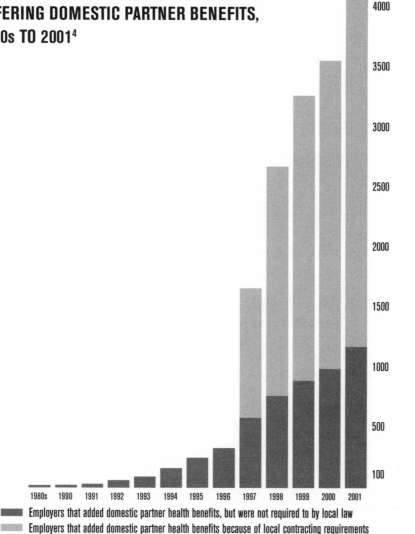

- ■ Employers that added domestic partner health benefits, but were not required to by local law
- ■ Employers that added domestic partner health benefits because of local contracting requirements

WHERE ARE THE BENEFITS?

THE MOST COMPREHENSIVE lists of employers offering domestic partner benefits, and municipalities offering domestic partner registries, are maintained by the Human Rights Campaign (www.hrc.org/worknet) in a database that can be searched online. Their site also provides sample affidavits employers can adapt, and strategies for organizing for benefits.

According to the Human Rights Campaign, over 4,400 employers offer domestic partner health benefits,[5] and over a quarter of Americans work for an employer that provides them.[6] Although this is still a minority, it's fast becoming the new norm. Nearly 90 percent of employers offering domestic partner benefits added them in the last five years, and 35 percent of large employers who don't already offer them are considering adding them in the next three years.[7] Current trends suggest that before long only a handful of employers will dare—or be able—to afford—to treat employees' partners differently from the way they treat spouses.

HOW A SINGLE CITY MADE 2,700 COMPANIES DO THE RIGHT THING

IN 1997, THE city of San Francisco implemented a law requiring every company that does business with the city to provide the same benefits to its employees' domestic partners as it does to employees' spouses. The list of employers affected by the law was a long one, from the printer that prints business cards for the office clerks, to the consultants that troubleshoot the city's computer network, to the airlines that fly into San Francisco's airport. Within three years, over 2,700 companies changed their benefits policies to include domestic partners. Although some were small, local companies, others were major national firms. No other single law has ever made such a profound impact on domestic partner benefits.

Since the San Francisco law passed, Seattle; Los Angeles; Portland, Maine; Broward County, Florida; and several other cities and towns adopted similar ordinances, leading over 3,087 employers to adopt DP benefits policies.[8] The Broward County law, less expansive than San Francisco's, gives a competitive advantage to contractors that bid on county projects if they provide domestic partner benefits to their employees.[9] We can only imagine how the landscape of employee benefits could change if other cities followed the lead of these fair-minded trailblazers.

MANY WAYS TO SET UP A DOMESTIC PARTNER PLAN

Not every employer that offers domestic partner (DP) benefits does it the same way. Some offer the benefits to both same-sex and different-sex couples, while others exclude different-sex couples (see more on this at "What If Your Employer Has a Gays-Only Policy, But You're Not Gay?," page 165). Some provide exactly the same benefits to domestic partners as to spouses, while others offer more limited benefits. Some allow employees to add a "dependent" to their health insurance, a broader category that could include a dependent parent, sibling, or partner. Others have created flexible "cafeteria benefits plans" to allow employees to decide how they want to spend their benefits dollars.

The definition of "domestic partner" varies from company to company. At some workplaces you just have to sign a simple affidavit stating that you live with a "spouse equivalent" or "domestic partner," while at other places you have to meet a long list of criteria and submit supporting paperwork in order to qualify for benefits. Some employers don't require partners to sign an affidavit at all in order truly to treat partnered employees the same as married ones. After all, they take married couples at their word that they really are married. At small workplaces where everyone in the office knows everyone else's family, an affidavit often isn't necessary.

Val ran into trouble when she tried to sign up for a benefit connected to her partner's university's community. She likes to tell the story of her solution:

> My partner Ken was a graduate student at the Massachusetts Institute of Technology. MIT makes available identification cards that give certain privileges to spouses and partners of MIT students. To get one, you need your partner's MIT number, your own photo ID, and proof of partnership. I went to apply for a partner ID, and brought a piece of mail addressed to me at our address, along with a piece of mail addressed to Ken at the same address. The woman to whom I presented my documentation was initially unwilling to issue me a card, on the grounds that I had not brought her anything which proved that Ken and I were partners. I explained that Ken and I had separate finances but that we were in fact partners, but she was unconvinced. Eventually, I offered to go get him and make love with him on the office carpet. She declined this generous offer and issued the ID.

Although employers' methods of determining who qualifies as a domestic partner vary widely, you can be reassured you won't need to do anything as risqué as Val's proposal. Below is a list of some of the requirements employers do impose. Keep in mind that most affidavits include some, not all, of these criteria.

- The partners share a primary residence. Some affidavits require partners to have lived together for at least 6 or 12 months, or to have a 6 or 12 month space of time before an employee is eligible to sign up a new partner.
- The couple have a committed relationship (described in some affidavits as "close," "caring," "long-term," "for mutual support and benefit," or some combination of these terms). Sometimes the criteria specify that the commitment should be similar to marriage.
- The relationship is expected to continue indefinitely.
- Some affidavits require that the partners be the same sex. The vast majority (90 percent), though, are "sex-neutral," open to both same-sex and different-sex couples.[10]

PERCENT OF EMPLOYERS OFFERING INCLUSIVE VS. LIMITED DOMESTIC PARTNER BENEFITS[10]

10% available only to same-sex couples

90% available to both same-sex and different-sex couples

- The partners are jointly responsible for each other's emotional and financial welfare, or are mutually responsible for basic living expenses. Some affidavits require that the couple attach (or be prepared to present, if asked) one or two items of proof in the form of wills or life insurance policies naming each other as primary beneficiaries; powers of attorney for health care and property; joint ownership of a motor vehicle; joint bank accounts or credit cards; joint mortgage or lease; joint utility billing statements; or domestic partner agreements.
- Neither partner is married to someone else or has declared another domestic partner relationship with someone else.

- The partners are not related by blood to a degree that would prevent them from getting married in their state.
- The partners are both of the age of consent in their state.
- The partners are mentally competent to enter into a contract.

Regardless of how domestic partner is defined, employees who receive health benefits for their partners must pay state and federal taxes on those benefits, unlike their married co-workers. DP benefits are counted as additional compensation, and their value is added to the employee's salary for tax purposes. The only exception to this is if the partner receiving the benefits is the employee's dependent.

CAFETERIA PLANS: AN ALTERNATIVE TO TRADITIONAL BENEFITS PLANS

CAFETERIA PLANS REPRESENT a slightly different approach some employers are taking to recognize their employees' differing family needs. Traditional benefits plans give the employee an umbrella of protection that extends certain benefits to him and his spouse and children. Domestic partner plans bring domestic partners, partners' children, and, in some cases, other dependents under the "family" umbrella.

It's been pointed out, though, that these types of benefits plans don't really adhere to the concept of equal pay for equal work. On average, benefits make up 30 percent of an employee's overall compensation.[12] Some argue that a married employee with six children who receives health insurance, on-site day care, and tuition assistance for all his children is receiving a substantially larger compensation package than his single, childfree coworker who needs only personal health insurance. Others say that's as it should be, since as a society we have an investment in raising the next generation.

To respond to the idea that different employees have different benefits needs, some employers now offer "cafeteria style" benefits plans. The idea is simple: Each employee is eligible to receive a set, equal amount of benefits, to be allocated as they choose. A married worker with children may already get health care benefits from his spouse's job, so he can choose to use his benefits to cover child care, while a childfree employee might invest more in her retirement plan since she won't have children to support her in her old age. A worker caring for an elderly parent could add the parent to his health insurance package, and a person in a multiple-adult family could do the same for more than one domestic partner. The flexibility of this type of plan allows each employee to create a benefits package that fits her situation.

DOMESTIC PARTNER REGISTRIES

Some towns, cities, and states have domestic partner registries where partners who meet certain criteria can pay a small fee, become "registered" domestic partners, and sometimes take home an official-looking certificate with their names. Often these registries offer no immediate benefits, but other entities, like employers or insurance companies, can choose to rely on the registry's information to decide who is eligible for domestic partner health benefits, different insurance rates, and other benefits. A few registries, like California's, provide some concrete rights like medical decisionmaking. Some couples register because it feels validating, which can be especially meaningful in a culture that too often fails to recognize unmarried relationships as significant.

These registries are not the same thing as domestic partner benefits, the focus of this chapter. At most workplaces that offer domestic partner health benefits, you do not need to go to a registry in order to sign up for benefits. And in most municipalities, registering as domestic partners will not automatically provide you with domestic partner health benefits. There are fewer than 100 domestic partner registries in the U.S.; you can find out if your town is one of them at www.hrc.org/worknet/dp/index.asp.

SO YOU WANT YOUR EMPLOYER
TO ADD DOMESTIC PARTNER BENEFITS?

Employers add domestic partner benefits because employees ask, argue, and advocate for them. As consultant Liz Winfield says, "It's pretty common that requests for domestic partner benefits will come from a single voice, whether it's a 10-person company or a 10,000-person company."[13] In a few cases, getting domestic partner benefits really has been as easy as asking the right person on the right day. Small employers or ones that already have fairly progressive policies and benefits plans may be sympathetic; perhaps they were already considering adding DP benefits and just needed a little encouragement.

In most places, though, employees have to organize. Usually, it's the human resources department or a high-up supervisor that needs to be lobbied. State and municipal employees have an even harder task, since changing their benefits plans usually means getting a new law passed. Forming a group of supportive employees is a smart organizing strategy. Employees in unmarried same-sex or different-sex relationships are likely to be supportive, and building coalitions between people of different sexual orientations can be a powerful approach. If your place of employment doesn't already have a group for gay, lesbian, bisexual, and transgender employees and their allies, this may be the time to form one. But historically, gay and lesbian employees have done more than their fair share of the work to organize for DP benefits, so it's important for heterosexual people to help. Labor groups and unions, women's groups, senior citizens' groups, groups for people of color, local political and civil rights groups, and other employee groups or organizations may also be supportive. You can broaden your base of support by explaining your goals to those who may not be directly affected by the new policy, including customers, clients, and married employees: The stronger and broader your coalition, the better.

Your group will have to do its homework if it wants to be effective. You'll want to make sure your employer includes sexual orientation and marital status in its nondiscrimination policy, find out what benefits are available to the spouses of married employees, and research which other employers in your field or geographical area already offer DP benefits. Once you know what you want, you can develop a plan for how to get it, which may include drafting a proposal, writing letters, and meeting with key managers, executives, or board members. Successful campaigns for DP benefits often include:

> *Legally recognized domestic partnerships carrying equal legal entitlements should be available to everyone.*
>
> **—Abigail "Dear Abby" Van Buren**[14]

- ▸ *Solid facts.* You may have to educate your higher-ups about what kind of costs they can expect and about the experiences of similar employers who have chosen to offer the benefits.
- ▸ *"Best interest of the company" arguments.* Domestic partner benefits can be a cost-effective tool for attracting and retaining top-notch employees. One survey of 279 human resources professionals representing nineteen industries found that domestic partnership benefits were among the top three most effective incentives for recruiting new hires. Partner benefits were said to be more effective than telecommuting options, hiring bonuses, stock options, and 401(k) plans.[15] *Fast Company* magazine reports, "High-tech recruiters tell us that 8 out of 10 job candidates always ask a prospective employer whether the company offers domestic partner benefits—not because they need the benefit, but because it shows the company is a true meritocracy that supports talented people from all walks of life."[16]
- ▸ *Personal stories.* Putting a personal face on the subject of health insurance can be the most powerful way to remind managers about the humans who need the benefits you're seeking. Tell the stories of employees whose lives would be touched by DP benefits, and explain how the benefits would affect the ones they love. Showing with words and photos that unmarried people are part of loving relationships and families can increase sympathy for your cause.

♦   *Tenacity.* Many employee groups organize for months or years before achieving their goals.

RESPONSES TO COMMON ARGUMENTS AGAINST DP BENEFITS

Once you've laid the groundwork, built a coalition, and prepared your arguments, you're ready to begin a conversation with the powers-that-be. If you encounter hesitation or resistance, be prepared to educate the decisionmakers about the truth behind their concerns. Here are some of the most common arguments against providing DP benefits, and answers for each.

Argument: They're too expensive.

Reality: Cost isn't the issue—fairness is. Sometimes it costs employers more to do the right thing, whether that's disposing of chemical waste responsibly or updating the company's sexual harassment policy. Discriminating on the basis of sex, sexual orientation, or marital status may save the company a few bucks, but it may also violate state and federal laws and, quite possibly, the company's own nondiscrimination code. Although some CEOs and small business owners struggle with the rising costs of insurance premiums, the solution is not to save money at the expense of unmarried employees. One labor union made the point using a mock want ad:

WANTED—ACCOUNT CLERK
Starting wage of homosexual or unmarried worker $9.02 per hour. For married worker $10.33 per hour. Apply at the County Personnel Office. Alameda County is An Equal Opporunity Employer.[17]

Still, there are those whose job it is to study the bottom line. They'll be pleased to learn that two decades of employer experience find the costs of adding DP benefits to be low. Studies of this issue have concluded that on average, costs increase between 0.5% and 3 percent.[18] Eighty-five percent of respondents to a survey done by the Society for Human Resource Management said that offering DP benefits resulted in no increase in their health care costs.[19] Fears that there would be extra costs involved in providing health care for domestic partner couples (particularly the assumption that gay men are likely to have HIV/AIDS) have been proven groundless.[20] In fact, on average domestic partner couples are younger and have fewer children than married couples,[21] which means their health care costs are likely to be lower.

One of the reasons DP benefits don't cost much is that not many people enroll. Most estimates find that enrollments increase between 0.5% and 5 percent, and one study found that 75 percent of companies with DP benefits reported enrollment increases of 2 percent or less.[22] Many employees' partners get health benefits through their own jobs. Some couples find that because DP benefits are taxed (unlike identical spousal benefits), it costs less for them to buy health insurance other ways. Although the actual number of people who sign up for DP benefits is usually small, the importance of the benefits to those people's lives is often profound. Some employers offer other benefits that similarly have a low cost for the employer and are enormously meaningful for a small handful of employees who use them; adoption and foster care benefits are one example. If your employer offers other benefits with this same logic, point out the similarity in reasoning.

If your employer isn't ready to offer DP health benefits because of cost concerns, you can encourage them to expand bereavement leave, family sick leave, and other important "soft" benefits policies to include partners. It generally costs little, if anything, to expand these policies, and some employers find they're a confidence-building first step. By tracking how many employees take advantage of soft DP benefits, the employer can estimate how many might be interested in DP health benefits, knowing the number in need of health benefits will be smaller.

Some human resources experts have found that contrary to fears about high costs, DP benefits actually have monetary benefits. Not only do they help recruit qualified employees, they are can also increase employee retention, reducing hiring and training costs.[23]

Argument: It will lead to fraud—people will try to get health insurance for their roommates.

Reality: The potential for fraud can never be entirely eliminated in any system, but experience shows there is little cause for concern: among the thousands of employers already offering domestic partner benefits, there have been no reported cases of fraud.[24] Employers with concerns about this can protect themselves by adding a fraud provision that explains the consequences for employees who make fraudulent claims or requires them to pay back their premiums if the information they provide is not true.

Since the existing system of spousal benefits rarely requires employees to submit their marriage licenses as proof that they are really married, potential for fraud is not limited to domestic partners. It is equally possible to marry one's roommate simply to secure health benefits for him or her, but this is rarely given as a reason not to provide health benefits for employees' spouses.

Argument: There's not enough interest among employees.

Reality: In a survey of 1,058 large employers, 56 percent of human resources professionals at companies without DP benefits said they don't offfer the benefits because employees aren't interested in them.[25] While the human resources departments content themselves with the lack of interest, the Alternatives to Marriage Project is bombarded with calls and e-mails from people who desperately want the benefits—but haven't told the human resources departments at their workplaces! Benefits are a perfect example of how squeaky wheels get the oil. In this case, though, the wheels that need oil are heavily stigmatized. It's common for gay and lesbian employees not to be public at work about their relationships because they fear it would reduce their ability to get promotions or be treated fairly. Employees with different-sex partners may not speak up because they don't want to confront other people's judgments of their personal choices or be forced to explain to every supervisor why they're not married. We give a special gold star to those rare employers that offer benefits of their own accord, without waiting for employees to make the requests, write the letters, do the research, and make the case. These gold star employers demonstrate a level of sensitivity and respect that is likely to result in a workplace that feels safer for all kinds of employees.

> Does someone have to recite marriage vows to get health insurance?
>
> —THINK AGAIN, "artists fighting injustice"[26]

Since we know that fewer than 5 percent of employees generally sign up for DP benefits, employers are mistaken if they're waiting for an overwhelming number of employees to begin pounding on the human resources department's door. The pounding may sound more like a tentative knock now and then as a potential new hire or a quiet employee asks about the health benefits policy. But whether they'll affect one employee at a small company or 100 at a large one, benefits often mean the difference between an employee staying at a job or leaving, being able to have one partner care for a child at home or putting him in daycare, or not living in constant fear that an accident could leave the uninsured partner without access to the medical care she needs.

Argument: It will undermine marriage and the traditional family.

Reality: The rules of the workplace are that employers must provide equal pay for equal work. Workplaces are not where marriage laws are defined or upheld.

Undoubtedly, the desire to protect marriage and the "traditional family" usually stems from sincere concern about the good of children and families. But denying health care benefits to certain families because they don't conform to one particular model hurts those families far more than it helps. When health insurance is denied to an employee's partner or her partner's children, the family is forced to buy expensive insurance on their own, resulting in fewer financial resources available for child-related expenses, or leave members of the family uninsured, increasing the risk of serious illness or death. Compensating employees fairly and equally regardless of their marital status doesn't hurt married people or alter the fact that most people will still choose to get married. It simply addresses the reality that unmarried families exist and are too often uninsured.

WHAT IF YOUR EMPLOYER HAS A GAYS-ONLY POLICY, BUT YOU'RE NOT GAY?

Only one in ten companies offering domestic partner benefits limits their availability to same-sex couples.[27] Unfortunately, though, this includes some large employers, including the major U.S. automakers and most universities.[28] The rationale for same-sex-only policies is that since same-sex couples can't get legally married, they need another way to secure equal benefits for their families. This "unable to marry" argument is a powerful one, and it's convinced many employers that offering domestic partner benefits is a fair and logical step to take. Many of those same employers think that since different-sex couples could marry, there's no reason to give them benefits.

But that logic misses the point, because an employee's marital status shouldn't determine their compensation as employees. There are plenty of reasons, many of them outlined in chapter 2, why committed couples would choose to delay marrying or not marry at all. The employer's role is not to judge the merit of individual reasons, but rather to compensate all employees fairly.

The idea that you should not be forced to marry in order to be eligible for health benefits has widespread support. The National Organization of Women, the National Gay and Lesbian Task Force, the American Association for Single People, and many chapters of the American Association of Retired Persons all support policies that define "domestic partner" in a sex-neutral way. Sex-neutral DP policies hold all employees to the same standard regardless of their sex or that of their partner. Once again, providing equal pay for equal work is the primary issue. Nate made this case successfully when he got a new job:

> I was hired at a company that already had a domestic partnership policy in place, but Elise couldn't be covered because the policy defined domestic partners as only same-sex couples. I approached the director of human resources and found him very receptive to my arguments. After a few conversations and one formal letter of request, the company expanded its policy and I was able to sign Elise up.

Historically, lawsuits have not been an effective way to win the expansion of same-sex-only domestic partner policies.[29] It is entirely possible that future cases could have more success, as many lawyers and legal organizations believe they have legal merit. But given recent negative court decisions, convincing your employer through organizing and negotiation is probably a better strategy. Here are some points you can make when arguing your case:

- Thank and congratulate the employer for offering DP benefits. Tell them—sincerely!—how much you appreciate working at a workplace that recognizes that employees should be treated equally regardless of their sexual orientation or marital status. The employer obviously understands that gay and lesbian relationships deserve fair treatment even though they're not legal marriages. If the employer has a nondiscrimination statement, remind them what it says and express thanks for it.

- Remind the employer that they have already done the work to establish standard eligibility criteria for domestic partners. Provide them with a list of the company's own criteria from its domestic partner affidavit, if it has one (excluding the same-sex requirement), and point out how these criteria recognize committed relationships.

- Describe, point by point, how you and your partner (or the people in the coalition you've built) meet or exceed all the criteria. Show the employer how their same-sex-only policy violates the principle of equal pay for equal work. Benefits are part of an employee's pay, yet the current benefits policy would provide different benefits to two employees in identical relationships. You should not be treated differently based on your partner's sex.

- Let them know that their DP policy is out of step with the national trend, since 90 percent of employers with DP policies include both same-sex and different-sex couples. If possible, provide some examples of competitors in the same field or employers that are similar in terms of location and size, that provide more inclusive DP benefits.

- Explain that commitment is not contingent on being married, and that people choose not to marry or to delay marriage for a wide variety of political, religious, philosophical, and financial reasons. If your employers' domestic partner criteria are quite detailed, and include requirements that the partners live together or share financial obligations, point out that these standards are actually higher than the requirements for marriages. Married couples do not necessarily have to live together or share financial obligations. Make clear that as a unmarried couple, you are not trying to take "the easy way out."

- Remind the employer of all the benefits they choose to offer employees (just about everything beyond minimum wage salaries) even though these are not required by law. Thank them for the many ways they are committed to creating a workplace where employees and their families are supported, and remind them how this has enabled them to attract and retain high quality employees.

Only twenty years ago, the concept of "domestic partners"—and the idea that they deserved certain rights and recognitions—didn't even exist. Now even our grandmothers know what domestic partner means. Every week more employers decide that families created by marriage aren't the only ones that should be eligible for health and other employment benefits. Many people are frustrated that their employers don't *already* recognize their relationships. This sense of injustice is proof of the profound cultural shift that has taken place—and it provides the fuel that will bring family recognition the acceptance it deserves.

DOMESTIC PARTNER BENEFITS RESOURCES

The Domestic Partnership Organizing Manual for Employee Benefits
This manual provides much more detailed information about organizing for benefits, including how to write a proposal, sample policies and affidavits, and advice on how to argue your case. The *Manual* is published by the National Gay and Lesbian Task Force, but the information contained within is applicable to people of all sexual orientations. It can be downloaded for free from the web:

National Gay and Lesbian Task Force
www.ngltf.org (see the publications section of the site)

The Alternatives to Marriage Project's Resources page (www.unmarried. org) is regularly updated with the best domestic partnership resources.

The American Association of Single People (www.unmarriedamerica.com/ dp-info.html) provides news articles, cost-analyses for domestic partner benefits, information about legislation internationally, and other resources.

EIGHT

WALKING DOWN THE AISLE:
Commitment Ceremonies and Rituals

PEOPLE TALK ABOUT weddings and marriage as if the two were inseparable. In reality, the desire to celebrate one's love is not always matched by an interest in matrimony. Those who appreciate the ritual and rite of passage may not have an accompanying yearning for the legal relationship of husband and wife. Luckily, you can have a wedding without getting married.

There's no reason why you can't wear the white dress, walk down the aisle, exchange I do's and rings, and dance the Electric Slide all night long. In fact, there's no reason that the decision to tie the knot legally or not, and the decision to have a ceremony or not, have to go together at all. Anyone can have a ceremony, including people who can't or don't want to make it legal. And even people who *are* getting legally married can make their ceremony as much or as little like the ones in romantic movies as they like.

When it comes down to it, the process of planning a ceremony is pretty similar regardless of whether you plan to sign that piece of paper or not. This chapter will explore the reasons people might want to have a ceremony, discuss the different decisions that go into planning such an event, share the stories of some ceremonies couples actually pulled off (and what kind of reactions they got), and at the end, point you toward resources where you can learn more. If you're one of the people who are thinking, "No thanks! I'm not getting married because I'm trying to *avoid* white dresses and monogrammed towels," we've got you covered here, too.

WHY HAVE ONE?

There are plenty of reasons why having a ceremony might appeal:

▶ For Public Validation

Weddings indicate that it's time to take a couple seriously. Ceremonies (particularly those with lots of guests) can serve the same purpose, softening the hearts of great-aunts who didn't approve of cohabitation, indicating to friends that you intend this partner to be The One, and giving your mother her day to be "mother of the bride."

For Priscilla and Joe, defining Priscilla's role in Joe's family was one of the most important reasons to have a ceremony. They explain their problem:

> *I have a lot of nieces and nephews, and most of them have known Priscilla their entire lives. But they weren't quite sure how to categorize her, because I come from a traditional Southern family, and no one conveyed to my nieces and nephews what it might mean that we're not married. My other siblings are all married. The spouses of my siblings are all called aunts and uncles.*
> *—Joe*

> *Unintentionally, Joe's brother and Joe brought their girlfriends down to meet the family at the same time, about eight years ago. So we met the family the same way, at the same time. And over the years, Joe's brother and that girlfriend eventually got married. And so she became an aunt. But there was still this question, what was I? The kids were worried about it, too—the issue would come up a lot. "Can I call Priscilla aunt, or not?" It never was clarified.*
> *—Priscilla*

After their commitment ceremony—which they nicknamed their "Commitzvah," a combination of commitment ceremony and mitzvah, or blessing—the nieces and nephews started saying Aunt Priscilla. But they weren't the only ones who acted differently; Priscilla described having the ceremony as "a crossing over of some sort." Joe says:

It was incredible how our stock went up with people all over the place, how much more status we have. There was a way in which we were legitimized and benefit from the privileges that people get when they get married. We're dealt with as a little more adult, more responsible. I think my family members feel closer to Priscilla, and the same for me and her family members.

Anneke and Jeremy believe "it takes a community to support a relationship," just as people say it takes a village to raise a child. At the ceremony that celebrated 10 years of togetherness, they stood in the center, surrounded by "the people we love and the people who love us," including their adult daughters. The high point came after they expressed the commitments they had already made to each other:

We asked our friends and family to commit to supporting us in who we are together, to be the best we can be as a couple and also the best we can be as individuals. If they felt they could commit to that, we asked them to express, "I do" any way they wanted to. They shouted it and stomped and clapped—it was wild. The energy in the room went sky-high. It made an incredible difference.

Even though these relationships may have already deserved adult respect and community support, it was organizing a ceremony—going through the steps of reserving a space, writing the vows, planning the food—that helped others understand. As a result of those public vows, many partners find they are ushered into the circle of couples whose anniversaries are noted, whose partners are included as real members of the family at the annual Fourth of July cookout, and who can count on the timely words of wisdom that help them survive the unavoidable rocky times ahead.

▶ To Strengthen Your Relationship

Some people find that making a public statement of commitment strengthens and deepens their bonds. If theirs was a relationship of considerable length, some are surprised to find that the day after their wedding or ceremony, they feel more connected to each other than ever. Historian E. J. Graff writes of her ceremony with her partner, Madeline, "To our utter surprise, the ceremony did bring us closer, pulling an invisible cloak around us that has warmed us during difficult times."[1] Wolfsong's experience was similar:

Myra and I were living together quite happily. But when we had the ceremony, it changed the tenor. It made a difference that we had publicly made a commitment. And people treat you differently, too. Once you have a commitment ceremony, and you invite your co-workers and friends and family, then people see you as married, and—they just treat you differently. We had done some thinking, worked on our issues, and struggled through creating something true to us. The ceremony was a real sense of commitment.

Relationship expert Pepper Schwartz says that's not uncommon: public recognition of your relationship can help keep you together during hard times.[2] Your family might be more likely to help you through. You might feel more comfortable seeking counseling from a clergyperson who blessed your relationship. You might simply feel it's too embarrassing to walk out the door, if all your friends and relatives heard you say you'd hang in through the hard times.

▶ For the Children

Some partners have a ceremony because they're planning to have a child without getting married, and hope the event will create a sense of respect and legitimacy both for relatives and for the child. In an unmarried stepfamily, having a ceremony that children witness or, even better, participate in, can work wonders for solidifying the idea that "we're a family now," and strengthen the child-partner (stepparent) relationship. Marvin and Roberta announced they were getting married and held a church wedding—even though they didn't get legally married—so that his children, ages six and eight, would understand Roberta's role in their lives. Marvin, who considers Roberta his wife, says that at one point before the wedding:

I referred to Roberta as "your stepmother," and one of the kids was astonished. He said, "I thought she was the cooking lady." Well, we thought, we'd better straighten that up. So we arranged with a Unitarian clergyman for a nice wedding. It was small. It was in a church, presided over by a clergyman. There were guests and witnesses, and afterward a luncheon. My wife had flowers in her arms. In the course of the ceremony, the minister three times referred to us as man and wife. He said, "I pronounce you man and wife." What he left out was the expression, "under the authority of the state vested in me." Because he was not doing this under the authority of the state. He referred to it as a service of commitment, but it was unmistakably a wedding.

Sherry and her partner held a commitment ceremony in their home to mark the beginning of their Brady Bunch–like blended family. Each of them brought three children from their previous relationships, so at the time they had their ceremony their new family included six children between the ages of 15 and 20!

It was very private, just me and him and the kids, no clergyperson. We made promises to each other, and we exchanged promise rings that we still wear. The kids gave their blessings on that commitment. And we made a commitment as a family. I'm committed to being the best mom and stepmom that I know how to be, and he did the same for my boys. Today, the kids are very close and consider themselves brothers and sisters.

It doesn't matter whether your nonlegal ceremony is a full-scale wedding or a private ritual your family does one evening after dinner, as long as the ceremony feels serious and meaningful.

▶ As a Ritual or Rite of Passage

In cultures throughout the world, rituals are used to mark rites of passage, and people tend to store the rituals they've experienced in their memory bank of "significant lifetime events." Some of the most common rituals celebrate "coming of age," or the transition from childhood to adulthood. In the Jewish tradition, bar and bat mitzvahs are celebrated when a child turns twelve or thirteen. Catholic children receive Confirmation in eighth grade. Many Latina girls celebrate the *quinceañera* when they turn fifteen, a ceremony with some similarities to a wedding, recognizing the girl's maturity.[3] Other rites of passage range from full-fledged debutante parties among wealthy socialites to things as common as high school and college graduation ceremonies.

In addition to coming of age, rituals also mark significant points in family life, from the birth of a baby (showers, blessings, baptisms) to those that help grieve the loss of a loved one (funerals, memorial services, wakes). Weddings are one of our culture's most visible rites of passage, and most of them contain ritualistic elements laden with centuries of meaning. Like other powerful rituals, weddings are memorable, and signify to people in attendance, including the bride and groom, that something deeply important is taking place. Having a ceremony to acknowledge and celebrate the relationship can create many of these same powerful, positive feelings.

▶ To Get Married in the Eyes of God

Lots of folks who wish they could marry face legal or financial barriers that make doing so unwise or impossible. There's no rule against having a wedding, though, and leading your lives in every other way as a married couple (sans marriage certificate). Many clergy agree that it is possible for God to bless a loving relationship that is not a legal marriage (for more on this, see page 67).[4] Your wedding can look exactly like every other wedding, except that the minister wouldn't sign a marriage certificate at the end. One Jewish organization, The Shalom Center, advocates for rituals to make unmarried relationships sacred and holy.

Same-sex couples currently can't legally marry in any state in the country. Many, however, choose to have commitment ceremonies, and some call themselves married. Senior citizens receiving pension benefits from a deceased spouse, and those who met late in life and want to keep their estates separate, are also likely candidates for ceremonies without legal marriage. "It just didn't make sense to get into any financial entanglements . . . but it was important to make a commitment to each other," says Ernie, a 76-year-old who became "partners for life" in a ceremony with his partner, Muff.[5] The ceremony included an exchange of rings, vows, and blessings from a minister. This situation is common in places with large senior communities, and clergy often form informal referral services to help couples locate ministers and rabbis who will perform spiritual weddings. "My phone never stops ringing [with requests for these]," says Reverend Wallace Tervin, a retired Methodist minister in Lake Wales, Florida.[6]

If Judy C. remarries before she's 55, she'd lose a substantial annuity she receives from her late husband's estate. Her partner, Michael, worried about what his parents would think if he cohabited. As Judy explains:

> He didn't want his mom and dad to know he was "living in sin," so we had a religious ceremony without the civil aspect of it. There were about 30 people there, and we consider it our wedding. We had a minister and everything. So in a religious sense we are married, but not in a civil sense. His dad never did know that we weren't married—he passed away about three years ago. I did eventually tell his mother. And everybody else knew the truth.

If you live in or visit one of the thirteen states that still recognize common-law marriage, you'll need to be careful with this approach so you don't find yourself having to argue that you didn't intend to become common law spouses (see page 147 for a list of states).

In fact, for most of history, if a couple said they were married, and their community and family agreed, then they *were* married. Nowadays, you need to get a marriage license to make it official, but that doesn't stop people having a wedding and calling themselves husband and wife.

▶ To Have a Party

When most people think about having a wedding, it's not the new protection from having to testify against each other in court that puts the sparkle in their eyes. Part of the joy of marriage is getting a day to be the prince and princess, to celebrate with friends and family. Weddings are the biggest parties most people ever host. They command the attention of friends and relatives, who are often more than willing to travel long distances and pay for airfare, hotel, and gifts (and even for the event itself, in the case of the bride's and groom's parents). As Marie says, that's an appealing reason to plan a wedding:

That's when my family gets together, for weddings. It's really hard to get my family together. I love my family. I know that if I told them all that I was getting married, I would probably get everybody to come here to Vermont. And that's never happened.

A ceremony can be a way to have the same sparkling (or subdued) event, surrounded by the ones you love, even if there's no marriage certificate being signed.

▶ Because You Always Wanted a Wedding

At seven you exchanged aluminum foil wedding rings in the schoolyard. At seventeen you signed up for that marriage class in high school where you got to plan and act out a mock wedding. At twenty-seven, your feminist side is appalled that you secretly splurge on brides' magazines the way others hoard Häagen Däzs. Go for it! It's OK to admit you want a wedding, even if you don't want a marriage. For some couples who disagree about getting married, this option is the key that unlocks years of conflict: the one who desperately wants it gets that "once in a lifetime" day, and the one who doesn't want to get married doesn't have to make it legal. (For more on this, see the Marriage Decision Tool, pages 232–239).

▶ To Get the Goods

We don't advise having a ceremony just to get presents. But many of the couples we interviewed at least joked about the idea. Let's face it: People who haven't had weddings are well aware that two-thirds of the things we admire in other people's homes—that gorgeous ceramic bowl, the funky art print, the really cool kitchen gadget that can peel and chop an onion all by itself—were wedding gifts. The situation can be vexing for unmarried folks who eat with mismatched utensils and sleep on sheets our parents received when *they* got married. Deborah and her partner have been pondering the gifts their friends receive when they get married, and laugh, "We were thinking of having a Yep, We're Still Not Getting Married Party and trying to get a whole lot of stuff."

NO CEREMONY? NO PROBLEM!

YOU DON'T LOSE any points if you decide that having a ceremony isn't your thing. Maybe you think the idea is corny, you hate big parties, or being the center of attention makes your skin crawl. Maybe religion, spirituality, and ritual don't play a big role in your life, or the people you would want to invite aren't supportive of your relationship.

Teri says that having a ceremony simply isn't at the top of her and her partner's to-do list.

> Part of the reason we get along is because we're not into big celebrations. We're both kind of uncomfortable being the center of attention. When we were first together we used to talk about having a ceremony. When would we have it? Who would officiate? Nothing fit our personalities, our lifestyle, our worldview. We don't want to use a ritual or ceremony from some other tradition that we don't have any personal investment in, so we would have to fabricate it all from scratch. It just hasn't been a major priority.

And Chris says that avoiding his family's expectations was the best reason not to have a wedding:

> They would want all the things they know. They would want a band, and they would want the Chicken Dance, and they would want the throwing of rice—they would want all that stuff.

Chris's partner, also named Chris, responds:

> I wouldn't object to any of those things. But they would also want a priest, and they would want vows of monogamy and life ever after. And that's what we've been talking about that we don't want. The Chicken Dance I could live with.

Americans have such a love affair with weddings that it can be difficult to convince people that you really don't need a wedding to be happy. Reporters are fond of asking Dorian, "Honestly, though, don't you dream about wearing that white dress?" Of course they don't believe the answer they get. Chances are, over the years of your relationship you'll gradually gain many of the things often associated with weddings and ceremonies, like a deeper sense of commitment or increased family support.

THINGS TO CONSIDER

▶ Who Will Be There?

Witnesses are not an essential part of a ceremony. You can tap into the power of ritual, mark a rite of passage (like moving in together or buying a house), make a formal commitment, or celebrate a relationship's resilience or longevity alone with just your partner by your side. This kind of ceremony need not cost much, if anything, but the occasion can be every bit as memorable and meaningful as an elaborate event.

The ritual referred to earlier, that Sherry, her partner, and their six teenagers held, was one example of a private ceremony. The guest list for Ted and Eileen's ceremony was even smaller: just Ted and Eileen. Ted said, "We held a private ritual in the woods before our creator, binding ourselves to each other and vowing to remain independent."

Tracey R. and Jane S. knew they didn't want to have a large ceremony with guests, but did want to do something to honor their relationship and make a commitment to each other. Tracey says a deserted beach at daybreak was just what they were looking for:

> One time when we were in Provincetown we woke up real early in the morning and sat on a lifeguard chair together on the beach. We said a few words to each other about how we felt about each other, honoring what we have, and what our hopes were for our life in the future. Then we went to a café and had a good breakfast. Part of what was fun about it was that it was spur of the moment. It felt true to our feelings, because this wasn't the day we were supposed to say nice things to each other. . . . It was our equivalent of going to Vegas.

Michaela and her partner, followers of the nature-based religion Wicca, planned a ritual around deciding to have a child.

> We decided to have our daughter together, and we thought we ought to really discuss what we thought about parenting and about our relationship. We wanted to have a formal sit-down discussion, and we thought it was important to do it in our sacred space for our own comfort level. Sacred space is such a different mindset, just like going into church is a very different mindset than walking down the street or sitting at home. You take things more seriously when they're done in that environment. It separates it from the rest of the world as something special that you need to really pay attention to. So we sat down in the presence of God and discussed having a child.

On the other hand, for many the appeal and power of a ceremony is linked to public recognition of their relationship. Whether your mom is itching to be the mother of the bride (or groom), or you want to convince your buddies to stop introducing you to their single friends, a ceremony with guests may be just the thing.

▶ Will It Look Like a Traditional Wedding?

If you want, your ceremony can be a wedding straight out of *Brides* magazine. You'll have no problem finding timelines and instructions on how to word the invitations, what to ask the caterer, and when to hire the photographer. Add blood tests and some paperwork and stir briskly to make it a legal marriage, or skip those last ingredients for a wedding without a marriage.

But you're also allowed to break every one of Martha Stewart's rules, either by modifying the standard wedding template or by inventing a new model entirely. The Resources section at the end of this chapter points you toward more places to find ideas. Just to give you a sense of the range of possibilities, the event you plan could:

- be designed like a party, with food and mingling, with just one official portion where you invite your guests to talk about relationships, share their best relationship wisdom, make wishes for your future, or create a group keepsake to leave with you.
- be a weekend-long retreat—in a beautiful outdoor place or your own house—with the people who are most important to you.
- have the guests seated or standing in a circle, to emphasize the participation of the community, rather than sitting in rows like an audience.
- eliminate the part where the bride's father "gives her away," the vows, the exchange of rings, or any other part of a "traditional" wedding service that doesn't resonate for you.
- have an appropriate role or ritual for each "group" of people present (parents, siblings, other relatives, childhood friends, co-workers, etc.).
- ask guests to take a formal vow to support your relationship, share the good times, and help during the hard times.
- be a truly private affair, with no guests at all.

Some partners are excited to celebrate with the elements of a traditional wedding ceremony, and others delight in the freedom to design their own. Kirsten and Tom have spent years brainstorming creative ideas for how to have a non-traditional ceremony. Kirsten says:

The last few weddings we've been to have been so somber and serious. It makes me think this whole white American approach to weddings is all wrong. It's all wrong! I would want our ceremony to be like a party, with people laughing and really celebrating. I throw pretty good parties, so I think it could be fun.

One of the ideas they joke about is a parody wedding that would play on all their least favorite parts of a traditional wedding. They both laugh as Tom describes their vision to us:

It would be a puppet performance. The grim reaper would serve as the minister, and Kirsten's dad would lead her up the aisle in a noose. I would place a body-sized ring of iron around her, imprisoning her as my act of love.

The possibilities are limitless, whether you walk down the aisle on your father's arm, in a noose (we hope not!), have the partners enter together from a different direction, or start out in the room with everyone else. Admittedly, the freedom can make your head spin, since there's a lot more work involved in planning an event if you can't pull the timeline out of a how-to manual. Wolfsong compares his experience having a traditional wedding to what it was like to plan a more personalized ceremony that did not include a legal marriage.

When I got married the first time I just basically showed up. I drove home for the weekend and put on a suit and showed up at the church on time. My fiancée was there waiting and our families were there, and we went down the aisle, said that ritual formula, signed a marriage document, and we were married. But this time, Myra and I actually had to sit down and create our own ceremony. We had to come up with the words that would define our relationship, the unique relationship between two individuals. It was a challenging process. We had some serious disagreements, and we had to work them through. But in the end we created a ceremony that fit with our spirituality.

Joe says that at times when they were planning their ceremony, they'd wake up in the middle of the night wondering, "Do people think we're crazy?" Priscilla agrees, "With a wedding, at least it's a play that everybody knows. So you may feel like an idiot up there, but you at least have the cover of tradition. But if you're up there and people don't know what you're going to do, you worry that you'll look silly." But Joe says that despite how vulnerable they felt during the planning process:

By the time we had actually done it, so many people came to us afterwards and said, "I understand now why you did it this way," and "I think it's really great that you did it this way," and "I'm really inspired that you did it this way." A lot of people said, "Now I wish that's what we had done," or, "That's what I would like to do." It was so exhilarating to know that it was possible.

Reverend Barbara McKusick Liscord's experience presiding over commitment ceremonies confirms Joe and Priscilla's experience, She says, "When you create a ceremony that is an honest expression of who the participants are—no matter how unique it is—it resonates for everyone there as a meaningful experience. Everyone is uplifted in ways they hadn't expected."

▶ Will You Have an Officiant?

Traditional weddings usually have someone who leads the service, whether it's a minister, a rabbi, a justice of the peace, or some other officiant selected by the

---

A COMMITMENT CEREMONY ABOUT COMMITMENT

THE CENTERPIECE OF Charley and Alison's ceremony was the section where the guests could share. Some people knew in advance that they'd be invited to speak, and others did not. Charley describes it:

We wanted an open and unstructured part of the ceremony where people would speak from their heart or their experience. We framed it as, "Talk about the meaning of commitment, any kind of commitment." And one thing we wanted to avoid was having it feel like being at your own funeral, where everyone talks all glowing and wonderful about you. And we got a little of that, but most people stuck with the idea of talking about commitment. My partner's uncle, who is Catholic, stood up and did this thing spontaneously about commitment—it was beautiful. My sister-in-law, who didn't know this was going to happen and is a reticent sort of person, stood up and said something and had everyone in tears by the end of it, it was so beautiful. We have a couple of friends who are musicians who brought their guitars and played a couple of songs. We had our parents end the open time by reading their things. I think my partner's Mom read the "On Marriage" section from Kahlil Gibran, and my parents had some kind of Celtic blessing that they read.

---

couple. Reverend Jory Agate says, "A minister, rabbi, or other religious professional can talk to you about what you want your ceremony to be and help you craft something that is meaningful. They can offer advice on what tends to work or not work in a ritual, suggest other ideas for creating the mood you want, and help you place your ceremony in a religious context if that is what you choose to do. Even if you do not have the clergyperson officiate, you may want to talk with someone when planning the ceremony." Although it certainly isn't a requirement, having an officiant can give the event a more official tone, which could be particularly valuable with skeptical relatives.

If your goal is to get married "in the eyes of God" or within your spiritual belief system, it *is* possible to find a minister, rabbi, or other clergy who will marry you without requiring a legal marriage. Clergy may be more willing to do this if they know you personally, have a sense of your relationship and situation, and understand your reasons for not wanting to or being able to get legally married. Some clergy of more liberal religions like Unitarian Universalism, Reform and Reconstructionist Judaism, the Religious Society of Friends (Quakers), the United Church of Christ, and paganism or Wicca may be more likely to support you, though clergy of many other faiths have also been known to perform religious weddings without a civil component. Most Unitarian Universalist ministers are respectful of people's own religious beliefs and backgrounds without requiring any "conversion" or agreement to a new set of beliefs.

A growing number of clergy regularly perform wedding ceremonies for GLBT couples, and these clergy can be a great resource for straight couples, too. Chances are they already understand the concept of blessing loving relationships in all their forms, and they certainly have experience with weddings that aren't recognized by the state. The website of the Partners Task Force on Gay and Lesbian Couples (see Resources section at the end of this chapter) includes an excellent section on Ceremonial Marriage, listing some of the religious denominations and specific congregations in each state that perform ceremonies for gay, lesbian, and bisexual couples.

Your officiant doesn't have to be a clergyperson. You can ask a friend or relative to lead your ceremony, since having a person who knows you well officiate can make the event particularly meaningful. And of course, you don't need to have an officiant at all. Gabe says he wouldn't want one:

You're still relying on someone else to tell you your relationship is OK, you're official now. I just feel that the relationship is personal between the couple. It shouldn't have to be sanctified by anyone else.

Maybe your ceremony will follow a model described on pages 189–191, with Quaker-style silent worship and the opportunity for your guests to speak if they are so moved. Or maybe you're excited about the chance to star in your own show, to address your guests and each other, explaining the meaning of each part of the ceremony you lead. If the event you've planned is small, a family commitment at the dining room table or a gathering of a few friends in a favorite café, you might feel no need for an officiant.

▶ What Will You Call It?

You might choose one of the old standards: *wedding*, *marriage*, or *commitment ceremony* (OK, "commitment ceremony" isn't really old, but it's fast becoming standard). Regardless of whether your marriage will be on file at City Hall or not, you can choose whatever term you like for the event. In *The Essential Guide to Lesbian and Gay Weddings*, Tess Ayers and Paul Brown compiled a helpful list of other terms people have used:

- Affirmation Ceremony
- Blessing of Love
- Blessing of the Relationship
- Bonding Ceremony
- Celebration of Commitment
- Ceremony in Celebration of Our Lives Together
- Ceremony of Heart
- Covenant of Love
- Handfasting
- Holy Union
- Joining
- Life Partnership Ceremony
- Lifelong Commitment Vows
- Lifelong Commitment
- Permanent Partnership Ceremony
- Relationship Covenant
- Rite of Blessing
- Tryst
- Union Ceremony[7]

Maybe this list inspires other ideas. The possibilities are limitless!

▶ How Will You Explain It?

Most different-sex couples who invite others to their commitment ceremony run into resistance from a friend or family member somewhere along the way. Charley and Alison said both their sets of parents at first had a hard time with the announcement that two years into their relationship, they were planning a ceremony, but wouldn't be getting legally married. Some parents grieve the confirmation that their child will not have a wedding, choosing instead to celebrate her love with a nonlegal ceremony.

> *Alison's parents went out to dinner with her, and Alison was trying to break the news to them. They're sitting in this small Chinese restaurant right next to this table of four women, one of whom is showing the others this huge engagement ring she had just gotten from her boyfriend. So Alison's trying to explain this totally newfangled idea literally next to the table with tradition incarnate. Alison said she was painfully aware of how distracted her mother was by the other table.*

But despite the challenges of the announcement, Charley says both sets of parents came around.

> *My partner's parents loved it. They thought it was great. I think the most ecstatic person was Alison's mom. She thought it was the greatest thing in the world. Alison's dad was fine with it, too. It was really touching, at the ceremony he got up and said he'd rather see commitment without marriage than marriage without commitment.*

DAKOTA AND CHRIS'S RELATIONSHIP CELEBRATION

DAKOTA DESCRIBES THE ceremony she and her partner Chris had about 14 years ago, before the birth of their first child.

"We had a relationship ceremony that celebrated who we were in our community and our commitment to one another. We had been together for about a year and a half, and I was three months pregnant and 33 years old. I had had a very checkered relationship history, and everyone who knew me knew that. Part of having a relationship ceremony was about saying, 'OK guys, this relationship is real. This is serious. It's time for you to accept the fact that I really was telling the truth when I said, 'This is it.' You've got to welcome this person into our family in the way that you would if we were getting married.' It was a way of getting their attention, making them pay attention to what was happening in my life. Everybody in my family came with the exception of one sister who lived too far away and couldn't travel. People did take it seriously.

"We began the ceremony with a lovely pagan blessing, which I really liked. Our closest friend, who introduced us to one another and is sort of the patron saint of our relationship, is Jewish, so he blew the *shofar* and gave a Jewish blessing. Then we had my sister, who's a born-again Christian, read a passage from Corinthians.

And finally, Chris's close friend offered a Humanist blessing. We really evoked a large sacred circle to hold our relationship and to hold everybody who was there in their own way of being connected to Spirit.

"After the blessings we called everybody to the circle. We started with the people who'd known us the longest. I had my family stand up first, my mother and father, then my brother, then my sisters down the line. Chris did the same with his family, pausing for a special moment to call his mother's sprit to join us. The next most recent people were two of Chris's friends from high school, then friends from college, then from his first work experience. People saw the rings of community. And everybody ended up knowing who everyone was—people were not mystery faces. There were 60 people total, a manageable size.

The heart of the ceremony were the beautiful vows that we said to each other, which we later renewed on our tenth anniversary. There were seven levels of commitment and we moved out through the levels, from personal to global. They began with this is my commitment to you as a person, to this is my commitment to you as a man/woman, to this is my commitment to you as a member of my family, my parenting partner, in a community of friends, in the world community. With each one, we alternated saying the actual commitment and then at the end we said together, 'To this we are committed.' It was powerful and meaningful for both of us.

"I think having the ceremony changed how people related to us, but it didn't change our relationship at all. We don't even remember the date of the ceremony. We celebrate our first night together as our anniversary, because that's when we knew who we were to each other. But I think it made it easier for my parents to deal with the fact that I was pregnant. For a long time my father called Chris my husband. I would keep correcting him, 'Dad we're not married.' He'd say, 'Oh, well, you know, in my mind you are.' He's definitely accepted Chris as part of his family, although he would still be delighted if we actually got married."

Even though those who survive their own ceremonies say the process of getting everyone "on board" has its challenges, they also agree that by the end of the ceremony, even the most skeptical guests are generally impressed. Many had the experience Charley did, where people would say, "You guys are married. Call it what you want, but you're married." And most partners agree that even if that wasn't the take-home message they'd been intending, it's good enough.

There are at least five ways to help baffled parents, cousins, and childhood friends understand what you're planning.

1. Understand it yourself.

Being forced to explain to others your decision to have a ceremony will require you to know exactly why you've made the decision. Joe said at the beginning, he and Priscilla weren't quite prepared for all the questions they'd have to answer. "Be really clear with yourselves, and with other people, why you're having a ceremony," he advises. "Know what you want out of it and why you're doing it a certain way."

2. Be prepared to explain, explain, and explain some more.

Most people who had ceremonies spent many accumulated hours talking with other people about their plans. Some even say they came to enjoy the opportunity to engage the people they loved in substantive conversations about marriage, weddings, and commitment. Joe said that throughout the conversations, he struggled to strike a balance: "You don't want to get too didactic or heavy-handed, and turn the whole thing into some ideological harangue that would crush the beauty of the thing. You don't want to alienate your audience. You want to bring them along, and find ways to make people feel comfortable." He and Priscilla found they needed to take different approaches for different people.

Some married people got a little tense about this choice, thinking that somehow by making this choice we were critiquing them. So we tried to be very gentle about it: "Getting married is your choice, but we don't want to define our relationship through marriage."
—*Priscilla*

And then some of our radical friends would say, "Well, why are you even doing this at all?" It was as if maybe we were pretending we weren't getting married, but we really were, anyway. And our lesbian and gay friends had two different kinds of reactions. One was, "If I were straight, I would get married. I don't know why you don't just go ahead and take that privilege." And others were excited about the idea that we were expanding the realm of possibilities.
—*Joe*

WENDY AND DAN'S RELATIONSHIP PARTY

WENDY AND DAN have each been married before, and between them they had lots of reasons for not wanting to do so again. But they decided to have a party to celebrate their anniversary, as Wendy describes.

"At the 10 year mark, we decided, OK, this has been a pretty good 10 years, so we had a relationship party. Our intention was to honor relationships of all kinds and their longevity, even though the form may change. So we had a nice dinner and about 15 or 20 close friends. We have a group of friends that are pretty close. It started as a support group in 1980 and we still meet every month. We call ourselves the Crazy Group.

"People were invited to bring a poem or a song or a gift or a little rite that would honor relationships, not necessarily us. Some people said nice things about us, and that was great, but they also did other things. One close friend was still grieving the breakup of her marriage, and she lit a candle and brought a picture of their wedding and put a scarf over it, sort of honoring coupledom. That was her way. And other people spoke or told a joke. We had a book, too, with blank pages, that people could write their thoughts or feelings about the evening or us or anything they experienced. We still have the book and what people wrote in it. I think it was affirming.

"The point was that relationships happen—certainly ours has been supported—in the context of community. We've had a really nice, easy relationship, but it would have been very different without this growing community, which we've invested almost as much energy in growing as our one-on-one relationship."

3. *Write something.*

Many partners found it helpful to explain their decision in writing in the invitation itself, in the ceremony's program, on a sign at the entrance to the event, or on a website. Amy G. and Roger B.'s wedding website included details about their plans, directions, photos of their new puppies, and a page that explained why their marriage would not have a civil component. Here's an excerpt of what they said:

Why We Are Not Applying for A License

We aren't applying for a marriage license because parts of the legal construct of marriage conflict with our core beliefs and ethics.

It's not because we're really first cousins.

We are having a ceremony because we want to celebrate our union and exchange vows in front of our family, friends, and our respective deities. We see marriage first as a personal commitment between two people in love, second, as a social construct where families are linked, third, as a religious custom where vows are made along the lines of a tradition, and finally, as a contract wherein rights are granted to the participants if the government's rules are met.

On May 28, we'll build the first three constructs described above in a thoughtful way, but we can't agree on the last one. The fact that there are political rules that prevent competent adults who are in love from getting married and receiving a basketful of special rights doesn't fit with our ethics. Three of the principles that inform our ethics are freedom, justice and integrity. Fortunately, we live in the U.S.A., so these principles aren't generally controversial. Unfortunately, marriage is a problem. Until the government allows same-sex couples to sign a marriage license, the system will be unjust. As long as the government withholds rights until the license is signed, the system limits freedom.

What This Means To You

Many of our friends are getting married right now and we're looking forward to attending or being attendants. We have no hard feelings towards people who choose marriage licenses for whatever reason. We can respect that choice. Each of us has to choose her battles. We chose this one, but there's plenty we haven't. Roger claims to enjoy animals, but he enjoys some best with BBQ sauce. We claim to value the ozone layer, but we get about five miles per gallon in the truck. Amy tends to think that kindergartners should work less than 16-hour days, but she still wears J. Crew clothes. Choosing this path has taken a lot of thought over the years and a good deal of resolve recently.

It's not a whim.

If we didn't care about what you thought, we wouldn't have invited you to the ceremony. We took a risk that we'd be rejected each time we mailed an invitation. So far, almost everyone who has taken the time to read this far has been supportive.

That's the story. Drop us a note or give us a call if you want to talk more.
—Roger and Amy

REGINA AND BARB'S
COMMITMENT CEREMONY

REGINA AND BARB met at a Women's Weekend retreat designed to help women learn to have successful relationships. A year later, they moved in together and, several months later, held a commitment ceremony that looked just like a wedding without the marriage certificate. About 100 guests attended their ceremony, where they vowed to be together for the rest of their lives. Regina describes what happened:

"Making a commitment and having a ceremony, and including our families in the ceremony, was important to both of us. We just felt like it was important to stand up and say it publicly, and ask everyone in the congregation for their support to keep us married.

"One funny thing was, the minister sent us an email message making sure that we knew that just because we were having what looked like a wedding, it didn't mean that we were really married by law. We said, 'Yeah, we know that.'

"We sent out traditional-looking invitations. The ceremony was at a Unitarian church. We had classical musicians, and they played Pachelbel's Canon. Barb's daughter, Lauren, and my niece were bridesmaids, and we also had our best friends as matrons of honor. Barb's brother walked her in and my brother walked me in, because my parents are deceased. We both wore different cream-colored dresses that were very pretty. We both carried bouquets.

"We honored the gift of the Women's Weekend by having our matrons of honor light a special candle and talking about how that was important in our lives. And then we honored Lauren, the child who's a part of our family, by giving her a necklace. And then we honored our two brothers and having men in our life, because of the importance of successful relationships between men and women. And we honored our families.

"Then we recited vows to each other, and I think we gave a brief kiss and a hug, and then we walked back up the aisle and out! It was great!

"We had a reception at a beautiful old estate with a house that's been turned into a function hall. We had caterers, and we had had our pictures taken by a professional photographer. We even had a first dance! We got out there, and it was a little bit scary but it was fun.

"The next day we went off on a honeymoon with Barb's daughter, Lauren, and a friend of hers. At the time, Lauren was 10. So we took them and we went to Disneyworld for about four days, and then sent them home and went off to California together.

"I think the ceremony was important to have. I think it's important to state your commitment in front of the people whom you care about, and make a public declaration of what you stand for. I wanted to make sure everyone knew that I was committed to this relationship, and I wanted to be surrounded by the people who loved me."

4. Give people roles they can feel good about.

Most weddings are planned not just by the couple getting married, but also by their relatives and friends. Tradition says the maid of honor plans the shower, the best man plans the bachelor party, the groom's parents host the rehearsal dinner, and the bride's parents foot the bill for nearly everything else. Even if you don't want to follow that pattern, letting people play a part in the process can give them a sense of ownership and convince them that you're not rejecting them, even if you are rejecting a marriage certificate.

Even though Joe didn't want a bachelor party, he agreed to go out for dinner and drinks with his male friends and relatives. Charley said his parents were excited to host "the equivalent of a rehearsal dinner the night before, so all of the out-of-town family from both sides had dinner together at a little restaurant." Dakota asked her born-again Christian sister to read a Bible passage during her ceremony. And "Alison and her mom had fun picking out potted plants as centerpieces for all the tables" at the reception her parents helped plan. Because Charley and Alison held their ceremony far from their parents and parents' friends, they made an effort to let each set of parents have their own party.

We did our "victory tour." We went to my partner's hometown, where her mom still lives and is actually the mayor of her town, and they had a barbecue and invited their friends over, so they got to come over and meet me and give us presents. It was fun, it was very nice. And my parents did the same thing. They were a good decade or so older than my partner's parents, so their friends were even more elderly. And so we had a luncheon-type thing at a restaurant. And my partner's parents came down for that, which was really neat.

PRISCILLA AND JOE'S COMMITZVAH

PRISCILLA AND JOE held their a commitment ceremony about seven years into their relationship. Joe said that during the planning process, "We were worried about how to make the event as meaningful to guests as it was to us, without making it look really cheesy or hokey."

Joe: We had it outside, at a sculpture garden of a small folk art museum. We decided to have my brother and Priscilla's sister emcee the ceremony. They're close to our ages. When people came they picked up a program, and picked up a bell—we'd gotten about 100 of these little Indian and Turkish bells—and came and sat down.

Priscilla: We had no aisle, and I didn't have a bouquet. We had an Irish fiddler playing, and we came down the back and just walked up toward everybody through this old pergola, which is a kind of vine-covered, rectangular structure. Everyone was sitting in a semicircle around us. My sister and Joe's brother welcomed everybody. We had two friends read poems, and another friend had written a short piece about us that he read. And then my sister and his brother said something that they had written, and also talked about having everybody here, naming the different places that we'd known all of these people and how they intersect with our lives. Because we really wanted to say how important it was that they came for this, and that them witnessing this is really what it's about.

Joe: We exchanged vows, which essentially said what it was about each other that we loved and that we got from each other. We said we want to grow old together. In a wedding, you have a certain kind of climax which is generally the exchange of rings. And we didn't have rings. And yet we wanted to do something, some kind of sharing. So we drank from the kiddush cup.

Priscilla: It's a cup that's used in different types of Jewish ceremonies or celebrations. We liked it because it was a sharing of some sort, but it wasn't really an exchange.

Joe: And then the last thing, we did an old Irish tradition. We'd given everybody little bells, and so at the end, my brother asked everybody to ring their bells on our behalf, and we had bells, too. So we all rang them, which was really fun.

Priscilla: Yeah, people loved the bells.

Joe: We had wanted to find ways to get the guests to endorse our bond. We wanted to ground the ceremony in the authority of our community as opposed to the state, and this helped them give a ringing endorsement. So everybody rang bells as we walked off, and then we met across the street for a reception of eating and drinking and dancing.

Priscilla: And we had a declaration of love and commitment. It was basically taken from a Quaker wedding idea, where there is a certificate or contract that the vows are written on, and then everybody who's present signs. So we asked everyone to sign it in the reception area, at some point during the course of the evening.

Joe: Along with normal wedding pressures, we really had the pressure of whether the event was going to seem legitimate, and work for people, and it did. People really seemed to love it.

5. Realize that in the end, people are likely to be supportive.

Nearly all stories about planning a ceremony follow the same pattern. Most of the invited friends and relatives are supportive, but a few struggle with the idea. There are some dicey moments when the partners wonder if deciding to have a ceremony was a huge mistake (remember, though, that the process of planning a wedding often entails similar family drama—these challenges are not restricted to nonmarriage ceremonies). Most of the naysayers change their tune before the big day arrives, and some even say remarkably touching things during the ceremony or in a toast afterwards. As Priscilla said, "Some people came and, I think, enjoyed themselves, and still felt like, 'I still don't know why they're not just getting married.' But at some point it was like, 'Enough of this already, let's just eat.'"

VINCE AND MARTHA'S WEDDING

VINCE AND MARTHA have been in a relationship for five years and have chosen not to live together. Their wedding became news in an unexpected way. The *New York Times* reporter who had been planning to write about their wedding for the *Times*'s Vows column (a short article that appears each Sunday about a recent wedding) decided to drop the story when she found out the couple was not getting legally married. The *Village Voice* ran an article about the whole episode, and we were able to track down Martha and Vince to interview them. Martha, who is a performance artist, describes how they came to have a wedding:

Martha: I was going to turn 50 and I was casting about for what I would like to do to mark this moment in my life, and hit upon this idea of a wedding, not a marriage, as a performance event. It's a performance that marks where the relationship happens to be right now, without promising that it's going to get anywhere tomorrow. We could walk tomorrow or it could be forever—we have no idea. Forever or not forever, that's not what's at stake here. What's at stake is that we're celebrating this moment now, and we'll worry about the future when the future arrives.

Vince: So many weddings—normal weddings—people are coming before their friends and the state and declaring themselves to be one unit and pledging for that to continue forever. In our society about 50 percent of the time it actually turns out not to be forever. We had no particular interest in making promises that we couldn't keep, because who knows who we will be next week? But I think otherwise our wedding was the same as most other weddings are. We have a relationship which we greatly enjoy. As far as we can see we're going to continue in this relationship for the foreseeable future, so we wanted to celebrate it with our friends. So we invited them all to come celebrate this relationship that we have and enjoy, and wanted to formalize it in some way, let our friends know they shouldn't set us up with somebody else. "Well, they don't look like they're gonna get married—maybe we should set 'em up with somebody else."

Martha: We sent out deceptively traditional-looking wedding invitations, but they had an asterisk on the front that said, "You are cordially invited to attend the wedding, asterisk, of Martha Wilson and Vince Bruns, Brooklyn Friends Meeting House," the date, and then you open the card and there's this statement that says that we have no intention of living together or paying joint income tax. And we don't want you to give us any presents, either. We're just gonna have a party, and you're invited to come. I had to send it back to the printer, because the printer didn't catch that vital little piece of information that we wanted the asterisk on it. He'd never done this before.

Martha: Vince sells fish for a living, so we decided to make fish the theme of the wedding. I asked another performance artist to design my wedding dress. She made me into a fish with this medieval hat with the point cut out so the mouth of the fish was at the top, and then the eyes are plastered on the side, and then the veil has bugs in it, and also the veil had scales on it, and it was quite fun. And then we made a school of fish—all the little kids were wearing little fish hats and blowing bubbles. It was in a Quaker Meeting House and I was raised Quaker. The idea was it was a silent meeting of worship, and we would write our own vows, and then everybody would stand up and say whatever they wanted. And that was the great success of the whole thing, which I can't believe we didn't figure out. It was a joy for the audience because they got to perform their views of our relationship.

Vince: The collection of people who were there was fabulous. Stuff from all different cultures. Some people had humorous things, some people had these very earnest things. It was beautiful.

Martha: We had women dressed as men, and women dressed as fish, and fairies. It was pretty enjoyable.

Vince: Since the ceremony, my parents will let me and Martha sleep in the same bed when we visit, which they won't do for my siblings who aren't married.

Martha: Everybody thinks it's a marriage except for us. Vince's family basically made me feel like I was a new member of the family, and the aunts and uncles have taken me out Irish dancing, and I have gone to the cousin reunion, and had gin and tonic with mean old Uncle Ed.

Vince: As old as I am, they were happy to see me make any kind of formalized relationship. "Okay, he's not gonna get married, but at least he did something like this."

CEREMONY RESOURCES

For better or for worse, wedding books are some of the most helpful resources for people planning relationship ceremonies. Although you won't (yet!) find a shelf in your bookstore on nonmarriage ceremonies, there are three kinds of books that can be useful:

1. *"Alternative wedding" books*, intended for engaged couples who don't want to rely on the standard wedding model, include advice on how to plan a nontraditional ceremony. It can be hard to read wedding books if you're not tying the knot legally—sometimes they seem awfully presumptuous to think that every reader who finds meaning in Ralph Waldo Emerson's musings on love intends to become a bride or groom. But many include great ideas for readings, vows, and rituals, and sample services from real couples with a variety of religious and cultural backgrounds.

2. *Gay and lesbian commitment ceremony books.* If you are heterosexual, it might feel strange to read a collection of lesbian ceremonies and apply them to your own life. But if you mentally make the appropriate corrections to the parts that don't apply to you—as gay and lesbian people do every day—you'll find these books rich sources of ideas.

3. *Collections of wedding vows and readings on love.* Whether you find the perfect vows in one of these books or use them to spark your own ideas, you'll be impressed by the sheer variety of loving vows. You might choose to stick with the "husband and wife" language, insert "partner" or another word you prefer, or select vows that commit to the individual without naming the relationship. Many collections of readings contain a variety of poems, prose, Biblical, and contemporary readings from Western and non-Western cultures. In addition to books written with weddings in mind, you'll also find wonderful readings in collections of love poems.

There are also excellent resources online:

Alternative Brides discussion list
http://groups.yahoo.com/group/alternativebrides/
Although most of the women on this list are planning some kind of nontraditional wedding, the group is very friendly to those who are planning nonwedding ceremonies.

Alternatives to Marriage Project
www.unmarried.org
AtMP's Resources page stays up-to-date with the best books, online lists, and websites, including a whole section on ceremonies and rituals.

Indiebride
www.indiebride.com
A website for the "independent-minded bride," including women who are getting married but "who have not, despite all of the cultural cues, been breathlessly awaiting their wedding day for their whole life."

International Commitment Ceremony Registry
www.unionoflove.com
If you submit your names and the date of your ceremony, it can get listed in their online registry. They also sell official-looking certificates of commitment.

Partners Task Force for Lesbian and Gay Couples
www.buddybuddy.com
Visit the Ceremonial Marriage section for lists of denominations and congregations that have supported ceremonies for GLBT couples.

NINE

UNMARRIED WITH CHILDREN:

Parenting Without a Marriage License

KIDS IN SCHOOLYARDS today still chant, "first comes love, then comes marriage, then comes a baby in the baby carriage." But that orderly progression isn't the case for a growing percentage of families. Baby carriages are increasingly pushed by unmarried parents, who may or may not go on to marry later. One in three babies in the U.S. is born to parents who are not married,[1] and although the phenomenon is often discussed as an increase in births to "single mothers," nearly all the recent increase has been because of unmarried couples having kids. Two-fifths of new so-called "single" mothers are single only in the legal sense—their children are born into two-parent cohabiting families.[2] This isn't only an issue of teenage parenthood, either: more than seven in ten unwed mothers are in their twenties, thirties, or forties.[3] More than half of unmarried different-sex couples with children are "stepfamilies," where the child lives with one biological parent and that parent's unmarried partner.[4] All told, about half of different-sex unmarried couples of childbearing age and 13 percent of same-sex cohabitors have children living with them. About two-fifths of children are expected to live in a cohabiting household at some point.[5]

Unmarried parents have a lot in common with married parents: They change diapers, read bedtime stories, kiss boo-boos, admire art projects, and beam at high school graduation. But they also face unique issues, such as coping with what others think of their marital status and ensuring that their family has the legal protections it needs. This chapter is designed to give unmarried parents and people considering parenthood information about issues like these, and to provide tools to keep their families strong. The first section, Considering Parenthood, is primarily for people who are considering forming a family through pregnancy, adoption, or stepfamilyhood. The second part, Making It Work, is for unmarried partners who are already parenting, as well as for others who are considering what might be on the horizon.

CONSIDERING PARENTHOOD

Maybe your partner has been bringing up The Baby Decision, or perhaps you've always liked the idea of adopting a child. Maybe you already have kids, or your partner does, and you've been thinking about whether you want to take on the joys and challenges of living together as a stepfamily. Regardless of how your family gets started, there's a lot to think about. The pages that follow will help you explore:

- whether forming an unmarried family fits your values
- whether your relationship is ready for children
- how you'll deal with parental, community, and societal approval (or disapproval)
- what children think about growing up in an unmarried family
- what legal protections extend to unmarried families
- talking to children about not being married
- the last name decision

► How Do You Feel about Parenting Together Unmarried?

Most people want to get married before they have children, even if they'd been happily unmarried before. Sharon's perspective is common: She and her partner were comfortable having an unmarried relationship as long as they were child-free, but saw things quite differently when they talked about parenting. "We've decided that when we do eventually have kids we're going to be married, because I think that's important," Sharon told us. "That's the only reason we would get married." Once they're pregnant, preparing to get pregnant, about to start the adoption process, or ready to blend a family with children from previous relationships, many cohabitors decide it's time for wedding bells. About half of pregnant cohabitors marry before their baby is born.[6] Cary and her partner agree that they want to be married before they have a child together, even if matrimony isn't a high priority otherwise:

> *Our decision to get married is largely based on our agreement that we'd rather be married when raising a child. If I didn't want to get pregnant, I'm not sure the marriage issue would be so important right now. I think more than anything, marriage might change the way people in the community view us. I'm hoping it doesn't change our relationship.*

Even if they haven't tied the knot by the time their bundle of joy arrives, half of unmarried couples get married within five years after having a baby.[7]

But the percentage of expectant unmarried couples who get hitched in a hurry is lower than it used to be. "Shotgun weddings," named for the literal or figurative shotgun pointed at an unmarried couple by the pregnant woman's father, are less common than they once were. The percentage of first babies *conceived* by unmarried women under age 30 has increased only a few percentage points since the 1930s. What has changed dramatically is the percentage of these couples who still haven't married by the time their baby is born, which fell from 54 percent to 23 percent over a 60-year period.[8]

While many want to marry when they're ready to become parents, not everyone can or does. For some who feel strongly about not marrying, the possibility of children doesn't change their opinions. Like Cary, above, Becky knew that having a baby was a high priority for her. Unlike Cary, though, being married in order to parent was less of a concern to Becky. She and her partner Mike together raised their son, now in his twenties, but never married.

> *I had thought I would want to be married to have a child, but then I had a good friend who didn't get married to have her child, and nothing terrible happened. That kind of opened my eyes. If Mike had said, "I don't want to have a child with you unless we marry," I probably would've married him. But I would have been less happy having been forced to marry. I think my being happier and comfortable with the way the relationship was must have had a positive effect on our child.*

PLAN FOR—OR AGAINST— PARENTHOOD

WITH A LIVE-IN lover, unmarried partners have plenty of access to sex. With countless nights of romantic romping, it's easy to become, shall we say, less careful about birth control than you used to be. If diaper pails and Lego's aren't your idea of home decorating—and you're a male-female couple who aren't absolutely confident your fertility chances are nil—promise each other you'll continue to be as diligent the hundredth night as you were on the first. Doubling up on birth control methods will help reduce the chance that some overeager little sperm will reach his destination. If not being a parent appeals to you for the long term, check out some of the Resources for Childfree Living on page 55.

And Michaela says that even though having a child made her pause to reconsider, staying unmarried still felt like the best decision for her.

> I'm slightly more inclined to think about marriage than I would have been previously, because having a child is such an incredible commitment to one another and to the child. I have thought, "Hmmm, I've made this huge commitment to share parenting with this person. What's the big deal about marriage?" And then I think, "No." All the reasons come back to me about why I was originally inclined not to be married.

For Paula and her partner, Suzanne, there's no marriage question to consider. As a lesbian couple, they are considered "single parents" even though they are raising their children together, as a two-parent family. Paula jokes:

> When Suzanne gave birth to our first child, Adam, I commented to her that she was now officially an unwed mother. When two and a half years later she gave birth to our second child, Julia, it occurred to me that she's now a statistic.

▶ Assess Your Relationship Readiness

Stability is one of the most critical things parents can guarantee their children. Anyone who's spent some time with kids knows they like things to stay the same. Children will beg to have the same book read to them 15 times a day, are delighted to watch the same video over and over, want to eat the same thing for lunch for months on end, and find comfort in a bedtime ritual that is identical night after night after night.

That's not to say that children can't also survive, and even thrive, in families where there's a divorce, separation, or a lot of moves and changes. But on average kids do best when their lives aren't filled with upheavals and losses—no surprise there.[9] If you're thinking about raising a child with an unmarried partner, a key consideration should be whether you can truly commit to sticking together for such a long-term project. As Sara McLanahan, one of the leading experts on unmarried parents, has written, "What matters for children is not whether their parents are married when they are born, but whether their parents live together while the children are growing up."[10]

If you're not married because you're uncertain about the future of your relationship and whether or not you'll be together a lifetime, that's a clear sign that this is not a good time to choose to have a child. Whether your intimate relationship lasts or not, having a child usually ties you to your child's other parent for a lifetime. Too many children who start life in a cohabiting family go on to see the end of their parents' relationship, and you need to do everything you can to make sure your child isn't one of them. If you plan to parent with a partner, being married isn't a requirement for doing it well. But having a strong, stable relationship, and confidence that you'll be able to stay together at least a couple of decades, should be.

Some people believe that having a child together can create commitment between the parents. It doesn't usually work that way. Parenting is a stressful project that can strain even the most committed relationship. But research suggests that the couples who are the most stressed and the most likely to separate are those who were having problems in their relationship *before* the baby arrived. Couples who weren't in agreement about whether they wanted to become parents in the first place are particularly high risk.[11]

Heartfelt introspection might lead you to conclude this isn't the right time to embark on parenthood or make your partner into a stepparent. But if you're already living with your child's other parent, use your commitment to being a great parent to motivate you to be just as committed to keeping your relationship working, if you can. Annie found that inspiration a couple of years after her son was born:

Two and a half years after Adrian was born my father died. It changed the face of the landscape of family for me. I think that since then I've been much more sober as far as feeling like there's only one biological dad. John's it for Adrian. I want to stick around. I want to be here to see that relationship. I want to be here to insert my influence over that relationship. I want to be in this conversation because I care about what happens to my child. I want him to have as much loving community as possible, but at the core I get that it's me and John who care the most about him, who have put in the most time, who are there every day after school. John and I took on this working relationship and I realize we really are partners in this. I feel like it's the most meaningful part of my life.

It was a similar commitment to stability for her children that led Ashton to decide *not* to create a blended family with her partner, Bob. Living separately for the first six years of their relationship made it easier for each of them to focus on their children, and eventually to merge their households when Bob's kids had left home.

The main reason we didn't move in together was that Bob's kids lived with him full-time and mine with me four days a week. I very consciously wanted to be able to devote all my energies to my kids when they were with me. I didn't want to choose between Bob and them, and I didn't want to spread myself thinner. Also, Bob and I have very different parenting styles and disciplinary priorities, and I just wasn't prepared to compromise on mine. He wanted to do the blended family thing early on and I said no. I'm sure many blended family parents will agree that the worst disagreements they have are over their kids, each bristling fiercely at criticism of their own spawn, and we are no exceptions. Since we could afford to live separately, I didn't want to have that many more things to negotiate and argue about. The kids are extremely close now, and I'm glad we didn't rush things.

And Skip knew she didn't want to commit to parenting, a great reason not to form a stepfamily.

When we started seeing each other, he had two small children. One was eighteen months old and the other was five. And I never did want to have children. I chose to have a career instead of children. I did not really want to be a mother to someone else's children. Alan had joint custody of the two kids with his ex-wife, so we shaped our relationship to be together on nights that he did not have the children. We basically figured once the kids were grown and gone, we would take a look at getting married. Now that they're grown, I have a lot more fun relating to them. I just don't have any interest in little kids.

If you *are* considering forming an unmarried stepfamily, it's important to consider carefully what impact that will have on your children. Once your kids learn to giggle at your partner's games, bond with his dog, and trust his authority, you don't want them to suffer a confusing loss if he later moves out. The stakes are higher when there are children involved, so you'll want to be extra sure that the stepparent your kids gain will be for keeps. The more you can define the new roles and predict what might be hardest for your child, the better prepared you'll be to help her through the transition.

You don't need to be married in order to create a nurturing, stable family. For many people, though, marriage can serve as an extra layer of "glue" to help hold their family together during hard times. If getting married is an option for you, your task is to make the most honest, well-informed prediction you can about whether marriage is likely to strengthen and stabilize your relationship, increasing the chances that your child will grow up living with the same parents he starts out with. If you're proceeding without marriage, you'll want to be sure your family has other kinds of strong "glue" for the long run.

▶ Consider Parental, Community, and Societal Approval

Even if you believe that being unmarried with children is the best decision for you, your family and friends may not share your enthusiasm. Depending on your circumstances, you might need to be prepared for questions, frowns, and outright hostility, especially at the beginning. That was Emily's experience nearly everywhere she went. She and her partner got married a year and half after their son was born, but before that:

> *I got everything from looks of pity in the supermarket when old ladies noticed my pregnant belly and naked ring finger, to people asking if my partner was really my son's father, because if he was, they'd ask, why we weren't married yet?*

Although grandparents-to-be don't wave shotguns anymore, in some families the intensity of the hostility to unmarried parenting leads couples to feel forced into marrying. Megan and Glen, both in their late thirties, had a 20-year unmarried relationship that was working well for them, and good relationships with their own families. But when they announced they were expecting a child, they were stunned by the vehemence of Glen's parents' opposition.

> *When we told Glen's parents we were pregnant, they weren't as happy as we expected them to be. They said they did not approve of our lifestyle, that the baby would be illegitimate. His parents called my parents—it was like we were 16 years old. They raised questions about whether Glen was really the father, and they sent us nasty e-mails and a letter. They said they thought the baby would be a bastard, that it would be despised by society. And they said they weren't going to have any contact with us or the baby if we didn't get married.*
>
> *I was scared. You are vulnerable when you're pregnant—you want to do everything you can to make sure everything goes safely and smoothly. For a couple of weeks, I felt really threatened—I thought about how this is what it's like if you're gay and your parents don't like your lifestyle. We panicked. So we went to a justice of the peace and got married. It took us 10 minutes, and cost $30. I didn't want to hurt people. I didn't want to hurt Glen's parents.*

In some cultures, including medieval Wales, the Andamon Islanders of India, and the Tiv of Nigeria, it's having a child, not having a wedding or legal document, that makes you married.[13] In places like this, most of the unmarried partners in this chapter would be considered married and fully "legitimate." In Puerto Rico, once an unmarried couple has a child they're more likely to refer to their relationship as an "informal marriage" rather than a cohabitation.[14]

Communities vary tremendously in how they perceive unmarried families. A family that's the subject of gossip in one neighborhood might not turn a single head somewhere else. In New York City, for instance, Martha says her son fits in perfectly.

When I was growing up, he would have been an illegitimate child. I used to think, "Gosh, that would be the worst thing you could do, have an illegitimate child. It'd be so awful for the child." But nowadays, the cultural mores of our society have changed. There is nothing illegitimate about him. There are loads of kids who have different kinds of families—they have two gay male parents and two gay female parents, or one black parent and one Jewish parent. He's certainly not an anomaly. In his school, there's nothing that makes him feel that he's an outsider or weird. This is the great joy of living in New York: it's a completely heterogeneous place to live and raise your kid.

Lyn has a similar comment about how her Massachusetts community differs from her family's worries. When she and her partner announced their first pregnancy, and their plans not to marry, their relatives were concerned:

I think our families don't understand that we don't live in the world that they lived in, both in time and also in community. We live in an urban center where families come in all different shapes and sizes. Nobody even questions that we're a family.

On the other hand, Sherry says that when she, her partner, and their teenagers first moved in together in West Virginia, they got a lot of questions.

The biggest obstacle we face is where we live. It's very rural and the mindset of the majority of the population is pretty narrow. When I say rural, I mean rural. We don't have street names. We give directions like, "Turn right at the big oak tree." Originally our family was a big deal. It's better now; I guess people accept things as time goes on.

Sherry's experience of things getting easier as time passes is fairly typical. Most unmarried parents agree that once the baby comes, previously worried grandparents usually melt and stop worrying about their children's marital status. Jodi and her partner are planning to get married soon, but they've already have a one-year-old daughter, Bailey. Even though Jodi says some of their relatives wish they had switched the order of these events, she says, "Bailey's here now—they're not going to send her back. They're all completely in love with her."

Different-sex unmarried couples who have children usually find that people they meet assume they're married. Many are pleasantly surprised to find that because of this assumption, their marital status is rarely, if ever, an issue when interacting with schools, teachers, and other officials. Anne says that the most difficulty she and her partner, Christopher, have encountered was when they got a passport for their son—it took a few extra minutes because the administrators were confused that his last name was different from both of theirs. In general, she says, parenting as an unmarried couple has been easier than she expected: "I mean, despite us having three last names, no one's ever asked us if we're married or not. Basically, my general sense is nobody asks, nobody cares." Charley agrees, and says that even though he and his partner never lie or pretend to be married, other parents are always surprised if they find out.

I don't really correct them unless it's the topic of discussion, like we're talking about weddings or something. I refer to Alison as my partner, so that gives people a clue that something's a little different here. I remember one time a friend I do a lot of parent things with said, "Oh my God, I didn't know you guys weren't married!" Other people seem to be thinking, "Hmmm, they seem awfully normal. . . . "

STICKS AND STONES AREN'T THE ONLY THINGS THAT HURT KIDS

CONTRARY TO THE nursery rhyme's claim about sticks and stones, names *do* hurt. Words like "illegitimate" and "bastard" have mostly been wiped out of contemporary vocabularies, thank goodness, but they haven't been completely eliminated. From time to time you can still catch a glimpse of them being used casually in political writing and conversation, like schoolyard bullies hurling hateful iceballs, pretending they're just playing in the snow. The conservative Heritage Foundation regularly discusses the problem of "illegitimacy" in its political analyses,[15] as do television and newspaper commentators each year when the latest statistics about unmarried births are released.[16] Fifteen states still have "illegitimate" or "bastard" in the language of their legal statutes.[17]

But at the same time, one in three babies is born to unmarried parents, and the most prestigious guides to the British aristocracy changed their policies to include the children of unmarried earls, barons, and lords.[18] Decades ago the United States stripped "illegitimate" and "bastard" of most of their legal meaning because people agreed that children should not be punished because of their parents' marital status. We understand these words' historical context. But as far as we're concerned, they are slurs that need to be banished to the archive of offensiveness, much like other words that insult people based on their race or ethnicity. If we believe that every individual child has value as a human being, it's time for those who claim to care about children to stop labeling them with outdated terms that say they're not genuine, not legal, and not acceptable.

▶ Will Your Kids Fit In?

It's entirely reasonable for parents to be concerned about whether their children will have problems socially because their parents aren't married. Many parents decide to marry for this reason, knowing that fitting in is important to kids. Abby says that for her and her partner, this was the number one reason to get a marriage license after so many years:

> We didn't want to subject our child to situations that he was put in because of our beliefs, not because of his—we didn't think that was fair. So we got married one month before he was born. I think if we hadn't had our son, we never would have gotten married. We had lived our lives together for 14 years without it.

Mark and Cary are also concerned about what their future child might wonder if they don't get married. Mark says:

> You follow a social norm so that your kids don't think, "Everyone else's parents are married, why aren't mine? Don't they love each other?" Kids are very literal, and they tend to jump to conclusions like that.

Other unmarrieds aren't as worried about what their children or their children's friends will think. Many in original parent families told us that if they live with a mommy and a daddy, children don't seem to notice whether their own or each other's parents are wearing wedding rings. Some, like Jodi, say that families come in so many shapes and sizes these days, parents who aren't married are hardly noteworthy.

> I think nowadays that things are so diverse that every kid has a different situation. There are all kinds of different families so that it's not so uncommon anymore. I can't believe that we would be the weirdest parents under the sky. Believe it or not, there's this guy at Julian's school who picks his child up every day with a casket in the back of his hearse. I don't think I can top that one.

And Arthur, who grew up with unmarried parents, says the only time the subject came up with his friends was when one of his schoolmates would assume his mother had his last name.

> Every so often, one of my friends would come over and say, "Can I have another glass of milk, Mrs. Prokosch?" She'd usually just kind of go along, and wouldn't really mind. Sometimes if it was a close friend that I saw a lot, she'd step in and say, "Well actually, Arthur's father and I aren't married," and give a brief

description why. And that didn't seem to be a problem. My mom was really sensible about it, it seems to me, and didn't make an issue out of it all the time.

Parents don't deny that kids sometimes get teased. But nearly all say that as far as they know, their not being married has not been the cause of the teasing. Tori said her son has a harder time because she doesn't let him play with toy guns. Arthur said growing up wasn't always easy because he was a smart kid who wasn't good at fitting in with his peers. "But," he continues, "I don't think it ever became an issue with other kids that my parents weren't married." Dakota sums it up well from the parents' perspective:

If you're choosing not to get married, then there's a very high likelihood that there are other choices that you are going to make that are going to put your kids at variance with their culture. Your kids are much more likely to get teased about those variances than they are about the marital status of their parents. For instance, we don't watch television. All our kids' friends do. Our kids are not supposed to be eating candy. All their friends do. My son gets more grief about the shoes he wears, because he wears Payless sneakers and not Adidas. He gets serious grief about that, and about the pants that he wears, that brings him to tears at night when he talks about it. These things actually impact our kids' lives a lot more than the fact that their parents aren't married. These are the things that parents have to help their kids learn to deal with. It isn't your marital status. It just doesn't come up very often. It's not what kids care about.

▶ What Will Your Children Think?

Because their situations are different, below we'll discuss children's experiences in "original families" and "stepfamilies." Of course, not every family fits neatly into these categories—for instance, some children of divorced parents split their time between two kinds of households, and some kids are adopted as older children.

Children in Unmarried Original Families[19]

Original families are those where children live with their original parents, the people who raised them from the beginning. Arthur grew up in one: Until he left for college, he lived with his two biological parents who never married. His comment is typical of the adult children of long-term unmarried couples: "It never seemed to me to be that big of a deal that my parents weren't married. I was just a kid. My parents were there. And so I never really thought about it that much." Most children in families like this agree that having parents in their lives was much more significant than whether they were wearing wedding bands. Arthur's mom, Becky, describes it this way:

We have a very traditional nuclear family—we joke that Arthur has had an abnormally stable upbringing. He's lived on the same street, lived in the same house, and slept in the same bedroom for 15 years. He's always had the same two parents who are actually his biological parents. How atypical and abnormal can you get in this country?

While Arthur's experience isn't exactly atypical—more than three in five children in the U.S. live with their two biological or adoptive parents[20]—Becky is right to point out that this consistency is part of what made growing up with unmarried parents not "that big of a deal" for him. The same is true for children in original parent gay and lesbian families.[21]

Dakota and her partner think their three kids, ages 8, 11, and 13, might benefit from the fact that they aren't married. They hope that their very conscious decision not to marry will help their children be independent thinkers.

I feel like we have the best of both worlds. We're a very intact, stable family, just like the best of married families. At the same time, we get to model for our kids that you can make choices that aren't what everyone else is doing. It can be not only OK but good. They're learning that it's important to stand up for what you believe in even if it makes you a minority.

Carmen's partner, Alex, is not her daughter's biological father, but since he's been part of her life since the day Jasmine was born, their family functions as an original family. Carmen and Alex had separated for a year, and Carmen dated someone else. But the baby's biological father wasn't interested in being involved, and Alex was. Six years later, he still is. Carmen says:

Alex was there since I was two months pregnant, all the way until my daughter was born. He said, "I love you and she comes with you. I love both of you." He bought her her crib, he bought her everything. He said, "That's my daughter." He wants to give her his last name. He is the one who is actually raising her, who has been there through thick and thin. When that girl has been sick—she's been hospitalized three times—he is the one who is always there. When she cries, he cries. When she is sick with any little thing, he just goes crazy. That's her daddy.

Children in Unmarried Stepfamilies

About three in five children in unmarried couple families are living in "stepfamilies," with one biological parent and that parent's partner, who joins the family sometime later.[22] Most of these families are heterosexual, though gay and lesbian people form stepfamilies, too, after a parent comes out and forms a same-sex relationship.

YOU DRIVE ME TO SOCCER PRACTICE, BUT WHAT SHOULD I CALL YOU?

ADULTS AREN'T THE only ones who stumble for words to introduce unmarried partners. Children, too, trip on the linguistic snags. In unmarried step-families, a conversation about what to call each other can smooth the road. Hillary, whose mom's unmarried partner lived in her family for most of her life, said that she saw him as one of her parents, and that their marital status didn't really matter to her. Knowing what to call him, though, was the hardest part:

> I guess when it came down to terminology it was kind of difficult to explain to other people what was going on. I think that's the main problem, that "mother's boyfriend" or "dad's girlfriend" doesn't really encompass the fact that they're there for a really long time and they're a big part of your life.

When it becomes clear that a parent's partner is more than "dad's girlfriend," families can have a conversation about what they want to call each other. Adults can tell kids that they are a family, just as some of their friends from school may come from families of different shapes and sizes. This allows the adult partner to tell the child how much he cares about him, and establish that he does not intend to replace other parents or stepparents. Children should be given some appropriate options based on their age, the stepparent-child relationship, and whether they have a relationship with their other biological parent. Most children call their stepparents by their first names. Kids whose biological parents are not part of their lives may want to call the partner a variation like "Papa" or "Daddy Ed, or even "Mom" or "Dad." Some might even be relieved finally to receive permission. Whatever you agree on, make sure the new name doesn't threaten the child's relationship with her biological parents.

Adults and kids can also jointly decide what to tell outsiders. Children should be allowed to decide if they want to describe the relationship to others as step-mom/stepson, dad/daughter, "my mom's girlfriend/partner/friend," or something else they come up with. Keep in mind—and point out to children—that there is no rule preventing unmarried families from using the language of marriage (stepmother, brother-in-law, etc.), and no apology or explanation is required. Often, it's the easi-est for outsiders to understand. Whatever words you use, it's important to respect children's wishes, since the way we refer to each other is highly personal. Just like adults, kids need to be able to choose language that works for them—as well as to change their minds in a given situation or as years go by.

Hillary ultimately concluded that "stepdad" summed up the relationship best:

> Sometimes I refer to him as my stepdad, because it's easier than trying to explain that he lives with us and has been around for 18 years but he's not

married to my mom. He did raise me, so he's sort of my stepdad. He is a father figure to me.

On the other hand, Skip did not play a major role in raising her partner's daughter, so she doesn't consider herself a stepmother. But she and her partner's daughter have a different kind of family relationship, with Skip's role perhaps more similar to an aunt or godmother. They've found lighthearted words to describe it:

If we meet people, I will refer to her as my "sorter daughter" [it rhymes] and she refers to me as her "other mother." But I think we have a more nontraditional relationship than a stepmother-stepdaughter thing. I think for her, I'm an older woman that she admires and considers a role model, and I'm very proud to fulfill that role for her.

Ultimately, what you call each other isn't as important as the relationship you have. But whether that relationship is as unique as Skip and her "sorter daughter" or as traditional as any parent-child pair, being able to explain it in words you both feel good about is part of making it work.

Tracey grew up in an unmarried stepfamily—her mom still lives with the man she considers her stepdad.

Being raised by an unmarried couple, it was like they were married, because they were together. They share household duties, they take turns cooking. There's a lot of humor in their relationship. My little nephews and nieces call him Poppa and Grandpa. He is their Poppa and Grandpa, even though technically he is not, because they're not married.

Victoria says that for her and her partner, Paul, the process of becoming a stepfamily has been a gradual one. Even though she and Paul aren't married, from her son's perspective, she says, Paul is definitely a stepfather.

As Paul and I became friends, my son got used to having him around. Since we went to the same church, we saw him frequently and casually. Then we shared a garden plot at the town farm and started sharing meals in one kitchen or the other. The first time Paul stayed overnight on a night my son was home was when Paul was ill and I wouldn't let him go home. It started to become clear we were a family-in-progress. We tried to let my son know at every step that he was an important and loved member of this family we were trying to create. It's very clear to all that my son has one mother, one father, one stepmother, and one stepfather. The poor kid had all of us, plus his grandmother, at his middle school graduation!

Some teenagers in unmarried step-families face challenges, possibly because the teen years are a particularly hard time for major changes.[23] When a new partner joins the household, having a new adult in the house isn't the only change: Often families move, kids start new schools, sometimes stepsiblings join the family. Unlike in married stepfamilies, teens may not know how to understand their relationship to Mom's new partner. Knowing this, parents of older children need to take the process of adding their partner to the family especially slowly and carefully. Minimizing moves and changes where possible can help, as can having explicit conversations about the roles and relationships of both the adults and the children in the household.

STEPFAMILY SUPPORT

THINKING ABOUT HOW to keep your unmarried stepfamily strong? The Stepfamily Association of America maintains an online forum, support groups, a magazine, and a comprehensive list of links to other groups and websites (including ones specifically for stepmothers, stepfathers, or children).

Stepfamily Association of America
650 J Street, Suite 205
Lincoln, NE 68508
800-735-0329
www.saafamilies.org

THE DEBATE ABOUT CHILDREN'S WELL-BEING

ALL PARENTS, MARRIED or unmarried, want their children to be happy, healthy, and to have the best shot at succeeding in the world. Given that common aspiration, it can be difficult for unmarried parents to know what to make of statistical claims that children fare better in married families. Here are some things to keep in mind when you hear about those kinds of claims:

1. *Most of the research doesn't look at all kinds of families, and it might not have considered yours.* Most research on how family structure affects children compares married couples to divorced couples, or two-parent families to single-parent families. It is extremely rare for a study even to include a sample of same-sex couples, different-sex unmarried couples, or any other kind of family for comparison. The differences this research finds among family structures tend to be small—as two researchers concluded, "The differences in children's and adolescents' adjustment *within* family types are greater than the differences *between* family types."[24] No study has ever specifically

focused on families where the parents are in committed, long-term un-married relationships.

2. *Most children in unmarried families do fine.* Overall, 70 to 90 percent of children in cohabiting families are not having problems, whether you're measuring by their report cards, their willingness to help clear the table, their friendships at school, or the number of fights they get in on the playground. Scanning the cheering section at the local Little League game, there's no sure way to tell which of the parents are married and which are cohabitors. But those researchers who *do* know which are which say that biological kids in cohabiting families are doing just as well, or nearly so, as kids in married families, and that only a minority of children in cohabiting stepfamilies are having a harder time than children in married stepfamilies.[25] As we've discussed before, talking about averages and relative risks misses the basic fact that most children do well regardless of family structure.

3. *Money matters.* There are mountains of evidence that family income is one of the most accurate ways to predict which children are going to have problems. The kids in these families show the effects of poverty—inferior schools, unsafe neighborhoods, second-rate health care, and stressed parents—serious problems, all of them, that deserve serious solutions. Yet many studies of family structure don't take socioeconomic factors into account. Almost three-quarters of different-sex cohabitors with biological children have a household income of less than $28,000 for a family of three (two times the poverty line).[26] Any conclusion about "average" children of cohabitors that doesn't take economics into account is really primarily a conclusion about poor children.

4. *All things are never equal.* Those who believe unmarried people shouldn't raise children often say something like, "All things being equal, kids do best in married families." But all things are never equal, and statements like that dramatically oversimplify the complicated world we live in. The truth is, children of well-off single moms tend to do better on standard measures of child well-being than children of poor married parents.[27] Children with divorced parents tend to do better than those in families where parents are constantly fighting.[28] Marriage is neither a one-size-fits-all solution, nor even an option for everyone. A more accurate conclusion would be that marriage is better for some families, and not a good fit for some, and not possible for others.

5. *Unmarried families that already exist need support.* Commentators who warn of the impact on children should be asked more often, "How does what you're saying help the children who are in unmarried families *right now*?" Condemning unmarried couples with children won't make them go away. And if following the "get married" advice isn't the right choice for a given couple, it doesn't provide them with anything constructive they can do to help their children succeed. Larry Bumpass, one of the most respected experts on cohab-

itation, says, "If we're concerned with the well-being of families with children, we may have to rethink our policies in ways that will allow us to provide adequate benefits for families that don't meet the formal marriage definitions that have prevailed in the past."[29]

The bottom line about what helps children thrive is what most people know from their own experience. Kids do best:

◆ if they have access to the financial resources to meet their basic needs (healthy food, health care, heat in the winter, etc.)
◆ if the adults who care for them are nurturing, attentive, predictable, and actively involved in their lives
◆ if the adults who care for them get along with each other most of the time
◆ if they have stable relationships with their caretakers.[30]

The challenge for parents everywhere is to figure out the best way to provide the above things, whether they're married or not.

MAKING IT WORK

So kids are already part of your unmarried life—yep, there they go, chasing the dog again. This second part of this chapter considers the issues that are particularly common or important for unmarried parents (no, convincing the children to leave the dog alone is not one of them).

▶ Legal Protections for Unmarrieds with Kids[31]

Unmarried parents' fears about legal protections for their children often dwarf any real legal threats. For the most part, biological and adoptive parent-child relationships are clearly defined in the law and well-protected—more clearly protected, in fact, than the legal relationship between unmarried partners. If you haven't already done so, having children should motivate you to create all the important documents we talked about in chapter 6. Despite the fact that children in unmarried families are not as legally vulnerable as many worry (especially if paternity has been established and/or there's a second parent or stepparent adoption in place), it's still too risky *not* to have the right paperwork prepared if a child is depending on it. Lyn and Billy heard all about this, as Lyn remembers:

Billy's family put on a pretty serious campaign when we were pregnant with Jordan. Billy's brother was calling us on the phone pretty regularly about the marriage thing. Billy's brother and his father are both lawyers. So I think we appeased them by going to a lawyer and writing up a will, giving each other power of attorney and health proxy and guardianship and all that. They were very worried.

Although these basic facts are standard, every state has its own approach to family law, making the U.S. a dizzying patchwork of frequently changing laws and precedents. Although it's impossible to provide state-by-state advice here, there are some general principles that apply to most unmarried families. To learn more, see the Resources section in chapter 6, or find a lawyer who specializes in family law. As we've said before, lawyers who specialize in working with gay and lesbian couples are often the best prepared to help unmarried heterosexual couples and multiple-partner families, because they have experience protecting families outside marriage.

For Two Biological Parents

The concept of "illegitimate" children is mostly meaningless as a legal category. A series of Supreme Court decisions in the late 1960s and 1970s made it illegal to treat children differently because their parents weren't married, and gave more equal status to fatherhood and motherhood regardless of marital status.[32] In one, the court wrote, "Obviously, no child is responsible for his birth and penalizing the illegitimate child is an ineffectual—as well as unjust—way of deterring the parent."[33] Because of these decisions, for the most part today the legal parent-child relationship is the same for every biological parent, married or unmarried. In order to be absolutely sure, there are three important legal steps to take if you're an unmarried different-sex couple parenting biological children.

1. *Put both parents' names on the birth certificate.* While that doesn't automatically establish paternity, it's a key first step to protecting the dad's legal rights. It's easy to do this at the time the baby is born; with rare exceptions, no one will ask whether you're married. If you missed your chance and want to add a parent's name to a birth certificate later, ask your state's Department of Health or Bureau of Vital Statistics how to make such a change. The National Center for Health Statistics (www.cdc.gov/nchs) provides contact information for the appropriate office in each state. You shouldn't lie about who the biological father is, even if you never saw him again and a much better guy will be co-parenting with you—this can cause all kinds of serious problems later.

2. *Establish paternity or parenthood.* As soon as he can, the baby's dad should sign a simple statement, or affidavit, that officially says he's the baby's father. If the baby is born in a hospital, the hospital will usually give the dad the appropriate form. This document protects the father-

child legal relationship; helps ensure the child will be eligible to inherit and receive life insurance, Social Security, and survivor's and other benefits from her dad; and protects the father's rights in case of a custody dispute later. Paternity can also be established by living with a child, welcoming her as your own, and showing parental responsibility.

If you haven't already signed a paternity statement, you can create your own easily. This can be either an acknowledgement of paternity (for dads only) or, even better, an acknowledgement of parenthood (for both parents). The statement should include:

- the name of the parents and the child, the child's birthdate, and the place of birth
- acknowledgment that the parents are the biological parents of the child
- a statement that the parents intend the child to be legitimate for all purposes, including the right to inherit from them
- acknowledgment of the duty to raise and support the child
- both signatures, dates, and notarization (notarization is recommended but not required).

Each parent should keep a copy of the notarized statement. In some states you can also file a copy of the statement with the same state agency that handles birth certificates (see above). If you have that option, it's a good idea to do so. As with birth certificates, lying about who is a biological parent is never a good move.

3. *Make a will.* If you've followed steps one and two, and if the father has acted like the dad by doing the things that dads do on an ongoing basis, the child should be able to inherit from his father without any problems. Some states don't protect the inheritance rights of the kids of unmarried fathers as strongly as they should, though. If you want to be absolutely sure your family heirlooms will make their way into your child's hands, name him in your will or other estate planning device.

It's also wise to write and sign a parenting agreement, where you formally state that you want to and plan to parent together, and that even if your relationship ends you both plan to continue co-parenting. While you're feeling loving and fair, you might even specify that if the relationship ends you intend to allow each other generous access to the children in terms of visitation, school access, and other situations. When a married couple's relationship ends, divorce courts make decisions about child custody based

The United Kingdom, France, Denmark, Finland, Norway, and Sweden all have a higher rate of births to unmarried parents than the U.S. does.[34]

TAX TIME

TAX FORMS ARE one place where the rules are different for families who aren't married. Since unmarried couples have to file separate tax returns, only one partner can claim your child as a dependent for tax purposes. The best strategy is to have the one who's in the higher tax bracket claim the child, since she'll benefit more from the savings. After you fill out your tax forms, you can split the savings on your own.[36]

on a set of assumptions about fairness and the children's best interest (though many question whether the system really works well for children or families). Family courts handle custody and visitation cases for both married and unmarried couples, but courts don't automatically make the same legal presumptions if a relationship without a marriage license ends. Putting your intentions in writing can provide added peace of mind for both parents. While there is no guarantee these agreements will be upheld by a court, the guidelines they provide can be enormously valuable.

If One Partner Is Not a Biological Parent

More than half of different-sex unmarried couples with children are stepfamilies,[35] and all same-sex couples with kids include at least one partner who is not genetically related to the child. In these families, the partner who's not related to the child has no legal connection to her. Even if the partner has packed a thousand school lunches and answered, "Are we there yet?" a million times, he doesn't have the right to authorize treatment in a hospital or visit the child if his relationship with the biological parent ends. In some situations, that's perfectly appropriate—there may be no reason why your partner should have additional rights. But other times, the lack of legal recognition for stepparents and their stepchildren can cause problems. If that's a concern for you, there are a few ways unmarried stepparents can gain some legal ties to the kids they help parent.

Stepparent adoptions are the most common kind of adoption done by family courts, and some states will allow an unmarried "stepparent" to adopt a child she's parenting. For the most part, though, courts will only allow a child to have two legal parents. So adoption is only an option if the child's other biological parent consents to give up his rights or has no parental rights—if he or she has died, or was a sperm or egg donor who signed away his or her rights, for instance. If the other parent is not involved in your child's life and doesn't pay child support, you can ask the court to terminate his or her parental rights, so that your partner, who truly performs a parenting role, can adopt. Once an adoption is final, an adoptive parent gains all the legal rights and responsibilities every other parent has. Because the laws and courthouse culture are different in every state, talk to a local attorney who's experienced with second-parent adoptions before pursuing one. When researching this kind of adoption, use the term "stepparent adoption" or "second-parent adoption" even though you're not married, because then lawyers and clerks will quickly understand what you're talking about.

Besides adoption, guardianship is the next closest legal relationship an adult can have to a child. A parent can name a guardian for his child in his will and, in some states, in a separate letter that can be used if the parent is living. To create an informal guardianship agreement (as opposed to a formal one, created by a court), the legal parent(s) and the guardian should sign and date a simple statement that includes:

- each of their names and addresses, and the child's date of birth
- a statement granting temporary guardianship to the designated guardian, giving this person authority to act in the place of a parent for (fill in these rights or others as appropriate for the situation): authorizing medical examinations, procedures, or treatments; communicating with and giving permission for school enrollment or activities; picking the child up from activities; etc. Some lawyers recommend that a document authorizing health care decisions be separate from ones granting other authority.

Give a notarized copy of the agreement to the school, and have extra notarized copies on hand for doctors, hospitals, or anyone else who might question the guardian's right to act as a parent. Sherry and her partner created a type of guardian agreement giving each of them some rights regarding the other's children:

We have a childcare authorization so Will has permission to act as a parent for my boys at school. It's the same for me with his children. Basically, it's just a signed parental statement that gives Will authority to take care of the kids if they need it and I'm not available. It gives him authority to act as a parent. We drew it up at home and gave copies to the schools. I checked with a friend who's an attorney and he said they were binding.

Even if adoption and guardianship aren't solutions for you, the child's parent can ask the child's school how to designate the stepparent as an additional adult with legal authority. The rules are different in different states and school systems, but at the very least the stepparent can be listed as an emergency contact person. Of course, even when an additional name is listed as having some permissions, the legal parents' or guardians' wishes will nearly always trump the stepparent's.

For Same-Sex Couples

Even though both people in a same-sex couple can't be genetically related to the child, some GLBT parent couples are more like biological parent families, where both partners decide together how they're going to become parents, both announce to their friends that they'll be moms or dads soon, and both paint the baby's room (or at least debate the color scheme). Other GLBT families are more like stepfamilies, where one partner joins the family later in a stepparent role. States vary widely in their recognition of same-sex couples as parents. Some allow second-parent adoptions that give non-biological parents and "stepparents" full status as legal parents, and some adoption agencies welcome gay and lesbian couples to adopt together. Other states explicitly ban gay couples from adopting (in some cases, gay and lesbian people aren't even allowed to adopt the children they already care for as foster parents or stepparents).

The key for GLBT parents is to get as many of the safeguards discussed above as you can in your state, and as are appropriate for your situation. If you can list both your names on the birth certificate or adopt jointly, do it; if you can get a second-parent adoption in your state, do that. Regardless of where you live, you can write a parenting agreement and a will. Get the best information you can from local lawyers with expertise in this area and from GLBT groups, and then do what you can to protect your family and yourself.

▶ Talking with Children About Not Being Married

There is clear consensus from unmarried couples who parent together that children don't care about marital status anywhere near as much as adults do. But that doesn't mean that children don't bring up the subject. John points out that nearly every kids' video seems to end with the two protagonists getting married, as if "saving the castle, saving the child at the top of the mountain, and getting married were all values on the same short list." Every unmarried parent whose children were old enough to understand said that their kids wanted to talk about marriage, and especially about weddings. Hillary, 19, used to dream of her mom and stepdad's marrying, but it seemed related to the fun of dressing up.

> I remember I used to wish Mom and Al would get married. I think it was mostly so I could be the flower girl. I just thought it would be really neat to have a wedding and everything. But I think that was from a very materialistic little kid point of view. I don't think it was an "I need a daddy" type of thing, because I already felt like he was one.

Most unmarried parents find ways of explaining their marital status to their kids in age-appropriate ways. Lyn's son is three, and just beginning to understand ideas about marriage and family.

> We've been talking with him for a while about how people who are romantically involved with each other are each other's family. So before Kira and John got married I would say to him, "You know Kira, she's John's family. They live together." And I still talk about her that way. When my brother was getting married he

asked, "What's 'married'?" We told him they were going to have a party to celebrate their relationship, and that some people decide that that's something they want to do. He said, "Did you do that?" and we said no.

Several people told us that other kids told their children parents *have* to be married, as if it were impossible to procreate without a ring on your finger. Some children are able to tell their friends that no, some parents are married and others aren't. Erica says their seven-year-old son, Remi, has been learning about reproduction. "If you asked him," she says, "he'd say, well, duh, you don't have to be married to have babies! You just need a sperm and an egg, and there you go." But others, like the six-year-old daughter of *Living Together* legal guide authors Ralph Warner and Toni Ihara, just didn't connect with her parents' explanation that, "Just like mama hamsters have baby hamsters without getting married, so, too, can Mom and Dad." After 19 years together the two decided to get married partly to ease their daughter's concerns.[37]

For similar reasons, some unmarried partners choose to have a commitment ceremony. Having a ceremony or ritual before a baby is born can increase relatives' acceptance of an unmarried birth and provide you with something to take the place of "wedding photos" to show future children. As Dakota says, "The fact that we had a relationship celebration made it easier for my parents to deal with the fact that I was pregnant." A ceremony can also be part of a conscious process of affirming an unmarried stepfamily. To read more about these ideas, see page 171.

Most parents of older kids are honest with them about why they're not marrying. Dakota has ongoing conversations with her three kids and told us, "If you're really, deeply comfortable with not being married, you'll think of a way to make your children comfortable with it. They will be comfortable with it because you are." But some parents, like Meredith, decide they need to approach the subject quite differently to protect their children from the stigma that remains in more conservative communities.

Our kids think we're married. We lie to them, because we don't want them to say something to their peers. We know it's important in the area we live in. Our daughter's Brownie leader is a born-again, fundamentalist Christian. We don't want the kids to be ostracized because of it. We'd rather mislead people or outright lie to them than get in a debate or discussion with someone whose opinion really doesn't matter. These people greatly influence the way our kids are treated.

As we talked about in chapter 8, some couples even have formal weddings so that their kids will think they're married, even though they're not getting legally married. No one sees lying to children is a strategy they prefer—it's something parents do out of desperation, usually because they can't marry for financial reasons but need to protect their children from harassment. In the long run, taking this approach can backfire, since the parental untruth is almost certain to be discovered eventually. The underlying problem here is not with a parenting decision, but with a culture that upholds married families as the only acceptable kind.

▶ Choosing a Last Name

Nearly every unmarried family has to confront the last-name dilemma. It's a quandary that affects plenty of married couples, too, but whereas 90 percent of married couples take the same last name[38], nearly all unmarried partners have different names. As adults, many unmarried people are comfortable, even pleased, to keep their own surnames. But when a child joins the family, you're forced to make a decision. There are no requirements about what last name you give your child—you can name him absolutely whatever you want. Will he get one parent's name, or the other, or both? How do you feel about not having a single family name in a culture where most families are unified by their surname? There are seven possible solutions, listed here in approximate order from most to least common.

1. Give the child the dad's last name.

This choice is the most traditional one, since in the U.S. surnames generally pass down the father's line. It's the option Becky and Mike chose, as Becky explains:

> We decided Arthur should have Mike's last name. I felt strongly about that because my claim to him could never be disputed as a biological parent, but putting Mike's last name on him, as well as having Mike on the birth certificate, make it clear that we both agree that he is the father. We just thought it would make it clearer to everybody, because since we're not married, people can wonder, "Well, is he Mike's kid, or did you have him before you met Mike?" So Arthur has Mike's last name, and my last name as a middle name. No hyphens.

Same-sex couples sometimes give their kids the last name of the partner who is not genetically related to the child, using similar reasoning.

2. Hyphenate the child's name.

Hyphenated names, which are becoming increasingly common, work best when the parents have relatively short, easy-to-spell last names. Some people worry that hyphenation is only a good solution for a single generation, since it could create tongue-twisters for two adults with hyphenated last names who want to hyphenate *their* names together or give their child a shared name. But there is something appealing about how clearly it links the child to both parents instead of just one. Erica and Tim gave their son a hyphenated last name, Neuman-Kelly. Erica says he's just old enough now to start talking about it.

> *Remi's now in second grade, and he's starting to have to write his last name, and he complained about how "it's really long." Tim and I talked about this when I was pregnant and we decided on the name. I said that when Remi's old enough, maybe when he's 10 or 12, if he decides the name is way too long and he doesn't like it, we will allow him to change it. He could pick one name or the other, or even a new one, and change it one time. So he brought up the issue the other day and I said well, you know, your Daddy and I decided a long time ago that if you wanted another last name you can decide that. He sat there and thought about it for a minute, and said, "Oh, no, I'll keep it."*

3. Give the child the mom's last name.

Some couples who are frustrated with the legacy of women "losing" their names when they marry decide to use a matrilineal system for a change, and give their children the mother's last name. Partners planning to have more than one child might agree that all girls will get their mother's name, and all boys their father's name, or vice versa. Others plan to alternate surnames with each child. Annie was very clear that she wanted her son, Adrian, to carry on her name:

"I guess we'd be considered a family. We're living together, we love each other, and we haven't eaten the children yet."

He has my last name, which was really important to me. Even if people do get married I bristle when the woman loses her name. I feel like it's one of the most blatant, outrageous examples of how the matriarchy has been obliterated through history. If George Bush had whatever his wife's maiden name was, who would he be? But John's last name is our son's middle name and I think that, for Adrian, it's really important for him to have his father's name as part of his full name.

4. Have the whole family take the same last name.

As we described in chapter 5, even if you're not married, it's perfectly legal for either partner to change his or her name to match the other's. Even if we didn't get married, Marshall Miller and Dorian Solot could become Marshall and Dorian Miller and then give our child the last name Miller. (Or we could do the same thing with the name Solot.) The family name doesn't have to belong to one of the partners, either. If you decide you want to be the Fishy family, you and your partner can each change your last names to Fishy, and then you can raise a whole school of little Fishys (or would that be Fishies?).

5. Merge your names.

Here's how Dakota and her partner Chris did it:

We have this lovely thing that we've been able to do with our names. I know not everyone has names that lend themselves to this, but it's worked great for us. My name is Butterfield, Chris' name is Cartter, and we've created Cartterfield as the children's name. So, we are the Cartterfield family, but I am Dakota Butterfield and Chris is Chris Cartter. What I love about it is that we both have a different name than our children but we both have part of our name in our children's name. The children love it. They get it. It really works for them on both a symbolic level and a practical level.

Depending on how many syllables are in your names, there are numerous ways to merge names. For an imaginary couple whose last names are Kimball and Sanchez, their kids could become Kimchez, Sanball, Kimsan, Ballchez, Chezkim, Ballsan, Sankim, or Chezball. (Even if you never use any of the merged options for your kids, making a list of your combinations can be great entertainment.)

6. Give the child a new name that the parents add to their names.

Beth, Drew, and Teresa are parenting their son together as a family of three adults. Before their baby was born they spent months pondering how to communicate

INSIDE ADVICE ON
UNMARRIED ADOPTION

THE WORLD OF adoption has come a long way from the days when the only people eligible to adopt were married couples with white picket fences. Today most adoption agencies welcome single people, and a growing number are willing to work with gay and lesbian couples. It's more unusual for unmarried different-sex couples to adopt, but in many places it's not impossible to do. Before unmarried issues became her full-time job, Dorian worked in the adoption field, where she specialized in helping nontraditional families navigate the adoption process. Here's her advice for how to begin, based on her insider's experience of what works.

First, figure out which adoption agencies, and which social workers within those agencies, are likely to be friendly to you. Straight unmarried couples can learn a lot by researching which agencies welcome gay and lesbian couples—they are more likely to be open-minded, and also to be accustomed to evaluating prospective adoptive parents who don't have a marriage license. Local gay parenting groups and ads in local gay publications are great sources of information, and networking can pay off. Ask that co-worker whose lesbian sister adopted last year to find out whether her sister would recommend the agency she used.

Once you have the names of some possible agencies—and ideally the name of a friendly contact person at each agency—start making phone calls. Ask lots of questions about how the adoption process works at their agency, whether someone in your kind of relationship (unmarried, gay, etc.) is eligible to adopt, whether they've ever worked with a family like yours before, and if it would be harder for your kind of family to be placed with a child (some agencies will charge you money to evaluate and approve you as adoptive parents, but never match you with a child). If they tell you they would consider an unmarried couple but have never worked with one before, ask how many children they've placed with single parents or gay couples in the last year to get a sense of whether nontraditional families are a regular part of their work or whether you'd stick out like a flamingo in a henhouse. That's the approach Meredith and her partner took when they pursued their adoption of two siblings from abroad:

I talked to about seven or eight agencies in the area. I never gave them my name right off the bat. I asked them if they had worked with single people. I asked if they were comfortable working with alternative families, and a lot of times they would say, "Well, what do you mean by that?" I would ask, "Have you worked with gay or lesbian clients? What about unmarried couples?" I just asked a lot questions about that. We just weeded our way through the list.

You may need to attend agencies' information meetings to get a better sense of them. Trust your gut on how the agencies answer your questions—you may learn more from their general attitudes than from the answers themselves. Your goal is to find a social worker who has experience getting kids placed in families that are different from the "norm" in some way, and who will be willing to advocate for you. Look for an agency you trust and will enjoy working with. You shouldn't have to settle for a business relationship that doesn't feel right.

If you're lucky enough to find an agency that's at least willing to consider you, different-sex couples should be prepared to be able to explain the reason they're not married clearly and compellingly. Expect to be held to higher standards than married couples in terms of the stability of your relationship and how long you've been together. Most agencies don't have a minimum number of years, but for good reason they'll want to be convinced that you'll stick together through the trials of parenting and the added stresses of adoption. Don't lie to your social worker—if your falsehood is discovered, it can put a quick end to your chances of adopting. Some agencies may say you can adopt as a single parent but not jointly, or impose other requirements because you're not married. As Meredith and her partner did, you'll have to sort out whether you can live with or work around these restrictions.

The state told our social worker that he couldn't write an affirmative homestudy [the document that approves a family to adopt] for us because there is a law in the state of Virginia that prohibits unmarried couples from residing together. They said, "Either you get married, or he has to move out, or she has to move out. They have to have separate residences." But things were moving so quickly that we were advised by our adoption agency not to get married at that time because the laws were in flux in the country we were adopting from. The social worker said, "You could get married but that could mean your kids could get stuck there for a year." What we ended up doing was, we leased a room from some of our friends who had a five bedroom house. Kevin had clothes in the closet and stuff there. The social worker was invited to come see the house if he chose. But the social worker thought it was a stupid law. He was supportive of us getting the kids.

Finally, consider a less traditional approach to adoption. The more willing you are to adopt a child who is considered "hard to place" because of his age (toddler or older), race, or disability, the easier it can be to adopt. Agencies seeking adoptive homes for school-age children with a history of abuse or neglect, sometimes misleadingly called "special needs" adoption, tend to be particularly open to considering all kinds of families. As an added bonus, this kind of adoption is generally free. Foster care is another path to adoption that works well for some people, since child welfare agencies usually give foster parents "first dibs" if a child in their care becomes eligible for adoption. But since foster parenting is by definition temporary, you'd need to be prepared for the likelihood that you'd provide a much-needed home to some children who are taken away from you before one becomes free for adoption. Before becoming a foster parent who hopes to adopt, make sure the agency would allow you to adopt—some agencies have stricter eligibility requirements for adoptive parents than foster parents.

that they're all related to him and to each other, without giving him three last names or completely changing their own names. They finally decided instead to give him a new last name that each of them would take. As Beth says, "He gave us our last name, instead of the other way around." They settled on the last name Eliot, a name that had personal meaning for all three of them. The baby's last name is Eliot, and each parent kept his or her own last name but added Eliot either before or after it.

Other families that use this approach hyphenate the parents' names but not the child's, figuring that hyphenation going *up* the family line is much more sustainable for the long-term than hyphenation going *down* the line. So for example, if Jack North and Jill South used this approach and decided to add the name East, Jack would be Jack North-East, Jill would be Jill South-East, and their child would just have the last name East.

7. Give the child a last name different than either parent.

There's nothing that requires you to give your child a last name that matches yours. Anne and Christopher didn't want their child to have only one of their last names, didn't like the way hyphenation is a "one-generation solution," and found their last names didn't merge well. They decided to give their son a name different from either of theirs and chose Anne's grandmother's maiden name, Ellinger, which had been lost through marriage. Although Anne and Christopher add Ellinger to their own names when they need one family name, she says, "That rarely happens. Other than occasional moments explaining to people why we have three last names, it doesn't seem to be a problem. When we ask our son if he would like us to take Ellinger, or if he wishes he had our names, he says he doesn't care." Anne points out that part of the reason this solution works for them is because their own surnames will be passed along by their siblings' children. "It might have been different if I were the last one left with my last name," she says.

Parenting without a marriage license is not for everyone. But it is a reality— sometimes a very good one—for growing numbers of parents and children. In order to be strong, unmarried families require both the kind of commitment to staying together often associated with marriage, and access to the same social support and legal recognition that married families receive. With these needs met, unmarried families can be stable, nurturing, places for children to grow.

TEN

SHALL WE MARRY?

Happily Ever After With

Wedding Bells or Without

LOOKING FOR A happy ending? We've got at least two for you. If you get married, you can live happily ever after, and if you don't, you can do the same, because the quality of your relationship matters far more than whether your partner shares your last name or gives you a gold band. In reality, married and unmarried relationships are much more similar than they are different. In fact, married people and cohabitors are usually the same people. Most cohabitors marry. Most marrying couples cohabit first.[1] Cohabitation and marriage are not an either-or decision, since most people today choose both.

This chapter is for partners who have the option to marry, but disagree about whether they want to get married, or just can't decide. If you're already in agreement about marriage—two thumbs up or two down—you can head straight for the wedding planning guides, or dive into nurturing your unmarried partnership.

TO WED OR NOT TO WED

It may seem like everyone has an opinion about whether you should get married: your mother, your best friend, maybe even your children. As Marshall discovered, our own marital status has become the subject of inquiry among politicians in the Boston suburb where we live:

> *I was out running errands just before a local election. A town official with whom I've chatted a few times before was campaigning in front of the post office. "Marshall!" he greeted me, in friendly small-town-politician fashion, and we talked briefly about the election. As our conversation drew to a close and I turned to leave, he called out, "Hey, are you married yet?" I laughed, "Not yet." Shaking his head and smiling, he said in a serious tone, "You gotta tie the knot, Marshall. You gotta tie the knot."*

We're not alone in getting advice. When Ethan sent a Christmas card to an old piano teacher, the reply informed him that he and his partner should "go together before God" and get married.

One couple became so fascinated with all the unsolicited advice about whether they should marry that they started soliciting it, compiling the results into the documentary *Wedding Advice: Speak Now or Forever Hold Your Peace.* In it, Karen Sosnoski and Fred Zeytoonjian asked their grandparents, friends, national experts, and even strangers in the park for their musings on whether they should wed and on the marriage institution overall. "We found that we are not alone in being ambivalent about marriage. Even people who have been married for years can feel that way," Sosnoski says. She and Zeytoonjian have been together for 18 years.[2]

We, too, find that people's feelings about marriage are complex. Some aren't even sure how they feel. Thinking about her relationship with Rodrigo, Valerie told us, "We both have very ambivalent feelings about marriage. We have a lifetime commitment to each other, but do we need to make that a legal one?" Daren says that after eight years, "We are leaning hard toward marriage. I can't give a good reason why we are not married. I guess I avoid the actual final decision."

Despite the complexity, over time people fall into five general categories when it comes to this decision, two types of "yes," two types of "no," and one right in the middle. On the yes side are When the Time Is Right couples who plan to get married someday, and For a Particular Reason folks, who marry when an external factor convinces them they should. The "no" side includes the Unmarried Forevers, who know deep down that matrimony is not what they want, and the Insurmountable Barriers group, for whom legal or financial factors prevent marriage. A fifth category, Undecided, includes people who truly aren't sure what they want as well as those who don't care and are happy to let their partner make the decision. Each of these categories overlaps with others, but the following descriptions may give you a sense of where you fit.

▶ I Do: When the Time Is Right

Like most unmarried couples, Robyn and Jeff are of the "When the Time Is Right" persuasion. Together for two and a half years, they recently bought a house together, certainly a sign of their commitment. Robyn says, "We talk about marriage quite a bit. We both want it, although we want to wait just a bit longer to take the plunge." Sarit, who is married now, says she and her husband waited:

> For many years, neither of us felt ready to get married. We had been dating for seven years and living together for five before we got engaged. We both knew that there was no question about our degree of commitment to each other, but for me, the issue was one of identity—I wasn't ready to be a "married person." The change occurred slowly. We first talked about it obliquely at a café on vacation in California, over a year before we actually got engaged. The process of moving toward our engagement was thrilling, full of excitement and promise for both of us.

Couples like these agree that marriage is what they both want. For other couples, "the right time" may arrive when the more reluctant partner agrees to marry. Carmen says she's happy in her unmarried relationship of six years, and questions whether it's worth it to spend money on a ring and a wedding. Still, it sounds like she wouldn't turn down a proposal from her partner:

> He says, "We will get married one of these days. You are the one." He says to me, "It's the same thing. It's like we're married, the only thing is we just don't have a ring on our finger, we don't have the document." He says one of these days we will. I'm like, "Well, what are you thinking of?" And he says, "One of these days when the time is right." Six years, when is the time right? We'll see. Maybe he'll surprise me one of these years. I don't think you have to go that extra step, spend all that money, just to show your love.

Some are waiting to be fully convinced that the match is the right one for a lifetime. Others are working through all the other issues associated with marriage. Many are waiting to marry until they are in a financial position to "do it right," able to afford a vision of married life that may include a lavish wedding, fancy dress, good job, house, and children. Stephen says, "We want to get married when the time is right for us. This includes my girlfriend getting into graduate school, and saving enough money for a nice ring and honeymoon. We are in no hurry to get married, but we know we will."

► I Do: For a Particular Reason

Sometimes the legal, financial, or social benefits can tip the scales in favor of marrying. Many in this category say they were leaning toward marrying anyway, but that a factor like health insurance or their plans for children finally convinced them. Alan and Pepper, for instance, considered themselves engaged but said they probably wouldn't have married "for quite a while" if not for a cancer scare Pepper went through. Though the breast lump turned out to be benign, the experience prompted them to move quickly, knowing that as her spouse, Alan could add her to his health insurance plan.

We'd had talks about getting married, and backed off, and talked about it, and backed off. As soon as her breast cancer scare was over, I said, "OK, I don't want to go through this again. I'm worried about whether you're going to get good health care. What are you doing Tuesday?" This was on Friday, so we had three business days to gather friends and family.
—Alan

He said, "You make the telephone calls, I'll cook the turkey." So I made all the phone calls, and Sunday we talked with the woman who was our minister. And we ended up having the ceremony at her house. The only time available was between 5:30 and 7:30 on Tuesday night, because everybody, including us, had things to do later on Tuesday night. So everybody who could made it by 5:30. We had the potluck marriage ceremony, and then by 7:15 all our friends were ready to go to where they needed to go.
—Pepper

Others who opt for the legal and financial protections say they would have preferred not to marry. Dakota, passionately unmarried at age 47, has been pondering what will happen when she's a senior citizen:

We're starting to think about being 60 or 70, and it's just really clear that it's stupid for us not to take advantage of my having access to his Social Security benefit. The only way I can get access to that is by getting married. I made him swear that if we do this, he will never refer to me as his wife, he will never say those words. He will say, "This is the woman to whom I am married."

Shaken by a hospital visit, Skip married her partner of 18 years:

I think what catalyzed this for me was when I had to go into the hospital for a day procedure. Alan took me because I was going to be having anesthesia, and some-

one has to drive you home. We sat in the admitting office together while I answered the routine questions that the nice lady was asking. She asked me my marital status. I can tell you that at this point in time I do not feel like I'm a divorced woman. I feel like I'm in a partnered, long-term, committed relationship. So when she asked me that question—I guess I hadn't been asked that question in quite a while—I hesitated, and I said single. Maybe because I hesitated, she said, "That means you've never been married." I said, "Well, no, I was married, but I was divorced in 1975." So she wrote down divorced. Then we get further along in filling out the form, and she asked for who to notify in case of emergency and I said Alan, and pointed to him. She said, "Relationship?" I responded, "Life partner." And she wrote down "friend." As small a thing as it seems, it was very catalytic in terms of my realizing how society perceives the relationship that we have.

The hospital staff ultimately welcomed Alan's presence, let him into the recovery room after Skip's procedure, and explained the results to him. But the two realized that in Alan's words, "that was the hospital's choice, as opposed to their obligation." Skip adds, "Had it been another hospital, or a different doctor, we would've faced the same situation as lesbians and gay men face. I don't like the vulnerable feeling."

▶ I Can't: Insurmountable Barriers

For many in this group, no matter how good the reasons are, marriage isn't an option. Like same-sex couples and those receiving certain kinds of pensions, disability, or survivors' benefits, people who fall into this category are sometimes saddened to hear about people who marry "for a particular reason," since it's a reminder of their own powerlessness to do the same. Others here find that although they theoretically could sign a marriage license, the legal or financial reasons not to far outweigh the possible benefits.

That doesn't mean that everyone in this group wants to marry. In fact, if Congress waved its magic wand tomorrow and removed all the legal and financial penalties to matrimony for the people in this group, they would scatter themselves among the other four categories. Sherry, who receives survivors' benefits that make marriage unaffordable, would run to the first group. "We would *love* to be married," she says. "We would like to be married now. But there's just no possible way." Chris, a gay man who's been with his partner for 16 years, says:

We both grew up with very conventional ideas of marriage and the assumption that we would marry. Part of coming out was dropping those assumptions. In a lot of ways, coming out was a very empowering experience. It made me feel like I could set the terms for my own life, since I'd already broken the "rules" by being gay. In some ways, I liked leaving that vision of how I would grow up and marry, and I think that's one reason why I'm not attracted to the idea of a marriage ceremony.

Raymond and Brian, another gay couple, would belong in the For a Particular Reason category, because they're concerned about property rights and hospital visitation.

▶ I Don't: Unmarried Forever

Jacquie is one of those who knows deep in her heart that marriage is not for her. Comparing her past marriage to her current unmarried relationship, she says this one wins hands down.

> *This partner that I have is good for me, but to marry him would be a disaster. The relationship would not be the same, and the trust with each other would not be the same. I don't care if all the marriage counselors in the world told me otherwise. The Pope could come and tell me that marriage would be the same. I say it wouldn't. The two of us know what is good for us.*

Christopher's conviction is similar. Just as marriage can be part of a sacred path for some, remaining unmarried has been an expression of his spiritual beliefs. The principle that inspires him, satyagraha, was developed and named by Mahatma Gandhi.

> *As I started exploring spirituality, I was inspired by the principle of satyagraha, truth-seeking. It literally means each being has a piece of the truth, and that you need to speak up for your truth and try to understand more of somebody else's truth. I feel like being a nonmarried couple is a form of cultural satyagraha. The wider culture tries to put commitment in a box, to say it can only exist if it's sanctioned with legal marriage. If we had gotten married just to fit in, I would have been backing down from adding my truth to the mix, which is that family, love, and long-term commitment can flourish just fine without a marriage certificate.*

After mulling over her disinterest in marriage for years, Rachel Fudge writes in "Why I Don't" that her gut-level truth is more important than all her attempts at explanations:

> *Ironically, my relationship looks a lot more like a marriage than like any of the other nontraditional family forms out there. So why is it so important to me that our relationship not become a marriage? What it really boils down to is this:*

Marriage feels wrong. My relationship with Hugh feels very, very right. Marriage is irrelevant to the daily hubbub of our relationship.[3]

As we discussed in chapter 2, Unmarried Forevers may make their decision for one of many carefully considered reasons—or simply because they see no compelling reason to marry. Some happily spend decades in this category before finding a tangible reason to marry, some eventually go their separate ways, and some remain unmarried to each other for the rest of their lives.

DOES GETTING MARRIED CHANGE ANYTHING?

It's only reasonable that those who are thinking about marriage wonder whether everything will look different if they walk down the aisle. There's no simple answer to this question—people's experiences vary widely.

Betsy knows that getting married improved her relationship. After living together for a year, her partner broke up with her. They were apart for three years, then started dating again and moved back in together. When they finally got married, she says the emotional and legal commitment made a real difference in her mind.

> *I wasn't very secure in our relationship, partly because he had already broken my heart one time. When we were living together, he would never say, 'We're going to be together forever and ever.' I saw getting married as him making a commitment to me—I knew he wouldn't abandon me again.*

Ruthie called in to a national radio show to say that even after having been together 10 years, getting married had noticeably positive effects.

> *The marriage made a big difference to us, and it was a very positive difference. There was something about saying publicly that we were committed to each other that really increased the security we felt, and really made us more willing to put a lot of work into our relationship. . . . And it made our relationship much more joyful.[4]*

Although some expect marriage to change their relationship for the better, just as many are surprised by the depth of the change. Even though they had a child together, Lisa refused to marry her partner until he cleaned up his drug and alcohol problems. They struggled along together for over a decade, and Lisa says, "If I had married him sooner I probably would've divorced him." But once he was clean and sober, she agreed to get married, and was surprised to see the relationship improve even further.

We had a rocky relationship. Now that we're married he has totally changed. He doesn't drink, he doesn't use drugs, he's more family oriented. It happened gradually. We view each other differently—we're more of a family. I had never thought marriage mattered, I hadn't thought it was a big deal. It turned out marriage was the best thing I could have done, but waiting was important. I had to wait for him to get to that certain step, reach that certain time in his life. He's a good guy now. Getting married absolutely changed our relationship for the better.

Some other cohabitors who get married notice less of a change. Some say there's a reason marriage is sometimes described as "just a piece of paper." Regardless of what others think, they haven't found their relationship to be better, rockier, or different than it was before they had that marriage certificate. Heidi and her partner lived together for two years before marrying. After their honeymoon ended, they returned to the house where they'd already been living. She says, "I don't think marriage was that much different. We got along really well. Living together we had learned how to do our finances together. Once we got married, I don't think much changed." Dennis and Marcia's relationship was thirteen years old when they married, and Dennis says, "Marcia and I have always had such a good time. Marriage didn't change the way we relate to each other." It doesn't seem surprising that couples like Dennis and Marcia, whose patterns of interaction were established over many years, may be less likely to find marriage brings changes.

Even among couples who say their relationship didn't change, most agree that other people viewed them differently once they were married. Ron's observation, that "there really hasn't been any difference other than how everybody looks at us,"[5] is a common one. Cheryl has noticed, "When you get married you become an adult. You sort of enter a big club. It may not be very tangible—it's not named and spoken out loud, but I think that it exists in our culture. I think you get taken more seriously and perceived as more mature if you can say you're a husband or you're a wife." Having a wedding may not change the relationship itself, but it is likely to change others' assumptions about the relationship—often for the better.

Then there are those whose experiences after marrying were less than rosy. Six years into their relationship, when Nikki was pregnant, she and Kyle got married in response to pressure from both their families. They agree their relationship immediately took a turn for the worse, and both suspect that if they hadn't married, they might still be together. Nikki tries to articulate what changed:

Living together was completely different from being married. We shouldn't have gotten married, we should have just lived together. We had the same bills as we had before, and we had the same kids, lived in the same place, but it was just harder. I had to become a wife. I was expected to make dinner. Before, it was like, "Oh, want to eat? Well, go ahead." But now I was expected to make dinner, I was expected to do the laundry, expected to keep an immaculate house. Not necessarily by Kyle, but by my mother, his mother: "Oh, you're a wife now." Kyle and I have not always been the conventional parents or the conventional couple, but we were expected to suddenly become this conventional husband and wife. It became hard.

Women aren't the only ones who can be changed by marriage. In an extreme example of this, becoming a husband changed the man Judy C. loved:

Getting married definitely made a difference. We lived together before we married, and there was a drastic change. Once we had signed the paper, my husband became very dominant and controlling. The first five years we were married I couldn't even go to the grocery store by myself. We worked in the same building and he absolutely monitored everybody who came into my office. It was pretty awful.

People whose relationships falter after they marry often point to assumptions about how "husbands" and "wives" are supposed to act as one source of the problem. Journalist Dalma Heyn calls this phenomenon "marriage shock," and wrote a book by that title about her research on how common it is for women's sex lives, communication styles, and division of household chores to change in gender-stereotyped ways after they married.[6] Some couples worry not about gender roles, but about taking each other for granted if they marry. Alice says the fact that "marriage can breed a kind of complacency" is one of the things that concerns her.

Fortunately, many of these negative experiences are preventable. You can prevent your relationship from suffering from complacency or marriage shock by talking about it before the wedding. Discuss with your partner what being a husband or wife means to you, and whether you expect your roles or your relationship to change once you're married. They key is to proceed consciously.

WHAT IF WE CAN'T DECIDE?

What happens if you're having a hard time deciding whether to get married or not? Maybe you're eager to get hitched, but your partner has dug in his heels. Perhaps you never wanted to be a bridesmaid, let alone the bride, but your sweetie gets all dewy-eyed when he talks about slipping a ring on your finger. Or maybe neither of you can decide *what* you want.

To untangle this knot, you'll need to dig deeper into your respective feelings for and against marrying. (Even though you arrive at different conclusions, you probably both see parts of matrimony that look appealing, and other parts that you'd happily forgo.) Is the partner who is reluctant to marry interested in staying in the relationship long-term without marrying, or is he concerned about your ultimate compatibility? If the real barrier to agreeing is an underlying relationship issue, you'll need to face that head-on before you can make a marriage decision. It might be helpful to use the Speaker-Listener Technique (explained on page 98), or work with a therapist, clergyperson, or other neutral third party to facilitate your conversation. If you do work with a third party, make sure this person sees both possible outcomes, marrying and not marrying, as valid and workable choices.

Chet and Laura arrived at their decision after many heartfelt conversations. When they first met, Laura said she never wanted to get married, didn't particularly like going to weddings, and was afraid marriage would mean losing her independence. Chet had positive feelings about marriage and the way it would be a public expression of commitment for each other. After talking at length to sort out their feelings, they decided to marry, but to do some things differently than most couples. They created their own wedding ceremony from scratch (in which Laura did not wear a white dress), and opted to hyphenate their last names, both taking identical ones. Six years later, both agree that they're pleased with their choices. Laura says, "Getting married has been really good. I have never regretted that decision."

Few people face a deadline for their marriage decision. You can decide to postpone the decision a while longer, and set a specific time when you'll check in again, to reassure the pro-marriage partner that her concerns won't be forgotten. Therapist Elizabeth Morrison suggests saying something along the lines of, "I understand that you can't give an answer about marriage right now. By next winter, I need you to let you me know. If you're still unable to decide, then I'll need to make a decision about what I'm going to do at that point." But Morrison warns, "Don't give an ultimatum that may hurt you, too!" If the deadline comes, and you're both feeling great about each other, don't end a perfectly good relationship because you set a deadline. Instead, says Morrison, have another conversation about how you're each feeling, and take it from there. Your partner might have inched closer towards marriage, or you might find yourself more comfortable with staying together unmarried. Not every couple manages to find common ground, but if you're lucky, eventually you'll find a place where you agree.[7]

Let's say you both want your relationship to continue for the long term, but you still disagree about getting married. In that case, your best plan may be to take your plates to the relationship buffet that we talked about in the introduction. Once you've sorted out all the different ingredients that make up the familiar marriage "meal," explore together whether you can choose those dishes off the buffet that will meet both your needs. To make your conversation easier, we've provided a sample Marriage Decision Tool (pages 236–239). Here's how to use it:

Step One: Do some serious thinking about marriage separately and together. Have a good, honest conversation about what is important to each of you about marriage or nonmarriage. Make lists of the things that are important to each partner. Be as specific as possible.

Step Two: Choose one item from one of your lists. Using our sample Marriage Decision Tool or one you create yourselves, consider whether there's a way for both of you to get your needs met for that item. For example, you feel like having the same last name would contribute to a sense of family unity, but your partner doesn't want to get married. Find the Marriage Decision Tool labeled "Potential Issue: Last Names." In the column on the left, locate the box that says, "It would mean a lot to me to have the same last name." That's where you are. Now read across to the far right column ("I don't want to get legally married")— that's where your partner is. Read the options in the box, and see if they might meet both your needs. In this case, the solution might be as simple as getting a legal name change. Even without getting legally married, you can take your partner's name, ask him to take yours, hyphenate your names, or choose a new name that you both adopt.

Step Three: Repeat Step Two for each item on your lists, as needed.

Step Four: Discuss how you each feel about the options you've generated. Do they meet your needs? Your conversation might result in new issues you realize are important to you. If so, write them down, and go back to Step Two.

www.CartoonStock.com

"Now that our kids are grown and the house is paid off,
what do you say we get married?"

A SAMPLE MARRIAGE DECISION TOOL

POTENTIAL ISSUE: Last Names	I WANT TO GET LEGALLY MARRIED	I DON'T WANT TO GET LEGALLY MARRIED
It would mean a lot to me to have the same last name.	◆ The woman can easily take her husband's name when she gets married. ◆ The man can take his wife's name by getting a legal name change (it's not quite as simple as it is for a woman, but it can be done). ◆ Both people can change their names to a hyphenated version or an entirely new name they choose together.	There's no rule against it. ◆ One partner can take the other's last name by getting a legal name change. ◆ Both people can change their names to a hyphenated version or an entirely new name they choose together. *(Read the section on name changes in chapter 5, pages 126–127.)*
It's important to me to keep my last name.	Get married but keep your own last names.	No action needed. Don't change a thing.

Potential Issue: Public recognition	I WANT TO GET LEGALLY MARRIED	I DON'T WANT TO GET LEGALLY MARRIED
Public validation or celebration of our relationship is important to me.	Plan a wedding.	Plan a commitment ceremony or ritual. If you like, call it a wedding, even if you're not getting legally married. *(Read chapter 8.)*
I don't want to have a big wedding or have people make a fuss over us.	◆ Have a quick ceremony at the courthouse or with a justice of the peace. Invite only your best friend, or no one at all. ◆ Elope.	No action needed. Spend the day at the beach.

Potential Issue: **Rings**	**I WANT TO GET LEGALLY MARRIED**	**I DON'T WANT TO GET LEGALLY MARRIED**
I want to wear a ring to symbolize our love and commitment.	Exchange rings at your wedding.	There's no rule to stop unmarried partners from wearing rings. You can: ◆ Exchange rings on your own. ◆ Exchange rings at a commitment ceremony where you don't get legally married. ◆ Buy yourself a ring that looks like an engagement ring or a wedding band, and wear it on your wedding ring finger.
I don't want to wear a ring.	◆ Don't exchange rings at your wedding—there's no requirement that you must do so. ◆ Exchange rings at your wedding, but after the event store them in a safe place instead of wearing them. ◆ Wear your ring on a necklace instead of on your finger, or find some other nontraditional way to wear it. ◆ Instead of rings, at your wedding exchange other tokens to symbolize your commitment.	No action needed. Display your bare ring finger with pride.

Potential Issue: **Legal Protections**	**I WANT TO GET LEGALLY MARRIED**	**I DON'T WANT TO GET LEGALLY MARRIED**
I'm very concerned about legal protections for us and/or for our children.	Get married, and also make a will. Consider working with a lawyer and/or estate planner to make sure you've covered the bases.	Take the time to complete the paperwork, including making a will, that will give you most, if not all, of the legal protections that are important to you. Consider working with a lawyer and/or estate planner to make sure you've covered the bases. *(Read chapter 6.)*
I want as few legal connections as possible.	Before you get married, hire a lawyer to draw up a prenuptial agreement.	No action needed. Relax with a pot of tea. *(But read Chapter 6 first to make sure there isn't some specific legal protection that is important to you, after all.)*

Potential Issue: **Language**	**I WANT TO GET LEGALLY MARRIED**	**I DON'T WANT TO GET LEGALLY MARRIED**
I want to be able to say "my husband" or "my wife" like everyone else does.	Get married. As soon as the officiant says, "I now pronounce you husband and wife," you're golden.	There's no rule against it. You can introduce each other as husband and wife and consider yourselves spiritually married, even if you're not legally married. *(Note: Read up on common-law marriages first, page 147. If you live in a state that recognizes common-law marriages, write and sign a statement saying you do not intend to form one before you represent yourselves as married.)*
I can't stand the thought of being called "husband" or "wife."	Get married, but find other words that work better for you like partner, mate, or spouse. *(See page 117 for a list of ideas.)*	Find and use a word that works for you, or use different words for different situations. *(See page 117 for a list of ideas.)*

OTHER ISSUES: Fill in Your Own Here	I WANT TO GET LEGALLY MARRIED	I DON'T WANT TO GET LEGALLY MARRIED

HOW IT WORKS OUT FOR ONE IMAGINARY COUPLE
(with a choose-your-own ending)

FOR MONTHS, TARA and Travis have been avoiding the issue of whether they will get married. Travis would like to propose to Tara, but from things she's said, he has the sense that she may not be enthusiastic about getting engaged. Tara is frustrated that Travis is always hinting about marriage—doesn't he see they already have everything they need to be happy? Travis is baffled as to why Tara always gets so upset when he talks about making her his wife. Aren't women always saying they want a guy to commit to them? If she really loves him like she says she does, why won't she marry him?

Tara and Travis finally decide to sit down separately and each make a list of some of the issues they've been thinking about marriage. Here's what their lists look like:

Why Travis Wants To Get Married

1. I want Tara to know how much I love her. I can think of no better way to show her, and the world, than to marry her.
2. I want to have children some day, and I want them to have the legal protections that marriage brings.
3. I want my parents to welcome and include Tara the same way they include my brother's wife as part of the family.

Why Tara Doesn't Want To Get Married

1. I love how romantic and fair our relationship feels. Somehow becoming Travis' *wife* makes me feel like I should spend all my time wearing an apron.
2. All my friends who got married ended up getting divorced soon afterward. As far as I'm concerned, if it ain't broke, don't fix it. I love Travis too much to risk ruining our relationship by getting married.
3. I am a total introvert, as Travis knows. I do not want to stand in front of all those people at a wedding—I'd probably faint before Travis got to kiss the bride.
4 Travis' last name is O'Hara—how will I ever be taken seriously with a name like Tara O'Hara?

Tara and Travis sit down together and read each other's lists. Tara is touched that Travis' list says he wants to marry her because he loves her, and because he wants his family to include her. Travis is surprised to see that Tara's list reveals that she loves him so much that she *doesn't* want to get married. And he had never even thought about the "Tara O'Hara" problem. Tara and Travis draw up a Marriage Decision Tool and get to work filling in the boxes and talking about the options they generate.

Choose Your Own Ending Number One

Tara and Travis read up on the legal protections for kids of unmarried parents, and Travis realizes that even if they don't get married, their children will have the same legal rights. They realize they can both be happy without getting married, if they have a small commitment ceremony but skip the marriage license. They'll hold it in a pretty field where they often walk near their house, and invite only their parents and siblings. After they exchange vows and rings, they'll take everyone out to dinner at their favorite Mexican restaurant. Tara is pretty sure she won't faint since the group is so small, and even if she does, she points out that the grass is so tall and soft she probably won't get a concussion. Travis says it never mattered to him whether Tara took his last name, so he readily agrees that they'll keep their different last names. Tara and Travis live happily ever after.

Choose Your Own Ending Number Two

Travis and Tara realize they could probably get married if they dealt with some of Tara's specific concerns. Travis reassures her that he'll continue to do the cooking if she'll continue to do the laundry, to maintain the balance they both like. They talk more about their friends who married and then quickly divorced, and Tara realizes that their situation is pretty different. She admits that she and Travis have known each other much longer than the friends who married and divorced, and that their own relationship has always been more stable. They decide to find a therapist who specializes in premarital counseling to help them talk through some of Tara's fears about the effects marrying could have on their relationship. Travis says it was never important to him to have a big wedding—in fact, they could go on a little vacation to some romantic, tropical place, have a little ceremony with just them and a justice of the peace, and only tell people about it after they came home. He knows his parents will be thrilled to hear that their son finally "did the right thing." Tara will keep her own name, though she says it would be OK with her if their future children are O'Haras ("as long as we don't name our daughters Sara or Clara," Travis laughs). They live happily ever after.

HAPPINESS ISN'T BASED ON WHETHER YOU MARRY

All the attention heaped on whether couples get married creates a false sense that the two marital statuses are worlds apart. In truth, whether or not you are married may matter very much to your mother, but it doesn't make much of a difference in daily life. Both married and unmarried partners benefit from having someone to remind them about a doctor's appointment or scratch the itch they can't reach. Both have to negotiate whether it's OK to squeeze the toothpaste tube in the middle and decide whether they're going to merge their bank accounts or not. The fact that people so often assume that unmarried different-sex couples are married reveals that when they walk down the street, the similarities between married and unmarried are more apparent than the differences.

There are plenty of valid reasons people don't marry—all the things in chapter 2. And there are plenty more valid reasons why people do. The point is to arrive at a decision that will feel right and keep your relationship going strong.

ELEVEN

FIRST COMES LOVE, THEN COMES LIVING TOGETHER:

Cohabitation's Past and Future

THE RATE OF unmarried cohabitation has skyrocketed over the last four decades. Where is it headed next? Will living together replace marriage as the preferred family form? Is cohabitation a temporary trend that can be reversed by those who oppose it?

Cohabitation is caught in a cultural tug-of-war. On the one hand, the general public has become increasingly tolerant, even blasé, about unmarried couples living together. Most neighbors don't bat an eyelash if a pair of unmarrieds moves in next door, and many parents encourage their children to live with a partner before getting married. At the same time, opponents of cohabitation have raised their voices loudly, blaming unmarried couples for the downfall of marriage and the family. Marital status discrimination remains a common occurrence. Too many couples and families—especially those who don't have the knowledge or forethought to take the kinds of steps described in chapter 6—are living lives absent legal protections.

What's missing amidst all the hullabaloo is a broader view of unmarried relationships. When one takes a step back to look beyond the United States and before the last 50 years, an entirely different picture emerges. In centuries and millennia gone by, as well as in other countries around the world today, relationships outside the definition of formal marriage were and are common. As many historians have documented, in most places and times, committed relationships were recognized as a valid form of intimate partnership. The historical precedent is clear: Cohabitation is not replacing marriage, nor is it a sign of the downfall of the family; it *is*—and always has been—a form of family.

THE PAST: SHACKING UP, A LONG TRADITION

To hear contemporary opponents of cohabitation explain it, you'd think living together and having sex before marriage were invented in the sexual revolution of the late 1960s. That is true only if you started paying attention in the 1950s. For most of the history of civilization, it really wasn't very clear—or very important—who was married. People have always had relationships and families, but before the invention of the marriage license, marital status checkboxes would have looked more like a hazy blur. Most, if not all, human societies had some concept of cohabitation that existed right alongside formal marriage. Today's unmarried couples who live together and *act* married would likely have been considered married—or at least had their relationship accepted as valid—in most communities of the past.[1]

For thousands of years, distinctions between cohabitation and marriage were made primarily when family interests or property were at stake. Differentiating between the two was important to wealthy families who needed to determine who would rightfully inherit a plot of land or a royal position, but it mattered less to most common folks.[2] In ancient Egypt, where there was no word for marriage and no religious or civil marriage ceremony, couples just moved in together, and that was that.[3] It wasn't much different for most couples in ancient Babylon: since the oldest legal system ever recorded specified that only the upper classes could marry, most people did not.[4] Ancient Romans chose between two kinds of marriage, both perfectly valid. While the more formal kind put the wife under the husband's control, the less formal variation gave women more independence, making it popular among the women of Rome. With no ceremony or license needed to declare yourself married, it would be difficult to say which couples were married and which cohabiting. The difference between the two statuses wasn't nearly as obvious or important as it has become today.[5]

Fine, you might say. Everyone knows about those decadent Romans with their banquets and baths—it's no surprise they were so laid back about marriage. But once the Christians and Jews came along, with their stone tablets and Bibles, surely things changed.

Actually, things didn't change anywhere near as quickly as you might guess. In early Judaism, couples married themselves, without any involvement by a religious institution. Committed unmarried relationships called *pilagshut* were considered a perfectly valid, upstanding alternative to marriage. Rabbis didn't get involved in wedding ceremonies until centuries later.[6] Likewise for Christianity, the Catholic Church wrote out its first formal rules about marriage in 774 A.D., and continued to debate and rewrite them for the next 500 years.[7]

Throughout medieval Europe, people had relationships, lived together, and raised families both within and without marriage. The Welsh would usually not marry until they had proof of compatibility from cohabitation, or proof of fertility from pregnancy.[8] Local community practices and traditions, not government edicts, determined which couples "counted" as married.[9] In places where marriage was restricted, unmarried relationships were considered perfectly acceptable. Even after the church began to regulate marriage in the twelfth century, people continued to make their own commitments, hold their own marriage rituals, and exchange tokens of love outside the control of any religious or state supervision. No one got married in a church until the fourteenth century, and even after that time, the law and many religious bodies treated couples equally whether they were married at a church wedding or through private agreements among the couple and their families.[10]

These private promises were so common that in one fourteenth century English town, 89 of the 101 marriages in the public register were created privately, like today's cohabitations, not with a public wedding. In the 1500s, between a third and half of Europeans were officially unmarried, but just like legally "single" people today, we know that many of them were living with a partner and having children.[11] In Scotland, England, and Wales, these long-term relationships, called "living tally" or "living over t'brush," were perfectly respectable among eighteenth century working-class families. Couples "married" themselves by jumping together over a broomstick slanted in a doorway. If things weren't working out, they could divorce themselves in the first year by jumping backward over the broom.[13] It was only in 1754 that England drew a clear line between marriage and cohabitation, by passing a law declaring the only valid marriages to be those established in churches by Anglican clergy.[14]

In North America during this time, informal marriages were also common among both Native American tribes and colonists. If a Lenape couple wanted to marry, they just set up a wigwam together. For Navajo, as long as the woman's family approved of the man, moving in with his wife's family was all it took to make a marriage official. And Tlingit couples along the Northwest coast routinely lived together before they were considered married.[15] Although each native culture was distinct, many shared broad acceptance of the idea that a couple's behavior and personal commitments were what married them.

Anthropologist Suzanne Frayser found that 28 percent of the societies she compared paid little or no public attention to marriage. In many, there was no way to distinguish between cohabitation and marriage.[12]

Among the colonists, neighbors and judges treated unmarried couples who lived together with the same respect they gave married couples. Sex before marriage wasn't unusual, and if a couple got pregnant, that was a good indication that they should start considering themselves married by making the appropriate verbal promises to each other. Communities and courts accepted these self-made marriages as equally valid as ones with church ceremonies.[16] During the Revolutionary era, a third of first children were conceived before marriage.[17] Some colonies recognized a form of quasi-marriage called "handfast" marriage, where a man and woman made promises to each other and then had sex. If she got pregnant within a year, their relationship automatically upgraded to a regular marriage. If not, they could end the relationship hassle-free if they chose.[18]

The 1800s ushered in the Victorian era, with its lacy romance and its passion for morality, as well as a small free love movement, complete with communes and antimarriage propaganda (more about them in chapter 2). While the two groups had wildly divergent views about the meaning and structure of marriage, both advanced the idea that love and affection should be the primary reason to have a relationship.[19] It was only during this century that the kind of marriage we take for granted today, where a couple must sign a marriage license in order to have their relationship receive legal recognition, became common. Church ceremonies rather than self-written promises became the standard route to matrimony.[20]

In the twentieth century, employment increasingly moved from farms to factories. The population of cities exploded, giving young people unprecedented social and financial independence from their families. There were so many profound changes to intimate relationships that the early 1900s came to be known as the "first sexual revolution." Dating as we know it was born, with courtship moving from front porches to dance halls and movie houses.[22] The use of birth control became widespread, and the generation born between 1900 and 1909 was the first in which most women in the United States had sex before they married.[23] Young people became increasingly free to work and play together without formal courtship.

At the same time, a new level of urgency emerged about making sure people got *properly* married, which meant making sure every couple who shared a home had a marriage license on file at City Hall. Following the new model of workplace regulations, government became increasingly involved in the regulation of marriage, working to distinguish it from other types of relationships. Reformers narrowed the once-broad definition of family so that only married couples would count, and courts began to require proof that couples' marriages were formally created. The concept of common-law marriage, where couples became married just by living together and considering themselves husband and wife, came under attack because it was like a do-it-yourself stamp of approval. One writer called common-law marriage "suspiciously near the borderland of illicit intercourse."[24]

While neither cohabitation nor sex before marriage disappeared entirely in the 1940s and 1950s, a unique set of social, economic, and political factors created a decade unlike any before or since. The post-war economic boom, generous government benefits and loans, and the development of the interstate highway system created opportunities for families to pursue the new American dream of a home in the suburbs.[25] The proliferation of television sets in American living rooms in the 1950s beamed images of *Leave It To Beaver* and *Father Knows Best*, creating a universal image of what was considered a "normal" family.[26] Marriage rates hit an all-time high, and the average age at marriage dropped to a 100-year low. Thanks in part to governmental and parental willingness to subsidize young couples' homes and educations, more couples no longer needed to wait until the man could afford to support the family.[27]

This unusual period did not last long. In 1968 when a Barnard College student moved in with her boyfriend, the school tried to expel her, and the story was so titillating it got covered on television, in *Time* and *Newsweek*, and in 11 different articles in the *New York Times*.[28] But by the late 1970s there were so many people doing the same thing that the Census Bureau realized the need to track this demographic trend. It invented the concept of "POSSLQ" (People of the Opposite Sex Sharing Living Quarters) to get estimated counts, although this POSSLQ category had no way to distinguish between roommates and intimate partners.[29]

By the early 1980s, cohabitation was so widely acceptable that many parents advised their children not to marry someone unless they'd lived together first.[30] A 1987 survey found that most high school seniors agreed that cohabiting before tying the knot was a good idea.[31] In 1990 the Census finally stopped guessing which "roommates" were sleeping in the same bed and added a new " unmarried partners" checkbox for a more accurate count.

Even if they tried, TV cameras could no longer keep up with the masses of people who move into their honey's apartments each day with toothbrushes, pets, and china collections in tow. While the change seems dramatic lined up next to the young brides and grooms of the 1950s, put today's cohabitors next to a couple of ancient Egyptians or medieval Europeans and you might just chalk up another one for the more things change, the more they stay the same. The Census says that 11 million people are living with an unmarried partner in the United States, a 72 percent increase since 1990.[33] Almost half of women under age 45 have cohabited at some point. Today, couples who move in together *after* the wedding are a minority.[34]

In Jamaica there are more cohabiting couples than married ones.[32]

Increase in Different-Sex Unmarried Couples in the U.S., 1960–2000[35]

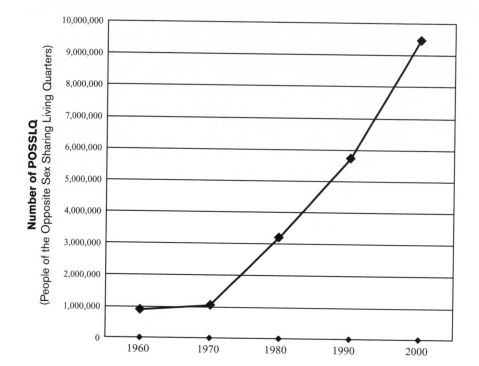

THE DEATH OF MARRIAGE
IS GREATLY EXAGGERATED

WE GET A lot of calls from TV producers who want us to be on shows with topics like "Is Marriage Dead?" They're often surprised to learn that, no, we *don't* think marriage is dead, nor do we have any interest in killing it. Most unmarried people want to get married, even if they live together first, and 9 out of 10 people marry at least once in their lives.[36]

But it turns out that fears about the future of marriage date back at least 500 years, and probably even further. For all we know, there could be cave art and Egyptian hieroglyphics warning that the institution is doomed if today's young people don't shape up and settle down. Below are some of our favorite examples of those who have prematurely written marriage's obituary in past and recent centuries. See if you can match the quotes on the left with the years they were written or spoken.

1522, 1859, 1907, 1933, 1977, 1985, 1995, 2002

1. "Will the family, that institution which we have long
   regarded as the unit of civilization . . . survive? . . .
   The home made by one man and one woman bound
   together 'until death do ye part' has in large measure
   given way to trial marriage." _____

2. "Marriage has universally fallen into awful disrepute." _____

3. "Marriage is under assault in our society. It is an
   institution in decline and even disrepute." _____

4. "The family, long supposed to be the best anchored
   of all social institutions, appears to have at last broken
   from its moorings" _____

5. "At no time in history, with the possible exception of
   Imperial Rome, has the institution of marriage been
   more problematic than it is today." _____

6. "The family, in its old sense, is disappearing from our
   land, and not only our free institutions but the very
   existence of society is endangered." _____

7. "Marriage is doomed and will be virtually extinct
   within 30 years, according to the country's leading
   relationship experts." _____

8. "By mid-[specific year] not one American family
   will be left." _____

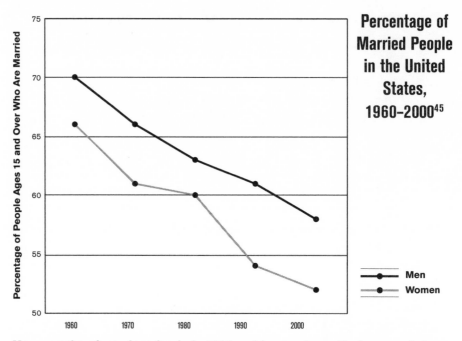

Percentage of Married People in the United States, 1960–2000[45]

Many graphs of marriage begin in 1960 and have a dramatic downward slope, apparently demonstrating marriage's impending demise. But one's perspective changes dramatically if you take a longer view. . . .

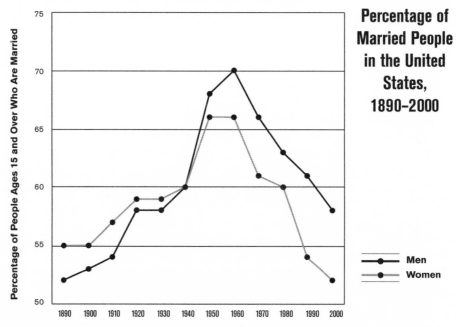

Percentage of Married People in the United States, 1890–2000

By graphing marriage since 1890, it becomes clear that today's rates may simply be a return to norms of a previous era.

THE PRESENT: COHABITATION BY THE NUMBERS

While we may all check off the same box on the Census form, the differences between cohabitors who clean their nose rings and those who clean their dentures isn't captured in a single number. Here's what the research says about all the households where people are unmarried to each other.[46]

- One in 10 are same-sex partners, and the other 9 are different-sex partners.[47]
- There are cohabitors in every age bracket. While more cohabitors are between 25 and 34 than any other age group; there are also many younger than 25 and between 35 and 64. As one would expect, the oldest generation doesn't cohabit as much, since in their day "shacking up" meant you'd ruin your reputation. But even there, things are changing: between 1990 and 2000 the number of senior citizen cohabitors tripled.[48] As younger generations age, they continue to be accepting of cohabitation, so in another generation or two there are likely to be significantly more gray-haired couples living together before, after, or instead of marriage.

Age of POSSLQ Householders, 1999[49]

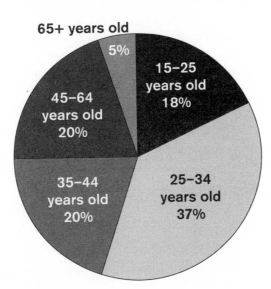

65+ years old
5%

15–25 years old
18%

45–64 years old
20%

35–44 years old
20%

25–34 years old
37%

- People of all races and ethnic groups cohabit. Caucasian, African-American, and Latino people live with their partners at about the same rates, and Asian-Americans at slightly lower ones.[50]
- Although the popular image of cohabitors is a childfree one, about half of different-sex unmarried couples of childbearing age are living with kids, as are 13 percent of same-sex couples.[51]
- More than half of unmarried partner households include at least one partner who has been married before.[52]

Cohabitation has become so commonplace that in a broad article summing up the research, sociologist Pamela Smock writes, "Instead of asking, 'who cohabits?' we might ask, 'who does not cohabit?'"[53] But living together means different things to different people. For same-sex couples, moving in together can signify the ultimate level of commitment, since "upgrading" to legal marriage isn't an option. More than three-quarters of different-sex couples who move in together plan to get married someday,[54] so for them cohabiting isn't a rejection of marriage, but a way of easing into it. Within five years of living together, about 53 percent of different-sex couples convert their cohabitations into legal marriages. Another 38 percent break up, realizing they're not a good match for a lifetime commitment.[55]

Ten percent of different-sex couples stay together and unmarried to each other five years or more, accumulating in the cohabitor pool so that one in five existing cohabitors falls into this "long-term" category.[56] Sociologists and demographers don't have much to tell this group about themselves, because there's so little data available on them that to this day no researcher has ever been able to focus on people in long-term unmarried relationships. Some of these folks are just taking the slow road toward marriage: Everyone seems to know somebody who got hitched after living together for 10 or 20 years. Lots of others have decided not to marry at all.

COHABITATION NATION

THE PERCENTAGE OF unmarried partner households grew in every state between 1990 and 2000. The most recent data shows that Vermont leads the country with the highest percentage of couples living together, while Alabama comes in last. Interestingly, the states with smaller percentages of unmarried partners, many in the South and Midwest, saw the greatest increases during the decade. This trend suggests they're playing catch-up to states that already have larger unmarried partner populations. The ranking below includes both same-sex and different-sex couples.[57]

Top Ten States: Highest Percentage of Unmarried Partner Households

1. Vermont
2. Alaska
3. Maine
4. Nevada
5. New Hampshire
6. New Mexico
7. Oregon
8. Arizona
9. Washington
10. Delaware[58]

Top Ten States: Largest Increase in Unmarried Partner Households Between 1990 and 2000

1. Arkansas
2. Mississippi
3. Tennessee
4. Kentucky
5. Idaho
6. West Virginia
7. South Carolina
8. North Dakota
9. North Carolina
10. Alabama[59]

THE FUTURE: WE ARE FAMILY

There's no question that both cohabitation and marriage are here to stay—most people say they want both, at different times in their lives. Given that cohabitation has been around as long as marriage has, it's not likely to be eliminated by any amount of moralizing. The question that does remain, though, is whether laws and social customs in the United States will recognize and support unmarried relationships, or continue to target them with stigma, prejudice, and discrimination.

Since the recent increase in cohabitation is an international phenomenon, other countries present two possible policy approaches. In the first category are Canada, France, and Sweden, which have already overhauled their legal codes so that references to "spouse" also pertain to unmarried partners, or so that partners who meet certain criteria can register and gain "marital" rights. Also moving toward this first category are Australia, Belgium, Ireland, Mexico, New Zealand,

MOST POPULAR CITIES TO LIVE TOGETHER

UNMARRIED PARTNERS LIVE everywhere, including remote rural areas, small towns, and suburbs. But cities, with their size and diversity, are where one finds the largest numbers of cohabitors. There are 311,442 cohabitors in New York City, 165,380 in Los Angeles, and 125,288 in Chicago. Of the 50 largest cities in the country, below are the ones with the highest percentages of unmarried partner households, and the highest percentages of cohabitors of various races. Both same-sex and different-sex couples are included.

Where Are the Cohabitors?

Cities with the Highest Percentages of Unmarried Partner Households Among All Households

1. Portland, OR
2. Seattle, WA
3. Minneapolis, MN
4. Long Beach, CA
5. Oakland, CA
6. Phoenix, AZ
7. San Francisco, CA
8. Fresno, CA
9. Sacramento, CA
10. Milwaukee, WI[60]

Where Are the Hispanic/Latino Cohabitors?

Cities with the Highest Percentages of Unmarried Partner Households Among Hispanic or Latino Households

1. Miami, FL
2. Fresno, CA
3. San Antonio, TX
4. Albuquerque, NM
5. Los Angeles, CA
6. El Paso, TX
7. Long Beach, CA
8. Tucson, AZ
9. Phoenix, AZ
10. Houston, TX[61]

Where Are the African-American Cohabitors?

Cities with the Highest Percentages of Unmarried Partner Households
Among African-American Households

1. Detroit, MI
2. Baltimore, MD
3. New Orleans, LA
4. Atlanta, GA
5. Memphis, TN
6. Cleveland, OH
7. St. Louis, MO
8. Washington, DC
9. Milwaukee, WI
10. Philadelphia, PA[62]

Where Are the Asian-American Cohabitors?

Cities with the Highest Percentages of Unmarried Partner Households
Among Asian-American Households

1. Honolulu, HI
2. San Francisco, CA
3. San Jose, CA
4. Sacramento, CA
5. Oakland, CA
6. Seattle, WA
7. Long Beach, CA
8. San Diego, CA
9. Los Angeles, CA
10. Fresno, CA[63]

Cohabitation isn't just limited to the big cities, though. In Peoria, Illinois there are 4,870 unmarried partners and in Biloxi, Mississippi 2,096. Even in Eldora, Iowa, a corn and soybean farming community with only 1,193 households in the whole town, forty-nine homes have an unmarried couple living together inside. It's easy to research how many unmarried partners live in your town, county, or state—we explain how to do it at www.unmarriedtoeachother.com/census/.

Norway, South Africa, Uganda, and the United Kingdom, all of which have either taken initial steps toward broader recognition, or are currently engaged in national debates about how to best reconcile the gap between the lives of real people and the laws on the books.[64] At the other end of the spectrum, countries like Nigeria and the United Arab Emirates still sentence women and couples to imprisonment, public floggings, or death by stoning for the crimes of cohabitation and unmarried sex.[65]

The policies of the United States lie somewhere in the middle. We don't flog unmarried couples in this country, thank goodness, but our legal system is still a long way from recognizing that, as the popular bumper stickers say, "Love Makes a Family." Every indication suggests the U.S. is moving toward increasing acceptance of unmarried people. Most children who play the card game Old Maid today don't even know what an old maid is, and "spinster" sounds positively quaint, a word from another era. There's widespread agreement that consenting adults should be allowed to have sex even if they're not married, that unmarried pregnant women should be allowed to keep their babies, and that children should be treated equally regardless of their parents' marital status.

According to a Harris poll, 90 percent of all people believe society "should value all types of families."[66] It shouldn't surprise anyone that most people believe supporting family diversity is inherently right. All they need to do is look around their neighborhoods, or their own kitchen tables, for the evidence that people in all kinds of relationships—married and unmarried, straight and gay, childfree and stroller-filled—can be happy, healthy, and productive. Even the ones who are bitterly opposed to cohabitation can't keep it from seeping into their personal lives. At a conference on marriage that Marshall attended:

> It was lunchtime, and I went searching for a place to sit to eat my boxed lunch provided by the conference. I saw an open seat at a table, sat down, and introduced myself to the others already seated there. Upon hearing about the work that I do, the woman seated to my left launched into a 20-minute monologue about the evils of cohabitation. I ate my lunch and listened to her quietly—and then when she was finished she added that her son is about to move in with his girlfriend.

Now that cohabitation has become the norm, it's difficult for anyone, anywhere in the country, anywhere on the political spectrum, to keep a distance from it. Living with the person you love simply feels intuitively right for too many people.

So the public overwhelmingly approves of cohabitation. Demographic trends have moved in this direction all over the world. Returning to an era where living together was scandalous and marriage was the only acceptable way for adults to organize their families seems about as likely as convincing people to give up their remote controls and return to changing the channel with a television knob.

Yet on a daily basis, unmarried people are denied access to health insurance, partners are shut out of hospital rooms, couples have faith communities slam doors in their faces, unmarried couples who are citizens of different countries are prevented from being together, and people lose their homes when their partner dies without a will. Although the Census counts married couples without children as "families," it groups equivalent unmarried partner households under the heading "nonfamilies," a symbolic act of exclusion. Similarly, some well-connected political groups, who have the ear of elected officials and policymakers, have framed the issue as if people forming loving relationships without wedding rings (for most of them, temporarily) are somehow a threat to family life. Some pundits openly recommend that parents, businesses, and government agencies discriminate against unmarried couples.[68] Some states have even begun to punish unmarried poor people and their children by making them eligible for fewer benefits and mandating they be counseled to marry.[69]

Fourteen percent of cohabitors under age 35 say they don't expect ever to marry anyone.[67]

It makes sense to assume that eventually, the U.S. will end up with a system less like Nigeria's and more like Canada's, which is working to treat most types of families fairly and equally regardless of marital status or sexual orientation. If that's where the U.S. is likely to wind up, what is the fastest, most effective route to ensuring fairness for all kinds of relationships, married or not? How can we use the momentum of demographics and popular opinion to create a society that treats people in unmarried families with respect and dignity? And how much more damage will be done to children and families in the intervening time before we update the archaic social and legal codes?

During the time that interracial marriage was illegal, many white and black people lived together in long-lasting unmarried relationships throughout the South.[70]

We unmarried folks have a lot to learn from other movements for justice and social change. Movements for the rights of African-Americans, women, and gay, lesbian, bisexual, and transgender people—driven by regular people who organized against the unfairness they saw in their lives—have changed the world profoundly in the last century. Each of these movements has broadened the way we think about families, so that interracial couples can now marry, women are legally and socially recognized as individuals regardless of whether they have husbands, and gay and lesbian couples can legally be considered co-parents. We owe a great deal to the accomplishments of these ongoing social movements. It's time for unmarried people to take the next step by recognizing marital status as a social justice issue, and working together to address it.

EXPANDING THE VISION:
UNMARRIEDS AROUND THE WORLD

SWEDEN IS UNDOUBTEDLY the cohabitation leader of the world. There, nearly every couple lives together before marriage—if they get married at all.[71] The Swedish marriage rate is half of ours in the U.S.[72] The Swedes even have a word, *sambo*, for which we have no equivalent in English: it means cohabiting partner. Fifty-five percent of Swedish babies are born to unmarried parents compared to one-third of American babies,[73] yet—in news puzzling to those who uphold marriage as the solution to poverty—Sweden's child poverty rate is one-seventh that of the U.S.[74] Low marriage rates and high cohabitation rates haven't caused the downfall of civilization there—quite the contrary. At least partly because Sweden makes supporting all children and families a priority, it has lower rates of rape and robbery, lower child mortality rates, and overall better health and longer life expectancies than the U.S.[75]

Anna Gavanas, a Swedish anthropologist who studies the marriage debates in the United States, says the people and governments of the two countries approach the subject of marriage entirely differently. "In Sweden, cohabitation is equivalent to marriage," she says. "Cohabiting couples have the same rights as married ones, and cohabiting couples are viewed as having made a commitment to each other." When asked whether Swedish people know they're different from the United States in this respect, she hesitates. "It's the Americans who are extreme in the modern world," she says. "It's not Sweden that's different—Americans should know that they are different. Nowadays most European countries have domestic partnership."[76]

Indeed, in the last decade marriage rates fell in Austria, Belgium, Bulgaria, France, Germany, Greece, Ireland, Italy, Portugal, Spain, and the United Kingdom, just to name a few.[77] In 2001 the Swiss marriage rate fell faster in a single year than it had in the previous 80 years.[78] The percentage of births to unmarried parents rose in fourteen of the fifteen European Union countries in the last ten years, and the percentage of births to unmarried parents is now 39 percent or more in a third of these nations.[79] Marriage rates are changing in other parts of the world, too: Australia, China, and Israel all had decreased rates over the last decade.[80] The number of unmarried parents in Japan grew 85 percent in the last five years alone.[81]

Although the demographic trends are similar, many countries have done far more to revise their law books to keep up with the changes. France, Hungary, the Netherlands, Portugal, and Sweden have all created systems that give unmarried same-sex and different-sex couples rights similar to married ones, and at least five other countries have partnership registries open only to same-sex or only to different-sex couples.[82] Whether the polices are called registered partnerships, de facto unions, common law marriages, civil solidarity unions, or some other term, policymakers around the world are finding ways to give unmarried families legal standing.[83]

Here in North America, when it comes to recognizing unmarried relationships, Canadians are nearing the finish line while Americans stand around arguing about which direction to run. The number of different-sex cohabiting partners more than doubled in Canada between 1981 and 1996[84]—in Quebec, one out of four different-sex couples is cohabiting. After a 1999 Canadian Supreme Court decision found that Ontario's family law discriminated against same-sex couples, Canada passed a law that makes unmarried same-sex and different-sex couples identical to married couples under federal law. Canada's provinces are in the process of making similar revisions, so that married and unmarried couples are treated similarly within the country's tax, pension, and criminal justice systems.[85]

While Canadian and European public policies are increasingly returning to a system that makes few distinctions between married and cohabiting couples, most American laws still cling to the differentiation. As Americans catch up, our challenges will be to recognize the overlaps and similarities between both kinds of relationships, as people have in most parts of the world throughout history.

▶ Taking Action

There is power in numbers, and there's no question unmarried partners have the numbers needed to bring change. With 11 million people—more than the populations of New York City and Chicago combined—we could be a voting block that would make politicians turn their heads. That is, if only we asked them to pay attention. Despite our huge numbers, unmarried people have only recently begun to recognize ourselves as a constituency with experiences and needs in common. At our speaking engagements, we have seen audiences of young feminists and senior citizens talk to gay couples and unmarried parents, discovering unexpected areas of shared experience based on their marital status. Talking with each other, learning from each other's perspectives, and identifying which issues are priorities for our community are essential first steps.

If you want to get people talking, start a local group. Spread the word about your first gathering among your friends, in the paper, to local colleges, and to organizations with overlapping interests. Once you have a few people around the same kitchen table or library meeting room, get to know each other. What draws each of you to this issue? What concerns are closest to your hearts? One group might decide they need to start with a discussion group; another might organize a letter-writing campaign in response to some pending legislation; a third might decide that an attention-getting Valentine's Day celebration of all kinds of loving relationships would be a great way to gain visibility. There's no one perfect plan of action; what matters, instead, is that all around the country, small groups of people are doing something. The impact of our collective action will make a difference.

WHAT LAWS NEED TO BE CHANGED?

THE U.S. HAS a long way to go to update its legal code to treat all families fairly. As a place to start, adopting the 10 changes below would be a giant step forward.

1. Equalize laws so that privileges, benefits, and responsibilities that impact spouses on the federal, state, and municipal levels apply equally to registered domestic partners.

2. Pass laws prohibiting marital status discrimination on the federal, state, and municipal levels, particularly in areas like housing, insurance, and employment. Ensure that these laws protect both married and unmarried people.

3. Amend federal and state income tax laws so that tax is not based on marital status. Eliminate both marriage penalties and marriage bonuses. Change the tax code so that domestic partner benefits are not considered taxable income, just as spousal benefits are not taxed.

4. Follow the lead of forward-thinking cities across the country by requiring employers who contract with states and municipalities to provide the same benefits (including health, pension and life insurance, and family leave) to the families of unmarried employees as they do to the families of married employees.

5. Establish some legal standing for co-parents and unmarried "step-parents" who live with a child, function as a parent, and have the consent of the child's legal parents to receive such standing. Ensure custody and visitation rights for these co-parents.

6. Remove all financial incentives and disincentives to marriage from federal, state, and municipal laws, so that individuals, not accountants, decide whether marriage is best for them.

7. Grant same-sex couples the right to marry and to have their marriages recognized in every state.

8. Repeal all laws prohibiting unmarried cohabitation, consensual sodomy, fornication, and other sex between consenting adults.

9. Require that any fee-charging company or agency (rental car companies, condominiums, etc.) charge same-sex and different-sex unmarried domestic partners the same thing that spouses are charged.

10. Use the same eligibility requirements and provide equal benefits to all two-parent families in low-income public assistance programs, regardless of their marital status, sex, and sexual orientation.

Even without a group, there's plenty you can do to advance the cause. Some of the most important activism can be done on an individual level by enlightening workplaces, modifying campus policies, helping friends at church understand, and advocating for other seemingly small, local changes that increase basic fairness and quality of life for unmarried partners. You can work toward changes of this kind during the informal interactions in everyday life.

Engage the people you know in conversations about what you've been thinking about, and speak up against marital status discrimination. Have a conversation with your boss in a meeting, with your friends over coffee or a beer, or with your extended family at dinnertime. Explain to the health club clerk why you think their family membership policy needs to be updated. Tell your doctor how adding a "partnered" checkbox on her patient forms would give her more accurate information and make you feel like you belong. Find out whether your workplace provides equal pay for equal work by offering the same benefits to employees' partners as to their spouses. A single conversation may not change the world, but if you're the third person this week to raise the issue at your doctor's office, she may just scribble a note to the person who designs the forms, "For next revision of patient intake form: add 'partnered' to marital status choices." You never know where you might create change until you try.

WHO IS FAMILY?

PART OF THE challenge to recognizing diverse family structures within the legal system is defining who counts as family. The Vanier Institute of the Family, a Canadian research and advocacy organization, came up with this wordy but wonderful definition, which could serve as a model for agencies trying to revise the old "marriage, blood, or adoption" system.

Any combination of two or more persons who are bound together over time by ties of mutual consent, birth and/or adoption placement, and who, together, assume responsibilities for variant combinations of some of the following:

- *physical maintenance and care of group members*
- *addition of new members through procreation or adoption*
- *socialization of children*
- *social control of members*
- *production, consumption and distribution of goods and services*
- *affective nurturance, love.*[86]

While you're thinking about small changes, don't forget about the government policies that shape our lives. Encourage your local legislators to expand the legal definition of family, so that families are recognized as people linked by emotional and financial care and interdependency, not limited to those connected by marriage, blood, or adoption. Make sure that when local politicians talk about "family values," they remember that *your* family is part of their constituency, too. When pending legislation would give state employees domestic partner benefits or repeal the state's law against cohabitation, find out how you can get involved to fight for its passage. Since there's no single law that could revise the definition of "family" everywhere at once, laws need to be updated one at a time.

Unmarried couples obviously stand to gain if our relationships are understood and recognized, but we're not marching alone under the family diversity banner. Some of the biggest supporters of the movement for fairness for all kinds of families are married people. Solo singles, who aren't in relationships, also have a major stake in whether or not unmarried people are treated fairly. And of course the coalition includes stepfamilies, divorced people, single parents, GLBT people, adoptive and foster families, and many others.

One of America's strengths is its diversity, which includes not only a wide range of races, ethnicities, creeds, abilities, genders, and sexual orientations, but also a range of family forms. At this moment in history we stand poised to decide when and how we will accept the challenge to respect, honor, and celebrate this diversity. As individuals and as a nation, it is our moral and ethical obligation to work toward creating happy, healthy, loving relationships and families for all people, married and unmarried.

In the fairy tales, all princes and princesses are married by the end of the book. In real life, marriage is the route to happiness for many, but others would rather ride off into rosy unmarried sunsets. Whatever your path, may your life be a journey toward happily ever after.

PERMISSIONS

Grateful acknowledgment is made for permission to reprint previously published material:

"Abelard and Heloise Surprised by the Abbot Fulbert" (detail) by Jean Vignaud, 1819. Reprinted by permission of the Joslyn Art Museum, Omaha, Nebraska.

"Agreement To Share Property" by Ralph Warner; Toni Ihara, and Frederick Hertz from *Living Together: A Legal Guide for Unmarried Couples*, 11th edition, copyright © 2001 by Toni Ihara and Ralph Warner. Reprinted by permission of Nolo.

Carlton Greeting Card #USA250 CV53823/2931010 by Carlton Cards. Reproduced by permission. American Greetings Corporation © AGC, Inc.

Cartoon MNO0238 by Marc Tyler Nobleman, copyright © by Marc Tyler Nobleman. Reprinted by permission of Cartoonstock.com.

"Johnny's Room" by Gunnar Madsen and Richard Greene from *My, I'm Large*, copyright © 1984 by Gunnar Madsen and Richard Greene. Reprinted by permission of Best of Breed Music.

"Number of Employers That Offer Domestic Partner Health Benefits, by Year" by the Human Rights Campaign Foundation, from *The State of the Workplace for Lesbian, Gay, Bisexual and Transgender Americans 2001*, copyright © 2001 by the Human Rights Campaign Foundation. Reprinted by permission of the Human Rights Campaign Foundation.

"Other Things You Can Call This Event" by Tess Ayers and Paul Brown from *The Essential Guide to Lesbian and Gay Weddings*, copyright © 1999 by Tess Ayers and Paul Brown. Reprinted by permission of Alyson Books.

"POSSLQ" from *There's Nothing I Wouldn't Do If You Would Be My POSSLQ* by Charles Osgood, © 1981 by CBS, Inc. Reprinted by permission of Henry Holt and Company, LLC.

Cartoon 24963 © The New Yorker Collection from cartoonbank.com. All Rights Reserved.

Photograph of Emma Goldman, courtesy of the Emma Goldman Papers, University of California, Berkeley.

ACKNOWLEDGMENTS

Unmarried to Each Other is a far better book thanks to the significant contributions of a remarkable group of our friends and colleagues. It took shape in the context of a community, surrounded by people dedicated to the idea that unmarried partners deserve supportive, useful, accurate information.

We are deeply indebted to Janie Fronek, who wrote us pages of insightful feedback on our earliest and final drafts, and had no idea what she was getting into when she innocently emailed, "If you guys have any specific research questions, I'd be happy to take a stab at them." We send heartfelt thanks to Ashton Applewhite for sassy wit and extraordinary wordsmithing in chapter after chapter. And our manuscript would not have been even *close* to on time if it had not been for Laurie Nelson, who arrived in our lives at exactly the right moment and brought the skills and willingness to chase down all the minutiae that needed chasing.

We were honored to have some of the smartest people we know share their insights and feedback on chapters. The extensive comments of Stephanie Coontz, Paula Ettelbrick, Abigail Garner, John Kilguss, Lockhart Steele, and Alice Yew shifted our thinking in profound ways, substantially improving the chapters they read. Others provided invaluable assistance in their areas of expertise, challenging us to think in more complex ways, pointing out confusing passages, correcting our errors, filling in our omissions, reassuring us that we were on the right track, and telling us honestly when we weren't: Rev. Jory Agate, Constance Ahrons, Thomas Coleman, Nancy Cott, Sarah Gibb, John Gillis, Ellen Hendriksen, Rev. Barbara McKusick Liscord, Wendy Manning, Carmen Morales, Pamela Smock, Karen Sosnoski, Tracey Rogers, Ralph Warner, and Dan Woog.

Ulla Figwer, Woody Glenn, Kirsten Isgro, Deva Kyle, Jeremy Pittman, Sarah Wright, and others named above have been by our side from the beginning as part of the Alternatives to Marriage Project board of directors, grappling with marital status as a social justice issue. Their vision has shaped ours, their language and political analysis have improved the way we talk and think about unmarried issues, and their enthusiasm is inspirational.

Nina Lanza, Wendy Layton, Anna Levin, and Pam Williams generously helped with the massive task of transcribing hundreds of hours of taped interviews, and Liesel Kuhr's assistance with launching this book was invaluable. Thank you to The Puffin Foundation for providing funding to offset the costs of our research interviews, enabling us to interview a racially, economically, and geographically diverse pool of cohabitors.

It was a joy to work with Shelley Roth, our agent, who was a perceptive reader of our earliest drafts, and without whom we would not have found Matthew Lore, our editor and publisher. Matthew was a writer's dream: He "got it" from the very beginning, made first-rate judgment calls, provided sage guidance, and most of all, allowed us the freedom to write the book we believed needed to be written. Sue McCloskey, the assistant editor at Marlowe & Company, was a true help in navigating our way through the publishing process, as was Blanca Oliviery with the publicity process. Special thanks to the many people who provided turns of the phrase, opinions, title suggestions, research articles, key bits of advice, and especially support to us. These people included Nancy Abbott, Kate Acheson, Josh Albertson, Anthony Arnove, Craig Bailey, Kirsten Barrett, Judy Bradford, Philip Bradley, Eric Breuninger, Deb Brewster, Melinda Brown, Daren Bulley, Denton Cairnes, Jill Chambers, Arthur Cohen, Barbara Cox, Annette Crowley, Merry Cutler, Christopher de Beer, Tom Durocher, Mel Epstein, Luigi Ferrer, Judi Fitts, Bernie Flynn, Libby Garland, Sue Gautsch, Anna Gavanas, Arza Goldstein, Sarit Golub, Melaina Governatore, Cary Hardwick, Frederick Hertz, Ken Heskestad, Brett Hill, Jonathan Kang, Kathleen Kiernan, Mark Koyama, John Kremer, Gail Leondar-Wright, Joanne Liljeholm, Wilson Lo, Karen Loewy, Elizabeth Lott, Sharon Maccini, Connie Malamed, Jim Maynard, Mike Mirarchi, Maureen Marovitch, Ryam Nearing, Barry Northrup, Michael Palmer, Barry Pateman, Heidi Pelletier, Adam Pertman, Catherine Reuben, Louise Rice, Barbara Solot, Jane Schwartz, Pepper Schwartz, Stephen Shapiro, Bob Stein, Valerie Tobin, Rodney VanDerwarker, Jeff vom Saal, Robyn Wood, Dean Yang, Fred Zeytonjian, and others too numerous to name.

We send loving thanks to our parents, siblings, and grandparents, Suzanne Miller and Walter vom Saal, Buck and Gene Miller, Marjorie and Theodore Nickles, Evan and Vicki Solot, Peter and Eileen Hill, Gwynn Miller, Julia Nickles, Aly Solot, Ryan Solot and Miki Takeda, Seena and Harry Dreisbach, Dorothy Nickles, Elizabeth Scheuer, and Goldie and Leslie Solot, as well as many other wonderfully supportive relatives. Many of them read and responded helpfully to chapters, and all of them cheered us on during the years we were writing and long before.

Finally, this book is brought to life by the stories of real people who are "unmarried to each other." The hundreds of married and unmarried people across the country who talked with us in formal interviews, surveys, the Alternatives to Marriage Project's online discussion list, and in our lectures and workshops taught us most of what we know about unmarried relationships. These include interviewees Nick Alexander, Adam Armstrong, Kurt Ashton, Chip August, Johanna Bates, Sue Bennett, Bettykay, Anita Marie Bozelli, Lydia Breckon, Billy Brittingham, Melinda Brown, Vince Bruns, Roger Buelow, Dakota Butterfield, Anneke Campbell, Tori Carson, Chris Caswell, Sharon Collins, Barbara Columbo, Janna Cordeiro, Drew Curtis, Emily Darling, Marie Davis, Debbie Deem, Laina Dicker, Skip Drum, Linda Dyndiuk, Kay Fatica, Phil Fitzpatrick, Judy Foster, Lyn Freundlich, Jean Gasbarro, Pat Gasbarro, Amy Glesius, Cevero Gonzalez, Dave Goss, Pepper Greene, Anna Grissom, Alan Gross, Hillary Gross, Alan Hamilton, Annie Hoffman, Teri Hu, Michaela Hutfles, Jeremy Kagan, Deborah Kaplan, Tim Kelly, Kathy Labrioloa, John Lapham, Amy Lesen, Ed Lesen, Leslie Levy, Mark Lott, Joe Lowndes, Jenna Marshall, Mike Martak, Pepper Mint, Sue Montana, Erica Neuman, Wendy Patterson, Allen Peterson, Becky Pierce, Clarice Pollock, Arthur Prokosch, Mike Prokosch, Jim Riley, Shannon Spicer, Dan Sullivan, Teresa Eliot Roberts, Tom Schicker, Beth Eliot Schultz, Stacey Slaughter, Duncan Smith, Lou Sortman, Marijah Sroczynski, 'Becca Stallings, Billie Jo Stoddard, Sean Sullivan, Kathryn Swain, Jennifer Taub, Kim Tilbury, Sebastian Toomey, Valerie White, Joan Walsh, Jodi Warner, Ethan Weker, Martha Wilson, Priscilla Yamin, and many others mentioned earlier or who prefer not to use their full names. We owe each of these people great thanks for their willingness to share their lives so openly. Some have words scattered in quotes throughout the pages of the book, and all have provided wisdom that runs through every page.

NOTES

Introduction

[1] U.S. Census Bureau. "Table DP-1. Profile of General Demographic Characteristics of the United States: 2000." Washington, D.C., 2000a. U.S. Census Bureau. "UC-1. Unmarried-Couple Households, by Presence of Children: 1960 to Present." Washington, D.C., 2001a.

[2] Bumpass, Larry and Lu, Hsien-Hen. "Trends in Cohabitation and Implications for Children's Family Contexts in the United States." *Population Studies*, 54: 29–41, 2000.

[3] Kaeser, Gigi and Gillespie, Peggy. *Love Makes a Family: Portraits of Lesbian, Gay, Bisexual, and Transgender Parents and Their Families*. Amherst, MA: University of Massachusetts Press, 1999.

[4] U.S. Bureau of the Census. Current Population Reports, Series P20-537, "America's Families and Living Arrangements: March 2000," and earlier reports.

[5] Kirk, Laura Meade. "ACLU Appeals Judge's Denial of Adoption." *Providence Journal-Bulletin*, 23 October 1997.

[6] For more stories from unmarried people's lives, see www.unmarried.org/storiestold.html.

[7] Intersex Society of North America, www.isna.org. Fausto-Sterling, Anne. *Sexing the Body: Gender Politics and the Construction of Sexuality*. New York: Basic Books, 2000. Fausto-Sterling, Anne. "The Five Sexes: Why Male and Female Are Not Enough." *The Sciences*. New York Academy of Sciences, March/April 1993, pp. 20–24.

[8] Kreider, Rose and Fields, Jason. "Number, Timing, and Duration of Marriages and Divorces: 1996." *Current Population Reports*. Washington, D.C.: U.S. Census Bureau, 2002, p. 15.

[9] Bumpass and Lu, 2000.

Chapter 1: Shall We Live Together?

[1] Bumpass, Larry and Lu, Hsien-Hen. "Trends in Cohabitation and Implications for Children's Family Contexts in the United States." *Population Studies*, 54: 29–41, 2000.

[2] Bumpass and Lu, 2000. Kiernan, Kathleen. "Cohabitation and Divorce Rates Across Nations and Generations: Continuities, Changes, and Inter-Relations." In Chase-Lansdale, P.L., Kiernan, K., and Friedman, R., eds. *Potential for Change Across Lives and Generations: Multidisciplinary Perspectives*. Cambridge: Cambridge University Press, forthcoming.

[3] Hiebert, William. Interview, 30 April 2002.

[4] Kollman, Maya. Interview, 15 April 2002.

5 This is different from the number who are separated. Fields, Jason. "America's Families and Living Arrangements 2000." Washington, D.C.: U.S. Census Bureau, 2001.

6 Saunders, Nancy. Interview, 22 April 2002.

7 Morrison, Elizabeth. Interview, 24 April 2002.

8 Kollman, 2002.

9 Blaisure, Karen. Interview, 27 April 2002.

10 Blaisure, 2002.

11 Fariello, Chris. Interview, 23 April 2002.

12 Blaisure, 2002.

13 Manning, Wendy. "Childbearing in Cohabiting Unions: Racial and Ethnic Differences." *Family Planning Perspectives* 33: 217–33, 2001.

14 Blaisure, 2002.

15 Fariello, 2002.

16 Fariello, 2002.

17 Weber, Julia. Interview, 21 April 2002.

18 Blaisure, 2002.

19 Kollman, 2002.

20 Le Bourdais, Celine. Personal communication, October 2000.

21 Inspired by sexuality trainers Pamela Wilson and Wayne Pawlowski's *Journey*. Metropolitan Washington, D.C., 1999.

Chapter 2: "Why Aren't You Married?"

1 April. "We Want To Be Able To Spend More Time Together, Be Closer, and Do More Together." *The Stories of Unmarried People*. 25 August 2001. www.unmarried.org/storiestold.html. (6 June 2002).

2 Bumpass, Larry; Sweet, James; and Cherlin, Andrew. "The Role of Cohabitation in Declining Rates of Marriage." *Journal of Marriage and the Family* 53: 913–27, 1991.

3 Cohen, Kate. *A Walk Down the Aisle: Notes on a Modern Wedding*. New York: W. W. Norton & Company, 2001, p. 65.

4 Bumpass, Larry. "What's Happening to the American Family? Interactions Between Demographic and Institutional Change." *Demography* 27: 483–98, 1990.

5 Duff, Johnette and Truitt, George. *The Spousal Equivalent Handbook: A Legal and Financial Guide to Living Together*. Houston: Sunny Beach Publications, 1991, p. 25.

6 Gillis, John. *A World of Their Own Making: Myth, Ritual, and the Quest for Family Values*. Cambridge, MA: Harvard University Press, 1996, pp. 149–50. Ingraham, Chrys. *White Weddings: Romancing Heterosexuality in Popular Culture*. New York: Routledge, 1999, pp. 28–9.

7 "We Have Been Trying To Save for a Wedding We Want." *The Stories of Unmarried People*. 20 May 2001. www.unmarried.org/storiestold.html. (6 June 2002).

8 Curtis, Elizabeth and Marquez, Joey. "We Are Both 19." *The Stories of Unmarried People*. 17 October 2000. www.unmarried.org/storiestold2000.html. (6 June 2002).

9 Bumpass, Larry and Lu, Hsien-Hen. "Trends in Cohabitation and Implications for Children's Family Contexts in the United States." *Population Studies*, 54: 29–41, 2000.

10 Gallup, George, Jr. *The Gallup Poll: Public Opinion 1996*. Wilmington, DE: Scholarly Resources, Inc., 1997, p. 211. National Survey of Families and Households. "Feelings About Marriage, Dating, and Cohabitation: Unmarried Respondents Aged 18–35 Who Are Not Cohabiting, by Sex." Madison, WI: Center for Demography and Ecology, University of Wisconsin-Madison, 1994. In Chadwick, Bruce and Heaton, Tim. *Statistical*

Handbook on the American Family. Phoenix: The Oryx Press, 1999, p. 195. Roper Starch Worldwide Inc. "The 1995 Virginia Slims Opinion Poll: A 25-Year Perspective on Women's Issues." *Tobacco Documents Online*. 1995. http://tobaccodocuments.org/pm/2070648486-8599.html. (29 June 2002).

[11] Gies, Frances and Gies, Joseph. *Marriage and the Family in the Middle Ages*. New York: Harper and Row, 1987, p. 23. Howard, G. E. *The History of Matrimonial Institutions*, I. London, 1904, p. 270. Thrupp, John. *The Anglo-Saxon Home*. London, 1862, pp. 49–70. As cited in Gillis, John. *For Better, For Worse: British Marriages, 1600 to the Present*. New York: Oxford University Press, 1985, p. 18.

[12] Clarkberg, Marin; Stolzenberg, Ross; and Waite, Linda. "Attitudes, Values, and Entrance into Cohabitational Versus Marital Unions." *Social Forces* 74: 609–34, 1995. Lye, Diane and Waldron, Ingrid. "Attitudes Toward Cohabitation, Family, and Gender Roles: Relationships to Values and Political Ideology." *Sociological Perspectives* 40: 199–225, 1997.

[13] Ross, Catherine. "Marriage and the Sense of Control." *Journal of Marriage and the Family* 53:831–8, 1991.

[14] Loosilu. 19 August 2001. *Why Would Anyone Still Toss Their Bouquet?* www.indiebride. com/kvetch/messages/91/93.html?1024084492. (16 June 2002).

[15] Sweed, Phyllis. "Building Bridal Business." *Gifts and Decorative Accessories*. April 1998. www.findarticles.com/cf_0/m3183/n4_v99/20497014/print.jhtml. (16 June 2002).

[16] U.S. Census Bureau. Unpublished Tables B Marital Status and Living Arrangements: March 1998 (Update). *Current Population Reports*, P20–514. Washington, D.C., 1998. As cited in Smock, Pamela and Gupta, Sanjiv. "Cohabitation in Contemporary North America." In Booth, Alan and Crouter, Ann. *Just Living Together: Implications of Cohabitation on Families, Children, and Social Policy*. Mahwah, NJ: Lawrence Erlbaum Associates, 2002a, pp. 53–84.

[17] Lach, Jennifer. "The Consequences of Divorce." *American Demographics*, October 1999, p. 14. Kreider and Fields, 2002. Sweet, James and Bumpass, Larry. *American Families and Households*. New York: Russell Sage Foundation, 1987.

[18] *The Letters of Heloise and Abelard*. Trans. Betty Radice. London: Penguin, 1974, p. 113, as cited in Geller, Jaclyn. *Here Comes the Bride: Women, Weddings, and the Marriage Mystique*. New York: Four Walls Eight Windows, 2001, p. 65.

[19] Taylor, Barbara. *Eve and the New Jerusalem: Socialism and Feminism in the Nineteenth Century*. New York: Pantheon Books, 1983, pp. 185.

[20] Spurlock, John. *Free Love: Marriage and Middle-Class Radicalism in America, 1825–1860*. New York: New York University Press, 1988, pp. 79–81.

[21] Spurlock, 1998.

[22] Pateman, Carole. *The Sexual Contract*. Stanford, CA: Stanford University Press, 1988, p. 161. "Harriet Taylor." *Spartacus Educational*. 7 Dec. 2001. www.spartacus.schoolnet. co.uk/Wtaylor.htm. (13 June 2002).

[23] Cott, Nancy. *Public Vows: A History of Marriage and the Nation*, Harvard University Press, 2001, p. 127.

[24] Goldman, Emma. "Marriage and Love." *Anarchism and Other Essays*. 2nd edition. New York: Mother Earth Publishing Association, 1911, pp. 233–45.

[25] Cott, 2001, pp. 32, 184–5. "Voters Remove Interracial Marriage Ban." *Birmingham News*, 8 November 2000.

[26] Graff, E. J. *What Is Marriage For?* Boston: Beacon Press, 1999, p. 202.

[27] Modern Bride. *The Bridal Market Retail Spending Study: A $35 Billion Market for the 90s*. New York: Primedia, 1994. As cited in Ingraham, 1999, p. 49. Calculation by Dorian Solot.

[28] Blau, Francine; Kahn, Lawrence; and Waldfogel, Jane. "Understanding Young Women's Marriage Decisions: The Role of Labor and Marriage Market Conditions." Working Paper 7510. Cambridge, MA: National Bureau of Economic Research, 2000. Lewis, Raphael. "Is That Love in the Air? More People Are Saying 'I Do'." *Philadelphia Inquirer*, April 19, 1998.

[29] United States. The White House. National Economic Council Interagency Working Group on Social Security. *Women and Retirement Security*. Washington, D.C.: 27 October 1998.

[30] Litvak, Simi. Personal communication, 27 November 1999.

[31] Hannon, Kerry. "Congress Trying To Change Marriage Tax Penalty." *USA Today*, June 19, 1998.

[32] Garland, Libby. "Weddings: A Custom of Our People." *CLAL on Culture*. New York: National Jewish Center for Learning and Leadership, 2000.

[33] Thornton, Arland; Axinn, William; and Hill, Daniel. "Reciprocal Effects of Religiosity, Cohabitation, and Marriage." *American Journal of Sociology* 98: 628–51, 1992.

[34] Some Jewish scholars disagree that the Torah commands people to marry, pointing to evidence of unmarried relationships called *pilagshut* that can also be legitimate and holy. See Winkler, Gershon. *Sacred Secrets: The Sanctity of Sex in Jewish Law and Lore*. Northvale, NJ: Jason Aronson Inc., 1998, pp. 78–96.

[35] Fisher, Helen. *Anatomy of Love: The Mysteries of Mating, Marriage, and Why We Stray*. New York: Fawcett Columbine, 1992, pp. 115–6. Parker, Stephen. *Informal Marriage, Cohabitation and the Law 1750–1989*. New York: St. Martin's Press, 1990, p. 26.

[36] Rindfuss, Ronald and VandenHeuvel, Audrey. "Cohabitation: A Precursor to Marriage or an Alternative to Being Single?" *Population and Development Review* 16: 703–26, 1990.

[37] Fisher, 1992, p. 66.

[38] Barash, David and Lipton, Judith Eve. *The Myth of Monogamy: Fidelity and Infidelity in Animals and People*. New York: W. H. Freeman and Company, 2001.

[39] These people are not necessarily gay or lesbian. Gay and lesbian people can get legally married, but not to same-sex partners. Some marry to hide or deny their sexual orientation; others marry for practical reasons like immigration or health insurance.

[40] U.S. Census Bureau. "PCT14. Unmarried Partner Households by Sex of Partners." Washington, D.C., 2000b.

[41] Institute for Gay and Lesbian Strategic Studies. "IGLSS study shows US census count of unmarried partners leaves out many." Press Release. Amherst, MA, 2001.

[42] Boswell, John. *Same-Sex Unions in Premodern Europe*. New York: Vintage Books, 1995. Brain, Robert. *Friends and Lovers*. New York: Basic Books, Inc., 1976. Demian. "Marriage Traditions in Various Times and Cultures." *Partners Task Force for Gay and Lesbian Couples*, 23 June 2000. www.buddybuddy.com/mar-trad.html. (2 July 2000). Pasternak, Burton; Ember, Carol; and Ember, Melvin. *Sex, Gender, and Kinship: A Cross-Cultural Perspective*. Upper Saddle River, NJ: Prentice-Hall, 1997.

[43] Grady, Denise. "No Genetic Reason To Discourage Cousin Marriage." *New York Times*, 3 April 2002.

[44] Brown, Vicki. "No 'Straight' Marriages Allowed?" *Bay Windows*, 27 November 1997.

[45] Wolfe, Leanna. *Women Who May Never Marry: The Reasons, Realities, and Opportunities*. Marietta, GA: Longstreet Press, Inc., 1993, p. 27.

Chapter 3: When Others Disagree

[1] Laumann, Edward, et. al. *Social Organization of Sexuality: Sexual Practices In The United States*; Chicago: University of Chicago Press, 1994, pp. 502–3.

[2] Laumann, 1994. Table 3.4, p. 88–9.

[3] Kennedy, Pagan. "So . . . Are You Two Together?" *Ms. Magazine*, June 2001, pp. 75–9. For more smart analysis of the significance of nonsexual friendships, www. celebratefriendship.org.

[4] Kollman, Maya. Interview, 15 April 2002.

[5] "Sexless Cohabiting." 6 July 2001. http://pub72.ezboard.com/ flivingtogetherunmarriedfrm1.showMessage?topicID=5.topic. (22 April 2002).

[6] Grace, Jim and Grace, Lisa Goldblatt. *The Art of Spooning: A Complete Guide to the Joy of Snuggling and Other Simple Pleasures*. Philadelphia: Running Press, 1998, cover flap.

[7] "On Living Together Without Sex—I'm Doing It!!" 4 April 2002. http://pub72.ezboard. com/flivingtogetherunmarriedfrm1.showMessage?topicID=5.topic. (22 April 2002).

[8] Alternatives to Marriage Project report, forthcoming.

[9] "Outline of Catholic Church Teaching on Sexual Ethics." *The Pro-Life Activist's Encyclopedia*. http://www.ewtn.com/library/PROLENC/APPENDA.TXT. (26 April 2002).

[10] This chapter focuses on responses to attacks on cohabitation based on Christianity, as these are the most common type of religiously grounded arguments against living together.

[11] Winkler, Gershon. *Sacred Secrets: The Sanctity of Sex in Jewish Law and Lore*. Northvale, NJ: Jason Aronson Inc., 1998, pp. 78–96. Bloch, Ariel and Bloch, Chana. *The Song of Songs: A New Translation with an Introduction and Commentary*. New York: Random House, 1995. Wink, Walter. "Homosexuality and the Bible." Chicago: Christian Century Foundation, 1996. Waskow, Arthur. *Down-to-Earth Judaism: Food, Money, Sex, and the Rest of Life*. New York: Quill, 1995, pp. 278–9, 307–18.

[12] Waskow, Arthur. "Sex, the Spirit, Leadership, and the Dangers of Abuse." *Building Community*. www.shalomctr.org/html/comm01.html. (1 June 2002).

[13] Maynard, Jim. Personal communication, 5 June 2002.

[14] Tobin, Joan. "Apology for Church's Attitude to Family." *The Irish Times*, 19 June 2000.

[15] Winkler, 1998, p. 78.

[16] Alternatives to Marriage Project report, forthcoming.

[17] This idea, also called "family of choice," was pioneered by anthropologist Kath Weston in Weston, Kath. *Families We Choose: Lesbians, Gays, Kinship*. New York: Columbia University Press, 1991.

[18] Waskow, 2002.

[19] Brown, Susan and Booth, Alan. "Cohabitation Versus Marriage: A Comparison of Relationship Quality." *Journal of Marriage and the Family* 58:668–78, 1996.

[20] Kenney, Catherine and McLanahan, Sara. "Are Cohabiting Relationships More Violent than Marriage?" Working Paper #01-02. Princeton, NJ: Center for Research on Child Wellbeing, Princeton University, 2001.

[21] Clarkberg, Stolzenberg, and Waite, 1995. Thomson, Elizabeth and Colella, Ugo. "Cohabitation and Marital Stability: Quality or Commitment?" *Journal of Marriage and the Family*, 54: 259–67, 1992. Lillard, Lee; Brien, Michael; and Waite, Linda. "Premarital Cohabitation and Subsequent Marital Dissolution: A Matter of Self-Selection?" *Demography* 32:437–57, 1995. Schoen, Robert. "First Unions and the Stability of First Marriages." *Journal of Marriage and the Family* 54:281–4, 1992. Seltzer, Judith. "Families Formed Outside of Marriage." *Journal of Marriage and the Family*. 62:1247–68, 2000.

22 Coltrane, Scott. "Fatherhood and Marriage in the 21st Century." *National Forum*, Summer 2000.

23 U.S. Census Bureau. "Table DP-1. Profile of General Demographic Characteristics of the United States: 2000." Washington, D.C., 2000a. U.S. Census Bureau. "UC-1. Unmarried-Couple Households, by Presence of Children: 1960 to Present." Washington, D.C., 2001a.

24 Cherlin, Andrew. *Marriage, Divorce, Remarriage.* 2nd ed. Cambridge, MA: Harvard University Press, 1992, p. 15. DeMaris, Alfred and Rao, Vaninadha. "Premarital Cohabitation and Subsequent Marital Stability in the United States: A Reassessment." *Journal of Marriage and the Family* 54:178–90, 1992. Teachman, Jay; Thomas, Jeffrey; and Paasch, Kathleen. "Legal Status and the Stability of Coresidential Unions." *Demography* 28:571–86, 1991. Wu, Zheng. *Cohabitation: An Alternative Form of Family Living.* New York: Oxford University Press, 2000, p. 144.

25 Forste, Renata and Tanfer, Koray. "Sexual Exclusivity Among Dating, Cohabiting, and Married Women." *Journal of Marriage and the Family* 58:33–47. Laumann, 1994, pp. 124–6.

26 Nock, Steven. "A Comparison of Marriages and Cohabiting Relationships." *Journal of Family Issues* 16:53–76, 1995.

27 Mirrlees-Black, Catriona. "Domestic Violence: Findings from a New British Crime Survey Self-Completion Questionnaire." Home Office Research Study 191. London: Home Office, 1999.

28 Kenney and McLanahan, 2001.

29 Gallup, 1997, p. 211. National Survey of Families and Households, 1994. In Chadwick and Heaton, 1999, p. 195. Ropert Starch Worldwide Inc, 1995.

30 Laumann, 1994, p. 502. Kreider, Rose and Fields, Jason. "Number, Timing, and Duration of Marriages and Divorces: 1996." *Current Population Reports.* Washington, D.C.: U.S. Census Bureau, 2002, p. 4.

31 Salmansohn, Karen. *Even God Is Single (So Stop Giving Me a Hard Time).* New York: Workman Publishing Company, Inc., 2000, pp. 1–2.

32 "My Partner and I Have Recently Passed the Three Year Mark." *The Stories of Unmarried People.* 15 May 2002. hwww.unmarried.org/storiestold.html. (6 June 2002).

33 Cohen, Kate. *A Walk Down the Aisle: Notes on a Modern Wedding.* New York: W. W. Norton & Company, 2001, p. 67.

34 Arizona repealed its law against cohabitation in 2001.

35 Thanks to Ashton Applewhite, Karen Kohfeld, Jay Sekora, and Stacey Slaughter. Also: Jim, Jr. "Why Aren't You Married Yet?" *JimJr's Classy Classic Collectibles.* www.qis.net/~jimjr/marr19.htm. (15 June 2002). Jim, Jr. "Why Aren't You Married Yet—II" *JimJr's Classy Classic Collectibles.* http://www.qis.net/~jimjr/marr77.htm. (15 June 2002). The Brunching Shuttlecocks. "Cute/Smart/Funny/Biting Responses." June-July 2001. www.brunchma.com/archives/Forum7/HTML/001774.html. (29 June 2002).

36 Whitehall Properties v. Anchorage Human Rights Commission. Alaska 874 P 2d 274. 1994. Chiang, Harriet. "Religious Landlady Loses Case: State Court Rules for Unmarried Couple." *San Francisco Chronicle*, 10 April 1996.

37 Foray v. NYNEX. New York 98 Civ. 3525. 1999.

Chapter 4: In It for the Long Haul

1 Hiebert, William. Interview, 30 April 2002.

2 Kollman, Maya. Interview, 15 April 2002.

[3] Gottman, John and Silver, Nan. *The Seven Principles for Making Marriage Work*. New York: Crown Publishers, Inc., 1999.

[4] Kollman, 2002.

[5] Gottman and Silver, 1999, p. 15. Emphasis in original.

[6] For more detail on how to use this technique, see Markman, Howard; Stanley, Scott; Blumberg, Susan L. *Fighting For Your Marriage*. San Francisco: Jossey-Bass Publishers, 1994. While this book was written for married couples, the techniques described within can and have been used for a wide range of types of relationships, including unmarried partners and nonintimate workplace settings.

[7] Weber, Julia. Interview, 21 April 2002.

[8] Kollman, 2002.

[9] Wile, Daniel. *After the Honeymoon: How Conflict Can Improve Your Relationship*. New York: John Wiley and Sons, 1988, p. 13.

[10] Hiebert, 2002

[11] Pransky, George. *The Relationship Handbook: A Simple Guide to Satisfying Relationships*. Blue Ride Summit, PA: Tab Books, 1992, pp. 31–2.

[12] Kollman, 2002.

[13] Saunders, Nancy. Interview, 22 April 2002.

[14] Morrison, Elizabeth. Interview, 24 April 2002.

[15] Fariello, Chris. Interview, 23 April 2002.

[16] Saunders, 2002.

[17] Morrison, 2002.

[18] Kelly. "I Have Never Before Felt Discriminated Against or Harassed . . . ." *The Stories of Unmarried People: 2000 Archives*. 7 Nov. 2000. www.unmarried.org/storiestold.html. (9 June 2002).

Chapter 5: "This Is My—Um, Uh. . . . "

[1] Gomez, Jewelle. "Otherwise Engaged: Marriage Is an Offer I *Can* Refuse." *Ms.* July 2000: 67–70, p. 70.

[2] Dunlap, David. "Special Thanks to My Um, My . . . ." *New York Times,* 26 March 1995.

[3] Campbell, Karlyn Kohrs and Burkholder, Thomas. *Critiques of Contemporary Rhetoric*. 2nd ed. Belmont, CA: Wadsworth Publishing, 1997. Fong, Mary. "The Crossroads of Language and Culture." *Intercultural Communication*. Ed. Somovar, Larry and Porter, Richard. 8th ed. Belmont, CA: Wadsworth, 1997.

[4] This word is based on the concept of symbiosis, in which two organisms function together for mutually beneficial reasons. Honeybees and flowers have a symbiotic relationship, where the flowers provide food for the bees while the bees pollinate the flowers.

[5] "Coming out" means to let someone know that you are gay, lesbian, bisexual, or transgender (taken from the phrase "coming out of the closet").

[6] Winkler, Gershon. *Sacred Secrets: The Sanctity of Sex in Jewish Law and Lore*. Northvale, NJ: Jason Aronson Inc., pp. 78–96. Waskow, Arthur. "Sex, the Spirit, Leadership, and the Dangers of Abuse." *Building Community*. www.shalomctr.org/html/comm01.html. (1 June 2002).

[7] Le Bourdais, Celine. Personal communication, October 2000. Marovitch, Maureen. Personal e-mail, 15 May 2002.

[8] Ni Chonghaile, Clar. "PACS Law Stirs Debate in France." *Nando Times*, 8 May 2000.

[9] Diehl, Andrea. Personal communication, 15 May 2001.

10 Elizabeth, V. "Cohabitation, Marriage, and the Unruly Consequences of Difference." *Gender and Society*. 14:87–110, 2000. Keilman, Nico. "Household Statistics in Europe: Consequences of Different Definitions." Prepared for 1991 Quetelet Seminar on the Collection and Comparability of Demographic and Social Data in Europe, Gambloux, Belgium, 2002. Nilsson, Ake. "Family Formation and Dissolution of Consensual Unions and Marriages in Sweden." Presented at EAPS/BIB seminar on Demographic Implications of Marital Status, Bonn, Germany, 1992.

11 Institute for Gay and Lesbian Strategic Studies. "IGLSS study shows US census count of unmarried partners leaves out many." Press Release. Amherst, MA, 2001.

12 Osgood, Charles. "POSSLQ." *There's Nothing That I Wouldn't Do If You Were My POSSLQ*. New York: Holt, Rinehart, and Winston, 1981, pp. 179–80.

13 For a detailed analysis of the historical problems with estimating the number of cohabitors, see Casper, Lynne and Cohen, Philip. "How Does POSSLQ Measure Up? Historical Estimates of Cohabitation." *Demography* 37:237–45, 2000.

14 In fact, if a woman is married at the time a child is conceived, her husband is presumed to be the child's father unless proven otherwise. In some states, like California, this presumption is "irrebuttable," meaning you're not allowed to prove otherwise, regardless of proof that the husband is not the child's biological father. Stanley, Jacqueline. *Unmarried Parents' Rights*. Naperville, IL: Sphinx Publishing, 1999, p. 59.

15 Burkitt, Janet. "More and More, People Are Defining Themselves by Changing Their Family Names." *The Seattle Times*, 4 December 2000.

16 Warner, Ralph; Ihara, Toni; and Hertz, Frederick. *Living Together: A Legal Guide for Unmarried Couples*, 11th edition. Berkeley, CA: Nolo, 2001, pp. 4/9–12.

17 Coleman, Thomas. Personal communication, 16 Sept. 1999.

Chapter 6: In the Eyes of the Law

1 Thank you to attorneys Paula Ettelbrick, Peter Hill, and Ralph Warner for their extensive help with this chapter.

2 The following states have laws against cohabitation (when two unmarried people live together and have a sexual relationship), sodomy (usually defined as oral and anal sex, although this varies state to state. In some states sodomy laws apply only to same-sex couples), and/or fornication (when an unmarried man and woman have voluntary sexual intercourse): Alabama, Arkansas, District of Columbia, Florida, Georgia, Kansas, Idaho, Illinois, Louisiana, Massachusetts, Michigan, Minnesota, Mississippi, Missouri, North Carolina, North Dakota, Oklahoma, South Carolina, Utah, Texas, Virginia, and West Virginia. States have not been included on this list if their sodomy law is still on the books but has been declared unconstitutional by the state's highest court. *The Right to Privacy in the U.S.* Washington, D.C.: National Gay and Lesbian Task Force, 2001. "Laws in the USA." *SodomyLaws*. 31 May 2002. www.sodomylaws.org (4 June 2002). Warner, Ihara, and Hertz, 2001.

3 "Indian American Activist Faces Legal Action." *Times of India*, 1 Sept. 2000.

4 "Judge Condemns Unmarried Couples." United Press International New Mexico Briefs. 26 Oct. 1998.

5 Levey, Bob. "Living Together, but Not on the Mailbox." *The Washington Post*, 25 May 1999, p. C10.

6 "Discrimination." E-mail. 16 Feb. 2001.

7 Winkler, Anne. "Economic Decision-Making by Cohabitors: Findings Regarding Income Pooling." *Applied Economics* 29:1079–90, 1997.

8 Seff, Monica. "Cohabitation and the Law." *Marriage and Family Review* 21:141–68, 1995.

9 United for a Fair Economy. "Estate Tax Talking Points." http://www.faireconomy.org/ activist/action_alert/Estate_Tax_Talking_Points.html. (6 June 2002.)

10 Connecticut's tax will phase out by 2005, and Louisiana's tax will phase out by 2004.

11 "Additional Driver Fees." *Renters' Guide.* 2001. www.avis.com/AvisWeb/JSP/global/en/ rentersguide/policies/us/US_Additional_Driver_Fees.jsp. (14 June 2002.)

12 Based on phone calls made to customer service representatives at Alamo, Avis, Budget, Dollar, Enterprise, Hertz, National, and Thrifty car rental companies in August 2000 and again in June 2002.

13 "AAA." *Service Partners.* 2002. http://www.hertz.com/partners_08/travelpartners/travel-partners.html. (14 June 2002.)

14 Note that in Canada, common-law marriage has a very different legal meaning than it does in the U.S.

15 When a month has two full moons, a rare event, the second one is called a blue moon.

16 Convey, Eric. "IRS Makes Tying the Knot an Expensive Proposal." *The Boston Globe,* 12 April 1999.

17 Convey, 1999.

18 "With This Wedding Ring, the IRS Thee Taxes." Editorial. *The Seattle Times,* 15 April 1999.

19 Goodman, Ellen. "Marriage Penalty Isn't What It Seems To Be." *The Boston Globe,* April 13, 2000.

20 In 1997 the U.S. General Accounting Office prepared a report listing the 1,049 federal laws that are affected by marital status. You can read the full report online or download a PDF version of it from http://www.buddybuddy.com/mar-feda.html.

Chapter 7: Equal Pay for Equal Work

1 Health Care for All—California. www.healthcareforall.org. 25 May 2002. (6 June 2002.)

2 Seligman, Jean. "Variations on a Theme." *Newsweek* (special edition) Winter/Spring. 1990, p. 38.

3 Holcomb, Desma. "Domestic Partner Health Benefits: The Corporate Model vs. the Union Model." In Hunt, Gerald, Ed. *Laboring for Rights: Unions and Sexual Diversity Across Nations.* Philadelphia: Temple University Press, 1999, p. 106.

4 Human Rights Campaign Foundation. *The State of the Workplace for Lesbian, Gay, Bisexual, and Transgender Americans 2001.* Washingron, D.C., 2001, p. 19.

5 Human Rights Campaign Foundation. "The State of the Workplace for Lesbian, Gay, Bisexual, and Transgender Americans: A Semiannual Snapshot." *HRC Worknet Report.* Washington, D.C., 2002.

6 U.S. Census Bureau. *County Business Patterns 2000.* Washington, D.C., 2002, p. 3. Society for Human Resource Management. *2002 Benefits Survey.* Alexandria, VA, 2002, p. 6. Calculation by Dorian Solot.

7 "Domestic Partner Benefits 2000." Lincolnshire, IL: Hewitt Associates, 2000.

8 Human Rights Campaign Foundation, 2001, p. 20.

9 Mills, Kim with Herrschaft, Daryl. *The State of the Workplace for Lesbian, Gay, Bisexual, and Transgendered Americans.* Washington, D.C.: Human Rights Campaign, 1999, p. 16.

10 Human Rights Campaign Foundation, 2001, p. 20. Calculation by Dorian Solot. We use the term "sex-neutral" rather than "gender-neutral" since most employers base benefits eligibility on legal sex, not gender identity. A person's sex and gender are usually the same, but not always.

[11] Human Rights Campaign Foundation. *The State of the Workplace for Lesbian, Gay, Bisexual, and Transgender Americans.* Washington, D.C.: 2001, p. 20. Calculation by Dorian Solot.

[12] Society for Human Resource Management. *2002 Benefits Survey.* Alexandria, VA, 2002, p. 40.

[13] Plaster, Gip. "Getting Your Company To Approve Benefits Can Be a Simple Matter of Knowing What To Say." *Bay Windows,* 25 May 2000.

[14] Van Buren, Abigail. "Dear Abby." Syndicated column. 28 May 1998.

[15] *Human Resources Management, Issues & Trends.* Commerce Clearing House, 16 June 1999.

[16] Breen, Bill. "Where Are You On The Talent Map?" *Fast Company,* January 2001, p. 106.

[17] Local 616 of the Service Employees' International Union. As quoted in Roberts, Patti. "Comments." In Cobble, Dorothy Sue, ed. *Women and Unions: Forging a Partnership.* Ithaca, NY: ILR Press, 1993, p. 352.

[18] Kohn, Sally. *The Domestic Partner Organizing Manual for Employee Benefits.* Washington, D.C.: The Policy Institute of the Gay and Lesbian Task Force, 1999. *Domestic Partner Benefits: A Trend Toward Fairness.* Washington: National Gay and Lesbian Journalists Association, 1997. *How To Achieve Domestic Partner Benefits in Your Workplace.* Washington, D.C.: Human Rights Campaign Worknet, 2002.

[19] *Domestic Partner Benefits Mini-Survey.* Alexandria, VA: Society for Human Resource Management, 1997.

[20] Badgett, M. V. Lee. "Calculating Costs with Credibility: Health Care Benefits for Domestic Partners." *Angles.* Washington, D.C.: The Institute for Gay and Lesbian Strategic Studies. Nov. 2000. "Domestic Partners and Employee Benefits." Lincolnshire, IL: Hewitt Associates, 1994. "Domestic Partner Benefits." *Employee Benefits Practices.* Fourth Quarter 1994, p. 4.

[21] Fields, Jason. "America's Families and Living Arrangements 2000." *Current Population Reports.* Washington, D.C.: U.S. Census Bureau, 2001. U.S. Census Bureau. "H3. Households with Two Unrelated Adults of the Opposite Sex, by Presence of Children Under 15 and Age, Marital Status, and Race and Hispanic Origin/1 of Householder and Partner: March 1999." Washington, D.C, 2001b. Black, Dan et al. "Demographics of the Gay and Lesbian Population in the United States: Evidence from Available Systemic Data Sources." *Demography* 37:139–54, 2000.

[22] "Report of the Domestic Partnership Study Group for the City University of New York," October 1993. Cited in Diagle, Christopher. "White Paper Re: Domestic Partnership Benefits." Tulane University, 1997. "Report of the Subcommittee on Domestic Partners' Benefits." University Committee on Faculty and Staff Benefits, Stanford University, 1992. "Employers Providing Domestic Partner Benefits to Same-Sex and Opposite-Sex Partners: Cost Analysis." Los Angeles, CA: Spectrum Institute, 1997. "Domestic Partner Benefits." *Census.* Brookfield, WI: International Society of Certified Employee Benefit Specialists, May 1995. *Executive Letter.* New York: The Segal Company. 17.1 and 17.2, 1993. "Interest in Domestic Partner Benefits Growing." New York: Towers Perrin, 20 November 1996.

[23] Badgett, 2000.

[24] Kohn, 1999. Ettelbrick, Paula. Personal communication, May 2002.

[25] Ross, Sherwood. "More Employers Weigh Domestic Partner Benefits." Reuters Limited, 28 September 1998.

[26] Postcard. THINK AGAIN. www.agitart.org. 1998.

[27] Human Rights Campaign Foundation, 2001, pp. 20, 39. Calculation by Dorian Solot.

[28] "Employers That Offer Domestic Partner Benefits." *Domestic Partner Benefits*. 2002. www.hrc.org/worknet/dp/index.asp. (9 June 2002).

[29] Cleaves v. City of Chicago. Illinois 98 C 1219. 1999. Foray v. NYNEX. New York 98 Civ. 3525. 1999. Irizarry v. Board of Education of City of Chicago Board of Education. United States WL 506985. 2001.

Chapter 8: Walking Down the Aisle, Married or Not

[1] Institute for Gay and Lesbian Strategic Studies. "IGLSS study shows US census count of unmarried partners leaves out many." Press Release. Amherst, MA, 2001, p. 247.

[2] Baehr v. Miike. Hawaii 91-1394. 1996.

[3] Menard, Valerie. *The Latino Holiday Book: From Cinco De Mayo to Dia De Los Muertos: The Celebrations and Traditions of Hispanic-Americans*. Marlowe & Company, 2000, pp. 54–6.

[4] Van Buren, Abigail. "Older Americans May Choose To Live Together." *Courier-Post*, 25 July 2000. Culver, Virginia. "Some Seniors Commit To Love, Not Marriage." *The Denver Post*, 12 June 2000.

[5] Culver, 2000.

[6] Deibler, Sherry. "Many Seniors Skip Altar to 'Marry.' " *Sharon Advocate*, 17 June 1998, p. 9.

Chapter 9: Unmarried with Children

[1] Martin, Joyce, et al. "Births: Final Data for 2000." *National Vital Statistics Reports*, Vol. 50 No. 5. Hyattsville, MD: National Center for Health Statistics, 2002, p. 2.

[2] Bumpass, Larry and Lu, Hsien-Hen. "Trends in Cohabitation and Implications for Children's Family Contexts in the United States." *Population Studies*, 54: 29–41, 2000.

[3] Martin, 2002, p. 46.

[4] Bumpass, Larry. "The Declining Significance of Marriage: Changing Family Life in the United States." Paper presented at the Potsdam International Conference, Potsdam, The Netherlands, December 1994.

[5] Bumpass and Lu, 2000. Black, Dan et al. "Demographics of the Gay and Lesbian Population in the United States: Evidence from Available Systemic Data Sources." *Demography* 37:139–54, 2000. U.S. Census Bureau. "PCT14. Unmarried Partner Households by Sex of Partners." Washington, D.C., 2000b.

[6] Manning, Wendy. "Marriage and Cohabitation Following Premarital Conception." *Journal of Marriage and the Family* 54:839–50, 1993.

[7] Graefe, Deborah and Lichter, Daniel. "Life Course Transitions of American Children: Parental Cohabitation, Marriage, and Single Parenthood." *Demography* 36:205–17, 1999.

[8] Bachu, Amara. "Trends in Premarital Childbearing 1930 to 1994." *Current Population Reports*. Washington, D.C., 1999, p. 2.

[9] Coontz, Stephanie. *The Way We Really Are: Coming To Terms With America's Changing Families*. New York: Basic Books, 1997, p. 101.

[10] McLanahan, Sara. "Growing Up Without a Father." In Daniels, Cynthia, ed. *Lost Fathers: The Politics of Fatherlessness in America*. New York: St. Martin's Griffin, 1998, p. 89.

[11] Cowan, Carolyn Pape and Cowan, Philip. *When Partners Become Parents: The Big Life Change for Couples*. Mahwah, NJ: Lawrence Erlbaum Associates, 2000.

[12] U.S. Census Bureau. "UC-1. Unmarried-Couple Households, by Presence of Children: 1960 to Present." Washington, D.C., 2001a.

[13] Fisher, Helen. *Anatomy of Love: The Mysteries of Mating, Marriage, and Why We Stray*. New York: Fawcett Columbine, 1992, pp. 115–16. Williams, W. Llewelyn. *Itinerary through Wales*. London, 1908, p. 195. As cited in Parker, 1990, p. 26.

[14] Landale, Nancy and Fennelly, Katherine. "Informal Unions Among Unmarried Puerto Rican Women." *Journal of Marriage and the Family* 54:269–80, 1992.

[15] Rector, Robert. "The Effects of Welfare Reform." Testimony Before the Subcommittee on Human Resources, Committee on Ways and Means. Washington, D.C., 15 March 2001. Fagan, Patrick and Rector, Robert. "The Effects of Divorce on America." *The Heritage Foundation Backgrounder*. Washington, D.C.: The Heritage Foundation, 2000.

[16] Fields, Suzanne. "There Goes the Bride." Column. *Washington Times*, 6 June 2002. Chebium, Raju. "U.S. Supreme Court Hears Constitutional Challenge to Portion of Citizenship Law." *CNN.com*, 9 January 2001. www.cnn.com/2001/LAW/01/09/scotus.ins. arguments/index.html. (8 June 2002.)

[17] "Most States Unjustly Stigmatize Children Born to Unmarried Parents." *American Association for Single People*. www.singlesrights.com/stop-stogma-list.htm. (9 June 2002.)

[18] "British Aristocrats More Red-Blooded Than Blue." Reuters, 17 May 1999.

[19] We use the term "original families" rather than "biological families" to recognize families formed by adoption. Most research on cohabiting and married families divides them into only two categories, biological families and stepfamilies. In many cases families with two adoptive parents are counted in the biological family category, so the term biological family is being used to mean original family. Families with one adoptive parent and one biological parent are counted as stepfamilies. In other cases adoptive families are removed from the sample, or it isn't clear how adoptive families are being counted. No system is perfect, since children join adoptive families from infancy to teenagehood, in so many different ways.

[20] Fields, Jason. "America's Families and Living Arrangements 2000." *Current Population Reports*. Washington, D.C.: U.S. Census Bureau, 2001, p. 4.

[21] There is nearly no research about children in multiple-partner families. Also, in order to analyze large amounts of data, quantitative research about families oversimplifies the realities of families. For instance, it is difficult for most research on child well-being to incorporate the fact that many children move in and out of different family structures at different times in their lives.

[22] Bumpass, 1994.

[23] Brown, Susan. "Child Well-Being in Cohabiting Families." In Booth, Alan and Crouter, Ann. *Just Living Together: Implications of Cohabitation on Families, Children, and Social Policy*. Mahwah, NJ: Lawrence Erlbaum Associates, 2002, pp. 173–87. Manning, Wendy. "The Implications of Cohabitation for Children's Well-Being." In Booth and Crouter, 2002a, 121–52. Manning, Wendy and Lamb, Kathleen. "Parental Cohabitation and Adolescent Well-Being." Center for Family and Demographic Research Working Paper 02-03. Bowling Green, OH: Bowling Green State University, 2002b. Thomson, Elizabeth; Hanson, Thomas; and McLanahan, Sara. "Family Structure and Child Well-Being: Economic Resources vs. Parental Behaviors." *Social Forces* 73:221–42, 1994.

[24] Alcock, Alan and Demo, David. *Family Diversity and Well-Being*. Thousand Oaks, CA: Sage Publications, 1994, p. 214.

[25] Brown, 2002. Manning, 2002a.

[26] Brown, 2002, p. 179.

[27] Stacey, Judith. "Dada-ism in the 1990s: Getting Past Baby Talk about Fatherlessness." In Daniels, Cynthia, ed. *Lost Fathers: The Politics of Fatherlessness in America*. New York: St. martin's Griffin, 1998, pp. 50–83, 1998, p. 70.

28 Amato, Paul; Loomis, Laura; and Booth, Alan. "Parental Divorce, Marital Conflict, and Offspring Well-Being During Early Adulthood." *Social Forces* 73:895–915, 1995.

29 *NPR Talk of the Nation.* National Public Radio, 11 November 1998.

30 Amato, Loomis, and Booth, 1995. Cherlin, Andrew. "Going to Extremes: Family Structure, Children's Well-Being, and Social Science." *Demography* 36:21–28, 1999. Jekielek, Susan. "Parental Conflict, Marital Disruption, and Children's Emotional Well-Being." *Social Forces.* 76:905–36, 1998. Vandewater, Elizabeth and Lansford, Jennifer. "Influences of Family Structure and Parental Conflict on Children's Well-Being." *Family Relations* 47:323–30, 1998.

31 Much of the information in this section comes from the Nolo website (www.nolo.com) and legal guides, *Living Together: A Legal Guide for Unmarried Couples*, by Ralph Warner, Toni Ihara, and Frederick Hertz (2001); and *A Legal Guide for Lesbian and Gay Couples*, by Hayden Curry, Denis Clifford, and Frederick Hertz (2001).

32 Gomez v. Perez, 409 U.S. 535. 1973. Levy v. Louisiana, 391 U.S. 68. 1968. Stanley v. Illinois, 405 U.S. 645. 1972. Weber v. Aetna Casualty & Surety Co., 406 U.S. 164. 1972. Carbone, June. *From Partners to Parents: The Second Revolution in Family Law.* New York: Columbia University Press, 2000.

33 Weber v. Aetna Casualty & Surety Co., 1972.

34 Eurostat. *100 Basic Indicators from Eurostat Yearbook 2001: The Statistical Guide to Europe.* Luxembourg: European Communities, 2001.

35 Fields, 2001.

36 "Parenting Issues for Unmarried Couples FAQ." *Law Centers.* 2002. www.nolo.com/law-center/faqs/detail.cfm/objectid/893B37A0-D0E8-4B7D-9FD90CE5DCBC3BE7. (8 June 2002).

37 Ihara, Toni and Warner, Ralph. *The Living Together Kit: A Legal Guide for Unmarried Couples*, 8th ed. Berkeley, CA: Nolo Press, 1997.

38 Brightman, Joan. "Why Hillary Chooses Rodham Clinton." *American Demographics* 16:9, 1994.

Chapter 10: Shall We Marry?

1 Bumpass, Larry and Lu, Hsien-Hen. "Trends in Cohabitation and Implications for Children's Family Contexts in the United States." *Population Studies*, 54: 29–41, 2000.

2 Sosnoski, Karen and Zeytoonjian, Fred. *Wedding Advice: Speak Now or Forever Hold Your Peace.* Alexandria, VA: SosZey Productions, 2001. Sosnoski, Karen. Interview, 11 May 2002.

3 Fudge, Rachel. "Why I Don't." In Corral, Jill and Miya-Jervis, Lisa. *Young Wives' Tales: New Adventures in Love and Partnership.* Seattle: Seal Press, 2001, p. 48.

4 *NPR Talk of the Nation.* National Public Radio, 11 November 1998.

5 *NPR Talk of the Nation*, 1998.

6 Heyn, Dalma. *Marriage Shock: The Transformation of Women into Wives.* New York: Villard, 1997. Also, see Mausart, Susan. *Wifework: What Marriage Really Means for Women.* New York: Bloomsbury, 2002.

7 Morrison, Elizabeth. Interview, 24 April 2002.

Chapter 11:
First Comes Love, Then Comes Living Together

1 Gillis, John. *A World of Their Own Making: Myth, Ritual, and the Quest for Family Values.* Cambridge, MA: Harvard University Press, 1996, p. 11. Graff, E. J. *What Is Marriage For?* Boston: Beacon Press, 1999. Wu, Zheng. *Cohabitation: An Alternative Form of Family Living.* New York: Oxford University Press, 2000, p. 41.

2 Gillis, John. *For Better, For Worse: British Marriages, 1600 to the Present.* New York: Oxford University Press, 1985, pp. 84–105. Gillis, 1996.

3 Graff, 1999, p. 89. Springer, Ilene. "The Egyptian Bride." *Tour Egypt Monthly,* 1 September 2000. www.egyptmonth.com/mag09012000/magf4.htm. (11 June 2002.)

4 Duff, Johnette and Truitt, George. *The Spousal Equivalent Handbook: A Legal and Financial Guide to Living Together.* Houston: Sunny Beach Publications, 1991, p. 37.

5 Graff, 1999, p. 210. Yalom, Marilyn. *A History of the Wife.* New York: HarperCollins Publishers, 2001, p. 28.

6 Graff, 1999, pp. 194–5. Winkler, Gershon. *Sacred Secrets: The Sanctity of Sex in Jewish Law and Lore.* Northvale, NJ: Jason Aronson Inc., 1998, pp. 78–96.

7 Graff, 1999, p. 195.

8 Williams, W. Llewelyn. *Itinerary through Wales.* London, 1908, p. 195. As cited in Parker, 1990, p. 26.

9 Bonnie Anderson and Judith Zinsser. *A History of Their Own: Women in Europe from Prehistory to the Present.* Volume I. New York: Harper & Row, 1988, pp. 119–124.

10 Bohannan, Paul. *All the Happy Families: Exploring the Varieties of Family Life.* New York: McGraw Hill Book Company, 1985. Gillis, 1985, pp. 7, 17, 84–105. Gillis, 1996, pp. 134–43. Graff, 1999, pp. 199–200.

11 Graff, 1999, p. 199.

12 Frayser, Suzanne. *Varieties of Sexual Experience: An Anthropological Perspective on Human Sexuality.* New Haven: HRAF Press, 1985. As cited in Pasternak, Burton; Ember, Carol; and Ember, Melvin. *Sex, Gender, and Kinship: A Cross-Cultural Perspective.* Upper Saddle River, NJ: Prentice-Hall, 1997.

13 Cott, Nancy. *Public Vows: A History of Marriage and the Nation,* Harvard University Press, 2001, pp. 35–6. Parker, 1990, p. 18. Kiernan, Kathleen and Estaugh, Valerie. *Cohabitation: Extra-Marital Childbearing and Social Policy.* London: Family Policy Studies Centre, 1993.

14 Quakers and Jews were exempted from these requirements. Gillis, 1985, p. 140. Graff, 1999, p. 203.

15 Demian. "Marriage Traditions in Various Times and Cultures." *Partners Task Force for Gay and Lesbian Couples,* 23 June 2000. www.buddybuddy.com/mar-trad.html. (2 July 2000.)

16 Cott, 2000, pp. 30–1, 39.

17 Shade, William. "A Mental Passion: Female Sexuality in Victorian America." *International Journal of Women's Studies* 1:16, 1978. As cited in Faderman, Lillian. *Odd Girls and Twilight Lovers: A History of Lesbian Life in Twentieth-Century America.* New York: Penguin, 1991.

18 Some couples today still get handfasted, a form of marriage or commitment ceremony that gets its name from the part of the ritual where the partners' wrists are symbolically bound together with a length of cord. Demian, 2000.

19 Peiss, Kathy. *Cheap Amusements: Working Women and Leisure in Turn-of-the-Century New York.* Philadelphia, PA: Temple University Press, 1986, p. 7

20 Gillis, 1996, p. 146. Katz, Jonathan ed. *The Invention of Heterosexuality*. New York: Penguin, 1995.

21 Manning, Wendy and Landale, Nancy. "Racial and Ethnic Differences in the Role of Cohabitation in Premarital Childbearing." *Journal of Marriage and the Family* 58:63–77, 1996.

22 White, Kevin. *The First Sexual Revolution: The Emergence of Male Heterosexuality in Modern America*. New York: New York University, 1993, p. 13. Coontz, Stephanie. *The Way We Never Were: American Families and the Nostalgia Trap*. New York: Basic Books, 1992, p. 194.

23 Mintz, Steven and Kellogg, Susan. *Domestic Revolutions: A Social History of American Family Life*. New York: The Free Press, 1988, 177–201. Peiss, 1986, p. 184. White, 1993, p. 15.

24 Graff, 1999, p. 204–5. Mintz and Kellogg, 1988, pp. 107–29.

25 May, Elaine Tyler. *Great Expectations: Marriage and Divorce in Post-Victorian America*. Chicago: University of Chicago Press, 1980, p. 55. Coontz, 1992, p. 29.

26 May, Elaine Tyler. *Homeward Bound: American Families in the Cold War Era*. New York: Basic Books, 1988.

27 Mintz and Kellogg, 1988, pp. 177-201. U.S. Census Bureau. "Table MS-2. Estimated Median Age at First Marriage, by Sex: 1890 to the Present." Washington, D.C., 2001c. Coontz, 1992, p. 39.

28 Skolnick, Arlene. *Embattled Paradise: The American Family in the Age of Uncertainty*. New York: Basic Books, 1991, pp. 75–6.

29 Casper, Lynne and Cohen, Philip. "How Does POSSLQ Measure Up? Historical Estimates of Cohabitation." *Demography* 37:237–45, 2000.

30 Rothman, Ellen. *Hands and Hearts: A History of Courtship in America*. New York: Basic Books, 1994.

31 Schulenberg, John et al. "Historical Trends in Attitudes and Preferences Regarding Family, Work, and the Future Among American Adolescents: National Data from 1976 through 1992." Monitoring the Future Occasional Paper 37. Ann Arbor, MI: Institute for Social Research, University of Michigan, 1994.

32 U.S. Census Bureau, International Data Base. "Table 047. Population by Marital Status, Age, Sex, and Urban/Rural Residence." 1997.

33 This number is often given as 5.5 million households. Each household contains a pair of partners, thus, 11 million individual people who live with a partner. U.S. Census Bureau. "Profile of General Demographic Characteristics for the United States: 2000." Table DP-1, 2000a.

34 Bumpass and Lu, 2000.

35 U.S. Census Bureau. "UC-1. Unmarried-Couple Households, by Presence of Children: 1960 to Present." Washington, D.C., 2001. The numbers here are slightly smaller than elsewhere in the book, because this chart uses POSSLQ data rather than unmarried partner data. We use POSSLQ numbers here because unmarried partner data collection began only in 1990. The Census has no estimates of same-sex couples prior to 1990.

36 Sweet, James and Bumpass, Larry. "Young Adults' View of Marriage, Cohabitation, and Family." In S. J. South and S. E. Tolnay, eds. *The Changing American Family*. Boulder: Westview Press, 1992. Louis Harris and Associates. "Generation 2001: A Survey of the First College Graduating Class of the New Millennium, 8." 1998. Kreider, Rose and Fields, Jason. "Number, Timing, and Duration of Marriages and Divorces: 1996." *Current Population Reports*. Washington, D.C.: U.S. Census Bureau, 2002, p. 16.

[37] Hawkins, Chauncey J. *Will the Home Survive? A Study of Tendencies in Modern Literature.* New York: T. Whittaker, Inc, 1907, as quoted in Graff, 1999, p. 88.

[38] Graff, 1999, p. 88.

[39] Council on Families in America. *Marriage in America: A Report to the Nation.* New York: Institute for American Values, 1995, p. 4.

[40] Graff, 1999, p. 114.

[41] Davis, Kingsley. "The Meaning and Significance of Marriage in Contemporary Society." In Davis, Kingsley, ed. *Contemporary Marriage.* New York: Russell Sage Foundation, 1985.

[42] Graff, 1999, p. 88.

[43] Harris, Sarah. "Marriage 'Will Be Extinct in 30 Years.' " *Daily Mail,* 20 April 2002.

[44] Etzioni, Amatai. "The Family: Is It Obsolete?" *Journal of Current Social Issues* 14 (1), 1977, p. 4.

[45] U.S. Census Bureau. "Series A 160-171. Marital Status of the Population, by Age and Sex: 1980 to 1970." *Historical Statistics of the United States, Colonial Times to 1970.* White Plains, NY: Kraus International Publications, 1989, pp. 20–1. Fields, Jason. "America's Families and Living Arrangements 2000." *Current Population Reports.* Washington, D.C.: U.S. Census Bureau, 2001, p. 10.

[46] Although many of the issues faced by unmarried partners are similar regardless of the sexes and sexual orientations of the people involved, most demographic studies consider only different-sex couples in their analysis. We present data on both same-sex and different-sex couples when we can, but some statistics count only different-sex couples.

[47] U.S. Census Bureau. "PCT14. Unmarried Partner Households by Sex of Partners." Washington, D.C., 2000b.

[48] Armas, Genaro. "Census: More Elderly Live Together." *Associated Press,* 30 July 2002.

[49] Source: U.S. Census Bureau. "H3. Households with Two Unrelated Adults of the Opposite Sex, by Presence of Children Under 15 and Age, Marital Status, and Race and Hispanic Origin/1 of Householder and Partner: March 1999." Washington, D.C., 2001.

[50] Bumpass, Larry and Lu, Hsien-Hen. "Trends in Cohabitation and Implications for Children's Family Contexts in the United States." *Population Studies,* 54: 29–41, 2000.

[51] Bumpass and Lu, 2000. Black, Dan et al. "Demographics of the Gay and Lesbian Population in the United States: Evidence from Available Systemic Data Sources." *Demography* 37:139–54, 2000. U.S. Census Bureau, 2000b.

[52] U.S. Census Bureau, 1998. As cited in Smock and Gupta, 2002a.

[53] Smock, Pamela. "Cohabitation in the United States: An Appraisal of Research Themes, Findings, and Implications." *Annual Review of Sociology* 26:1–20, 2000.

[54] Smock, Pamela. Personal communication, 27 April 2002b.

[55] Bumpass and Lu, 2000.

[56] Bumpass and Lu, 2000. Bumpass, Larry; Sweet, James; and Cherlin, Andrew. "The Role of Cohabitation in Declining Rates of Marriage." *Journal of Marriage and the Family* 53: 913–27, 1991.

[57] U.S. Census Bureau. "Table DP-1. Profile of General Demographic Characteristics, 1990 and 2000." Washington, D.C., 1991 and 2000a. Calculations by Dorian Solot.

[58] U.S. Census Bureau, 2001b. Thanks to Laurie Nelson for her research assistance with the Census data in this chapter.

[59] U.S. Census Bureau. "Table DP-1. Profile of General Demographic Characteristics: 1990" for each state, and equivalent data for 2000. Washington, D.C., 2000a.

[60] U.S. Census Bureau, 2001b.

61 The Census data on race is based on the race of the person who identifies him or herself as the householder. The Census states that Hispanic/Latino people may be of any race.

62 This data is from the Census race category "Black or African-American." U.S. Census Bureau. "PCT22. Unmarried Partner Households and Sex of Partners [7]—Universe: Households." Washington, D.C., 2000.

63 This data is from the Census race category "Asian." U.S. Census Bureau, 2000d.

64 Gibb, Frances. "Gays Call for Married Couples' Status." *The Times*, 24 October 2000. Dombey, Daniel. "Belgium Approves Tax Reforms." *Financial Times*, 5 July 2001. "To Love Outside the Law." *The Irish Times*, 17 April 2001. Lloyd, Marion. "In Mexico, a Mass Gay Wedding." *The Boston Globe*, 16 February 2001. "NZ Gay Couples Win Divorce Rights." *PlanetOut*, 22 November 2000. Solholm, Rolleiv. "Obligatory Mediation for Cohabitants." *The Norway Post*, 7 February 2002. *ANC Daily News Briefing*. "Concourt Judgment Welcome: Commission on Gender Equality." 3 December 1999. Balongo, Faith. "Perils of 'Come-We-Stay' Marriages." *The Nation*, 23 January 2000. "Partners' Hopes for Equal Treatment Rise." *The Telegraph*, 6 February 2002.

65 "Unwed Couple Flogged in Afghan Stadium." *Zenit News Agency*, 24 May 2001. "Another Unmarried Woman Faces Trial for Adultery in Sokoto." *Daily Trust*, 7 January 2002. Nazzal, Nasouh. "Preacher Lashed, Deported for Cohabitation." *Gulf News*, 24 June 2001.

66 Coontz, Stephanie. *The Way We Really Are: Coming To Terms With America's Changing Families*. New York: Basic Books, 1997, p. 94.

67 Sweet, James and Bumpass, Larry. "Young Adults' View of Marriage, Cohabitation, and Family." In S. J. South and S. E. Tolnay, eds. *The Changing American Family*. Boulder: Westview Press, 1992.

68 Gallagher, Maggie. *The Abolition of Marriage: How We Destroy Lasting Love*. Washington, D.C.: Regnery Publishing, Inc., 1996. Waite, Linda and Gallagher, Maggie. *The Case for Marriage: Why Married People Are Happier, Healthier, and Better off Financially*. New York: Doubleday, 2000. Wilson, James Q. *The Marriage Problem: How Our Culture Has Weakened Families*. New York: HarperCollins, 2002.

69 NOW Legal Defense and Education Fund. "State Marriage Initiatives." *Welfare and Poverty*. www.nowldef.org/html/issues/wel/statemarriage.shtml. (17 June 2002).

70 Cott, Nancy. *Public Vows: A History of Marriage and the Nation*, Harvard University Press, 2001, p. 45.

71 Kiernan, Kathleen. "Cohabitation in Western Europe: Trends, Issues, and Implications." In Booth, Alan and Crouter, Ann, eds. *Just Living Together: Implications of Cohabitation on Families, Children, and Social Policy*. Mahwah, NJ: Lawrence Erlbaum Associates, 2002, pp. 3–32.

72 Eurostat. *100 Basic Indicators from Eurostat Yearbook 2001: The Statistical Guide to Europe*. Luxembourg: European Communities, 2001.

73 Eurostat, 2001. Martin, Joyce, et al. "Births: Final Data for 2000." *National Vital Statistics Reports*, Vol. 50 No. 5. Hyattsville, MD: National Center for Health Statistics, 2002.

74 Bradbury, Bruce and Jantti, Markus. "Child Poverty Across Industrialized Nations." *Innocenti Occasional Papers: Economic and Social Policy Series No. 71*. 1999

75 Prescott-Allen, Robert. *The Wellbeing of Nations: A Country-by-Country Index of Quality of Life and the Environment*. Washington, D.C.: Island Press, 2001.

76 Gavanas, Anna. Interview, May 2002.

77 Eurostat. "First Results of the Demographic Data Collection for 1999 in Europe." *Statistics in Focus*. European Communities, 2000.

78 "Swiss Wedding Bells Fall Silent." *Swissinfo*, 10 February 2002.

[79] Thirty-three percent of U.S. births are to unmarried parents, compared with 39 percent in the UK and Finland, 41 percent in France, 45 percent in Denmark, 49 percent in Norway, 55 percent in Sweden, and 63 percent in Iceland. Eurostat, 2001.

[80] Cauchi, Stephen. "Tying the Knot Not What It Used To Be." *The Age*, 9 January 2001. Gang, Deng. "Marriages Down, Divorces Up." *People's Daily Online*, 25 April 2001. Sofer, Barbara. "Looking Around: The Singles Among Us." *The Jerusalem Post*, 26 October 2000.

[81] Tatsuta, Keiko. "More Women Daring To Be Single Mothers." *Japan Today*, 29 December 2001.

[82] There are some differences in some cases between the rights given to married versus registered partnership couples. Kiernan, 2002. "A Global View: Domestic Partnership Laws in Other Nations." *American Association for Single People*. www.singlesrights.com/dp-vermont-global.html. (12 June 2002). Jensen, Steffen. "Recognition of Gay and Lesbian Partnerships in Europe." www.steff.suite.dk/partner.htm. (12 June 2002).

[83] Graff, 1999.

[84] Wu, Zheng. *Cohabitation: An Alternative Form of Family Living*. New York: Oxford University Press, 2000.

[85] One remaining difference is that unmarried couples must live together for a year before the law affects them, while married couples are affected immediately. Smock and Gupta, 2002a.

[86] Owens, Anne Marie. "Pinning Down the Concept of Family." *National Post*, March 3, 1999.